Always a

BADGER

The Pat Richter Story

John —
Best Badger wishes
and hope you enjoy the book
On Wisconsin!

VINCE SWEENEY

TRAILS BOOKS
Black Earth, Wisconsin

Library of Congress Control Number: 2005926362
ISBN: 1-931599-62-9

Editor: Mark Knickelbine
Designer: Colin Harrington
Front Cover Photos: Courtesy of University of Wisconsin Athletic Department;
photo of Pat Richter with football courtesy of The Washington Redskins.
Back Cover Photo: Courtesy of Larsen Photography

Printed in the United States of America by Sheridan Books, Inc.

09 08 07 06 05   6 5 4 3 2 1

Trails Books, a division of Trails Media Group, Inc.
P.O. Box 317 • Black Earth, WI 53515
(800) 236-8088 • e-mail: books@wistrails.com
www.trailsbooks.com

To my wife Sharon, and our daughters,
Kelsey and Keara.

—Vince

TABLE OF CONTENTS

FOREWORD

by Donna Shalala

The first time I met Pat Richter I was struck by how graceful he
was and how quietly he made his points. It was the fall of 1987 and I was just arriving at the university. An outsider, I knew little of Wisconsin's traditions or heroes.

I had just come from visiting the University of Michigan. I was a friend of
the then president, Harold Shapiro, who had offered to fill me in on the Big Ten
and big-time research universities. It was a very useful tutorial. I stayed over for
the Michigan-Wisconsin football game. That was useful too but in another way.
The Badgers looked like a high school team compared with the Wolverines. But the
crowd and the enthusiasm of the game were impressive. I put into the back of my
mind to check out our lack of competitiveness.

I didn't attend another game until the fall of 1988—by then our fans were
scarce and frustrated. There was a lot of grumbling. Most of the university faculty
and staff had given up and decided that Wisconsin's high academic standards
made a competitive team impossible. Pat Richter was not one of them. He was
convinced that leadership could make a difference. The rest, as they say, is history.

Vince Sweeney, a fine writer and knowledgeable observer and participant in
the recovery of Wisconsin's program, is the perfect person to tell Pat's story. Every
state has its Golden Boy—some are stories of tragedy and some of glory. This is the
latter. Pat Richter had the golden touch from the time he was a boy. But more than
that, he had character. When I asked him to come back to save the athletic program
his only hesitation was about his responsibilities as a husband and father.

I played a small part in his story, and it was a time I treasure. I learned a lot
from Pat about pride, tenacity, courage, and grace under fire. More than anything,
I learned about loyalty to your alma mater—fierce loyalty. He is a Badger's Badger,
this son of Wisconsin. And now, thanks to Vince Sweeney, we have Pat's story.

ACKNOWLEDGMENTS

Her name was Sonja Christensen, and she was by far the best administrative assistant I had ever encountered. On this day, she had answered my call to her boss, Pat Richter, and as she had done for so many others, she had politely noted that Pat was unavailable to speak with me at the time. He would be happy to call me back, or I could try later, or leave a message. Sonja had done it again. She had screened Pat from my non-urgent phone call and somehow made me feel good about not getting through.

It was mid-February 1990 and I was calling to congratulate Richter, who weeks before had begun his new job as director of athletics at the University of Wisconsin–Madison. I was living with my wife, Sharon, and our two-year-old daughter, Kelsey, in Mission Viejo, California, and was in my first year as assistant sports editor of the Orange County edition of the *Los Angeles Times*. It was an unlikely place for us to be living; Sharon and I were both born and raised in Madison, where we attended Blessed Sacrament Grade School, went on to Edgewood High School, and graduated from the University of Wisconsin–Madison. We both had family in the area, and except for the drudgery of the cold and gray Wisconsin winters, we were quite content to be living in Madison. But 12 years into my career working for such daily newspapers as the *Madison Press Connection*, the *Milwaukee Journal*, the *Milwaukee Sentinel*, and most recently, the *Capital Times*, there would be a higher calling, so to speak. It was Bill Dwyre, sports editor of the *Los Angeles Times*, calling to encourage me to pursue a job as an assistant sports editor.

Initially, we resisted the lure of the sunshine, beaches, and warm weather. But eventually I fell victim to California dreaming, and I gradually convinced my wife to do the same. In 1989, we headed west for a new life in sunny California and a great job at one of the finest newspapers in the world.

I did not know the new UW athletic director well, but growing up in Madison, you always felt you knew Pat Richter. He represented all that was good about the Madison sports scene. He was one of our own who had gone on to be a great collegiate athlete and a solid professional football player. In later years, he became a well-respected executive at one of Madison's great companies, Oscar Mayer Foods.

I had met Pat on several occasions as his athletic and professional careers advanced. Like every other Badger fan, I admired the skill, poise, and talent that he displayed during his athletic career, particularly that record-setting performance in the dramatic 1963 Rose Bowl. I had watched closely as my older brother, Dennis, played baseball with Richter, Jim Bakken, and Dale Hackbart as a member of the legendary Monona Grove Lakers baseball team. And in later years, while covering local sports for the *Capital Times*, I had run into Richter at a number of UW sporting events and banquets in Madison.

For some reason, I felt compelled to place a call from California to Pat Richter that February day to offer my congratulations on his being named athletic director at Wisconsin.

Pat returned my call, and I wished him the best of luck in his new role. He asked me about my new job and if I ever ran into *LA Times* columnist Jim Murray, whom he had met at the 1963 Rose Bowl. He also asked about Dwyre, the Sheboygan native who left his job as sports editor at the *Milwaukee Journal* to become sports editor at the *LA Times*. And then he asked how I liked California. I paused just long enough for Pat to understand. "I remember when we were out east," Pat said. "It just kind of hits you that you want to get back. Renee and I decided that we liked where we were living, but if the right opportunity ever came along, we'd like to get back to Madison. That's our home."

Pat couldn't see my reaction, but I was nodding my head in agreement. We knew we would like California and the *Los Angeles Times*. But we also knew that if the right opportunity ever came along, we'd jump at the chance to return home, too.

In one brief conversation, Richter had managed to listen, understand, and provide insight and direction. It was emblematic of a personality and a management style that served him so well for many years.

Unfortunately, the right opportunity didn't come along in a timely manner. I resigned my position and we returned to Madison. I didn't have a job, but I did have big plans to open my own public relations firm, helping clients deal with the media and other public relations assignments. Among the many people I met to discuss the new venture was Linda Weimer, who served as the director of university relations for UW chancellor Donna Shalala. It was Weimer who called and asked if I could assist her office in preparing some background information on trademark licensing, which was becoming a controversial local issue. The UW Board of Regents had an upcoming meeting to discuss the issue, and Weimer needed some assistance to brief the Regents in time.

It would be the last consulting assignment for my new public relations firm. In the weeks following that initial assignment, Weimer assigned additional work, and eventually she and vice chancellor for legal affairs Melany Newby hired me in December 1990, to be the school's first director of trademark licensing.

Nine months later, an even better opportunity came along. Shalala's efforts to help the Athletic Department rid itself of debt had taken shape with the addition of a student fee and campus parking surcharge, both of which bolstered a staggering financial picture for UW athletics. Additionally, she designated the revenues from the trademark licensing program to be used for athletics, and when the Athletic Department wanted to create a new marketing position, it turned to Newby and Weimer for permission to use some of that licensing money to fund the position in Athletics.

I suggested to Newby, and ultimately to Richter, that they didn't really need to hire another new person for the job, that I could handle those additional marketing duties. They both agreed, and in September 1991, I was named the Athletic Department's first director of marketing.

During my first week in Athletics, I found myself standing next to Al Fish, the department's chief administrative officer. It was just prior to kickoff on a sunny autumn afternoon, when the football Badgers were playing host to Western Illinois in their 1991 home opener. In those days, walk-up ticket sales were a key component in the athletic department's budget. A rainy day would dampen the walk-up crowd and would have a major negative impact. A sunny day would enhance and improve those sales and brighten the financial picture.

On this day, the walk-up numbers were significant. From our perch in the Communications Center, we could see long lines forming near the portable ticket booths in Lot 18 on the southeast side of Camp Randall Stadium. With kickoff time fast approaching, it was obvious that the ticket office staffing was not sufficient to handle the last-minute walk-ups. Moments later, Fish and I had left the press box, tracked down ticket director Tim Van Alstine, grabbed a handful of available tickets, and were circulating throughout the parking lot, selling tickets to the hundreds waiting in line. It was an unorthodox way for a Division 1-A football program to be selling tickets and clearly was a state auditor's nightmare, but at the time it seemed like the most logical way to address the situation.

It was the beginning of an exciting run with UW Athletics. In the previous 15 months, Richter, Fish, Joel Maturi, Cheryl Marra, and others in the athletic department had made significant strides. Barry Alvarez had given new life to the football program, and consequently, the entire department. Shalala's endless energy and unwavering support had presented bountiful opportunities. There continued to be significant challenges ahead, but it was clear that things were moving in a positive direction.

Over the next 13 years, my roles changed in Athletics, as I moved from director of marketing to associate athletic director to senior associate athletic director. During that entire time, I was fortunate to work closely with Pat Richter as he brought the UW Athletic Department back to life. He did it with style, grace, and dignity. He moved forward with creativity and a reliance on good common sense at every turn. He showed respect for all and the ability to listen and to understand.

In the weeks that followed Pat's February 14, 2003, announcement of his pending retirement, it occurred to me that the story of Pat Richter was one that needed to be told. His was a story of natural greatness, about remarkable accomplishment, and about doing things the right way. It was a story worth sharing and one that deserved to be passed along to future generations of Badgers.

I approached Pat in the fall of 2003 and told him that I wanted to write his biography. Initially, he showed no desire to move forward; in fact, he seemed surprised that I would even consider his life a topic for a book. "Who would want to read about that?" he asked.

In subsequent conversations, I reminded him of the fun and accomplishment that characterized his life, and how great it would be to share the story with Badger fans. Eventually, he agreed to go along with it. In the year that followed, we conducted approximately 25 interviews together. In each interview, Pat was open, honest, and frank about all of the events and topics we discussed. He talked with great pride and satisfaction about a journey, which to that point, to use his words, had been a wonderful life. Those extensive conversations, and our 13 years of working together in the UW Athletic Department, form the basis of this book.

There were other important conversations as well. Donna Shalala took time from her duties as president at the University of Miami not only to be interviewed but also to write a foreword for the book. Barry Alvarez was in his first year of juggling his new athletic director duties with his job as head football coach, but still found time to talk to me about his days with Pat Richter. Former UW Athletic Board chairs Roger Formisano and Jim Hoyt and retired sportswriter Tom Butler were generous with their time and their memories, as were Cheryl Marra, Al Fish, and Pat's wife, Renee Richter.

The staff at the archives division of the Wisconsin State Historical Society was quite helpful as I spent many months poring through the state's newspapers for the many stories about Richter. Dave Zweifel, editor of the *Capital Times*, and Dennis McCormick, the Cap Times' librarian and historian, were helpful in securing photos for the project, as was Bernie Shermetzler from UW-Madison Archives.

I greatly appreciate the opportunity that Pat Richter provided me in 1991, for in the years that followed, I had a great seat from which to watch one of Wisconsin's greatest sports legends conduct one of the most remarkable turnarounds in the history of collegiate athletics. It was a wild ride, and I enjoyed every minute along the way.

I want to thank Linda Weimer and Melany Newby for taking a chance on an unemployed journalist and hiring me as director of trademark licensing in 1990. I want to thank Donna Shalala for her great vision and leadership at Wisconsin. And I want to thank Fish, Maturi, and Marra for working their way through those difficult early times and building a solid foundation for those who followed.

I thank Coach Alvarez for all the hard work that he and the Badger football family put forth to make things better, and in later years, for allowing me to continue this ride as part of his senior administrative staff at the UW.

And thanks to Steve Malchow for reviewing the manuscript of this book and taking the time to listen to this rookie author throughout my book-writing journey.

Thank you to Lee Larsen of Larsen Photography in Madison for permission to use his photo portrait of Pat Richter, and to my editor at Trails Media Group, Mark Knickelbine.

A special thanks to the late Sonja Christensen and the late John Sheffield, two of my coworkers who are no longer with us to celebrate Richter's achievements and the success of the Badgers. Both Sonja and John had character and charisma and spirit, and we dearly miss them.

And I am grateful to my late father, Vince Sweeney Sr., who was born on a farm in nearby Fitchburg, Wisconsin, moved to the big city of Madison, married his sweetheart and raised a family in the shadows of Camp Randall Stadium. For decades, he and my mother, Ruth, rarely missed a home Badger football or basketball game. Thanks Dad, for setting a shining example to follow and for helping me appreciate the value of a hard day's work, good sportsmanship, and a hearty laugh.

And thank you to my mother, Ruth, who—in addition to her love for the Badgers—has been my biggest fan at every turn along the way. Mom, your seven children will forever be grateful for your undying love and devotion.

To my wonderful wife, Sharon, and our beautiful daughters, Kelsey and Keara, thank you for your continued love and support. Our journey together has been exhilarating. Thank you for always being there for me. You're the best!

Finally, a huge thank you to the hundreds of thousands of Wisconsin Badger fans whose support and loyalty have been nothing short of remarkable over the years. While it truly has been a pleasure to work for Pat Richter, it has been an even greater pleasure to work for you.

I hope you enjoy reading this book as much as I enjoyed sharing it with you. On Wisconsin!

—*Vince Sweeney*
Madison, Wisconsin
April, 2005

There are two things you can say about Pat Richter. He is from the East Side of Madison. And he is a Wisconsin Badger.

—*Former UW Athletic Board chair*
Roger Formisano

INTRODUCTION

Bear with me because you go through these only once in your life. I am talking about retirement. I have decided to step down and retire as of April 1, 2004 . . . I would like to thank Donna Shalala for the opportunity to serve as athletic director at the University of Wisconsin. I would not be doing this at any other school in the country. I love this university and the people that support our mission to be the best. Growing up in Madison, I always wanted to be a Badger and was fortunate enough to be given that opportunity. I enjoyed being a student-athlete and a Badger.

> —*Pat Richter's opening comments at*
> *February 14, 2003 press conference*

Growing up in Madison during the late 1950s and 1960s, if you had any kind of interest in sports, then Pat Richter was likely one of your local heroes, a superb athlete who was the center of sports conversations at the city's playgrounds and schoolyards.

He began making a name for himself on the local sports scene at Madison East High School, where he helped the Purgolders win the 1958 WIAA state basketball championship, edging city rival West, led by future Badger teammate Jim Bakken, in the semifinals.

A year later, Richter's list of accomplishments grew as he earned all-city honors in both football and basketball at East.

Later, there was the time when Richter, while playing for the Monona Grove Lakers in the city's summer baseball league during his early college days, was said to have hit a home run at historic Breese Stevens Field that reached the

football scoreboard in deep left field on one bounce. The scoreboard was estimated to be 500 feet from home plate.

Or the time when Richter, a sophomore making his much-anticipated first
appearance as a University of Wisconsin football player, stepped in, caught seven
passes, and set a school record against host Stanford University.

Or the time that Richter hit a two-out, two-run home run to defeat Michigan
and prevent the Wolverines from winning the Big Ten Championship.

Or the time Richter caught 11 passes for 163 yards and one touchdown in
what is still remembered today as one of the most entertaining football games
ever, the Badgers' 42–37 loss to USC in the 1963 Rose Bowl.

Or the time Richter scored a 73-yard touchdown to lead the College All-Stars
to a 20–17 victory over Vince Lombardi's Green Bay Packers.

The stories continued to grow, as did the legend of Pat Richter.

Years later, Richter would interrupt an advancing corporate career at Oscar
Mayer Food Corporation and accept the job of director of intercollegiate athletics
at the University of Wisconsin. He would take over a program that was $2.1 mil-
lion in debt and struggling to stay afloat in the Big Ten Conference. Nearly 15 years
later, he would leave behind a program that had eliminated its huge debt and built
$7 million in reserve, achieved unthinkable results in football and men's basket-
ball, and remains among the nation's leaders in overall fan attendance.

To those who remember some of those long-ago stories about Richter's
younger-day accomplishments, his success as a college administrator did not
come as a surprise. Even so, the extent of that success was quite remarkable.

Some say that part of Pat Richter's legacy was this: No matter what the situation, Pat usually found a way to achieve success. More often than not, the
things that Pat Richter touched turned to gold.

In the weeks leading up to a March 2, 2004 retirement dinner in salute of
Pat Richter, UW officials were working hard to make the necessary adjustments
to the program planned for that night, where nearly 700 would gather to salute
the retiring Richter and his wife, Renee. The event date was selected because it
proved to be the only time prior to Richter's April 1 retirement date that former
chancellors David Ward and Donna Shalala could be present. The problem,
however, was that the men's basketball team had a game scheduled that night at
Michigan State. Big Ten Conference officials had yet to notify the UW of the
starting time of the game, so the event planners had two different plans, one for
an early start of the game, another for a late start. Less than two weeks before
the event, it was learned that the starting time would be 6:00 p.m.

With television screens set up throughout the Monona Terrace Convention
Center's exhibit hall, those gathered to honor Pat and Renee Richter were total-

ly focused on watching the underdog Badgers fight hard to stay close to the mighty Spartans. The excitement grew as the minutes passed. A Michigan State victory would earn the Spartans at least a tie for the Big Ten Conference championship and eliminate the Badgers' hope for the same.

As the game grew longer, event planners were concerned that the evening's program was being pushed back much later than anticipated and they were anxious to get the event moving. Yet, they knew that they had to wait until the game had been completed. The delay continued as the Badgers sent the game into overtime, much to the delight of the well-dressed and upbeat Badger fans at Monona Terrace. Finally, the place erupted in celebration as the Badgers completed the overtime upset of the Spartans.

As the program began, UW officials made arrangements for Badger coach Bo Ryan to call the Monona Terrace to address the crowd and salute the Richters.

It was a night when a lot of things could have gone wrong. A late start to the program along with a disappointing loss to the Spartans could have led to a long night at Monona Terrace. Instead, as master of ceremonies Marsh Shapiro proclaimed to the crowd as they sat down for dinner after the Badger victory, "How's that for good planning!"

It was vintage Pat Richter—it couldn't have turned out any better.

Earlier in the day, the feisty *Capital Times*, Madison's evening newspaper, not known for lavishing praise on the university for its modern-day movement into "big-time" college athletics, published the following editorial:

Pat Richter is a true son of Wisconsin and a true son of Madison.

So it should come as no surprise that so many Wisconsinites, and so many Madisonians, are so very excited about joining in tonight's celebration of Richter's long and distinguished career.

Wisconsin's soon-to-be retired athletic director will be honored at a gala dinner and program at Monona Terrace, during which his nearly 15 years at the helm will be recalled and toasted as they should be.

Richter is the quintessential success story, the local boy who made good. But he is more than that. He is the local boy who proved that a great university can also have a great athletic program. That was the charge handed to him by the UW–Madison chancellor at the time, Donna Shalala, when she lured him from his comfortable job at Oscar Mayer in 1989 to take over a debt-ridden and demoralized Athletic Department.

When Shalala tapped Richter, it was a popular choice. Wisconsin sports fans had keen memories of him—from the days when the teenager from Yahara Place was an All-State multisports star at Madison East High School, to his three-sport career at the UW itself, to his professional football days with the Washington Redskins.

Of course, the popular choice does not always turn out to be the right choice. But in Richter's case, the popular choice happened to be possessed of administrative skills that allowed him to quickly and ably tackle the daunting task that faced him.

Richter started by hiring an assistant Notre Dame coach named Barry Alvarez to take over the football program. That hire was crucial because the financial well-being of the entire department rested on it. Three Rose Bowl victories and six other bowl appearances once again filled the stands and put the Athletic Department in the black.

The Alvarez hire was not dumb luck. Richter hired three great basketball coaches—Stu Jackson, Dick Bennett, and Bo Ryan—and they turned a mediocre program into a nationally prominent one.

Richter raised the bar not only on the fields of play, but around them. The basketball team now plays in a state-of-the-art arena, there's a new track and softball facility and Camp Randall's renovation is well under way.

There's been a price, of course. Seat licensing and ticket prices have skyrocketed, but that's the cost that universities must pay if they are to compete in a culture that overemphasizes the importance of sports. Richter dealt with those issues openly and fairly.

To be sure, there were bumps along the way, including the overblown "Shoe Box" scandal that brought the UW sanctions because athletes received discounts on shoes at a store 25 miles from campus, and the time Richter gave bonuses to his coaches without first getting the chancellor's OK. But those incidents pale in comparison to the cheating and payola scandals that have marked many NCAA programs through the years.

This newspaper still feels that his decision to drop baseball as a UW sport was wrong. But Richter deserves praise for finally equalizing men's and women's sports opportunities, a long and frustrating endeavor that got the school out from under a cloud.

Above all, it is important to note that Pat Richter is a principled and honorable leader. He never let his successes or position go to his head. He accepted speaking engagements, volunteered at school and community functions, made himself accessible to fans from all walks of life, and made us all proud that he was a part of our university.

He and his wife, Renee, have earned a happy and long retirement and best wishes from a grateful city and a grateful state. But, knowing Richter, we fully expect that he will still make a little more history. He does not seem to know how to stop contributing. So it is our bet that, even in retirement, Pat Richter will continue to be a star.

CHAPTER ONE
GROWING UP
IN MADISON

As he grew up on Madison's Near East Side, Sundays were special for young Hugh Vernon Richter Jr., later to be known by most as Pat. That's when Pat, his two sisters, and their parents would visit his grandparents' house on East Johnson Street, just across from Emerson School. It was there that Pat's grandparents, Henry and Nellie Richter, would serve up a special treat for the entire family—Canadian bacon, fresh from Oscar Mayer Company.

The Oscar Mayer Company, founded in Chicago in 1883 and moved to Madison in 1919, was one of several growing companies that helped expand Madison's job base beyond state government and the university. Years later, the company would play a key role in young Pat Richter's professional life, as it had first played a key role in the life of Pat's grandfather, Henry Richter, who worked for several years in the peddle truck sales area at Oscar Mayer. The grandson says he doesn't remember all of what grandpa Henry did at Oscar, but he does recall that he once was honored for safely driving his Mack truck over 700,000 miles without an accident. Pat also remembers Henry showing him several Weinermobile whistles and pencils with Oscar Mayer logos. Promotional items like that are commonplace for many businesses these days, but not so in the late 1940s and early 1950s; a young Pat Richter was impressed.

Grandpa Henry Richter, also known as "Hank," was born in Montfort, Wisconsin, a farming community 55 miles west of Madison. He would marry Nellie Bjerke, also of Montfort. The youngest of their three children was Hugh Vernon, born on Saint Patrick's Day, March 17, 1918. That birth date led not only to Hugh's nickname of Pat, but would also lead to the same nickname for their future grandson.

In the mid-1920s, when Hugh Vernon Richter Sr. was in third grade, the Richters moved to Madison, where he would grow up to be an accomplished athlete on Madison's growing East Side. At Madison East High School in the 1930s, he played football, basketball, and baseball. At East, he was an All-City and All-State football player, as well as an accomplished ice boater. Unfortunately, he lost sight in one eye as a result of an injury suffered in a basketball game. At one time, he had plans to attend the University of Wisconsin and play football for Coach Harry Stuhldreher. Instead, Hugh graduated mid-year from East in 1935 and went to work in the foundry at Gisholt Machine and Foundry Company on Madison's Near East Side.

At East, Hugh Vernon Richter met Mary Alice Thompson, who lived near Marquette School on nearby Baldwin Street, just west of the Yahara River. Her father, Arthur Thompson, was an accomplished amateur golfer who worked for Rayovac. Her mother, the former Gladys Scott, had a great uncle named Bill Scott. In later years, Pat Richter would remember that family discussions often surmised that the he and his family were descendents of the legendary Sir Walter Scott.

Hugh Vernon and Mary Alice married and would live on Rutledge Street, just east of the Yahara River. Their first child, Hugh Vernon Jr., was born on September 9, 1941. One year later, daughter Randi was born, and five years later, another daughter, Jane, was born in 1947.

Hugh Vernon Richter Jr.—who would come to be known as Little Pat—first remembers playing sports at age seven, when his father—Big Pat—installed a low basket on the family's garage. As the years passed, Richter would alternate between playing basketball in the family's driveway and at the playground area between Yahara Place and Lake Monona. He signed up to play youth baseball in the Madison School District's City League program, and moved at age 10 from the competition in Midget League to the higher-level Junior League.

In those days, baseball was king among sports-minded youth during a Madison summertime. A well-organized program operated by Madison School & Community Recreation had youngsters playing baseball at city parks throughout Madison. The program's organizers also had a plan to supply the city's newspapers with scores and highlights, and as a result, the coverage was extensive, with articles and photos as a regular feature in the sports section on the days following competitions.

Friends and neighbors would form teams, register with the league's headquarters, and then try to solicit a sponsor that would provide the team with money to purchase T-shirts, bats, and balls. One of Richter's classmates was Lester Thomsen, whose father, P. B. Thomsen, had purchased Schoep's Grocery in 1940 and began wholesaling ice cream throughout the Midwest. During that time, the teams sponsored by Schoep's always had the reputation of being the best on the East Side, and young Pat Richter was thrilled to join the squad.

When the team won its games, the players rode their bikes over to Schoep's, where the victory celebration included a free Popsicle or Drumstick for each of the players in attendance.

The summer youth baseball season culminated with playoffs, and ultimately, with the best-of-three meeting of east-side champion versus west-side champion at beloved Breese Stevens Field. For city youth, it was their Williamsport, their World Series.

At the time, Breese Stevens Field was one of the finest municipal athletic facilities in the Midwest and an impressive sign of Madison's continued growth and economic expansion. Built in 1925, the facility's original grandstand was designed in a Mediterranean Revival style. The walls around the facility are constructed of sandstone, which, according to the Madison Trust for Historic Preservation, was quarried from the former city quarry at Hoyt Park on the city's Near West Side. The walls and concrete bleachers were added in 1934 and the wooden press box was built in 1939. For several decades, the facility served as Madison's major athletic complex, hosting high school football, professional wrestling, and All-City fast pitch softball championships. As recently as 2000, it was the site of the state high school soccer championships.

More importantly for Pat Richter and the other youngsters now privileged to play there in the city youth league baseball championship, Breese Stevens Field also served as the city's premier baseball site. That's where the city's best baseball players competed. In the early 1940s, it served as home for the Madison Blues, a semipro team. For at least one year, the team was an affiliate of the Milwaukee Brewers of the American Association. On rare occasions, major-league baseball came to town when the Chicago Cubs would travel to Madison and play an exhibition games at Breese Stevens Field. Its short right-field fence, bordering on East Washington Avenue, gave the park a unique characteristic, much like the legendary Green Monster in left field at Boston's Fenway Park.

In 1952, Pat Richter's youth baseball team advanced to the city championship series at Breese Stevens. Richter's east-side teammates on the Schoep's team that year included the likes of Dave Goff, Dickie Karls, Don Hahn, Sonny Hill, Alan Pauls, Ron Hastings, and Donny Pond. Their west-side opponents—Borden's—included flame throwing right-hander John Braun, who years later would sign a professional contract with the Milwaukee Braves organization. All of the participants were provided a sneak preview of Pat Richter's athletic future, as the 10-year-old blasted a triple to the right-field wall and helped his team defeat Borden's to win the city championship.

Baseball continued to be important to a young and impressionable Pat Richter. The following year, he was asked to serve as batboy for the Bowman

Dairy team, a collection of the city's finest amateur baseball players. Their coach and general manager was Gene Calhoun, who years later would become a key advisor to Richter. In 1953, Bowman Dairy won the state championship and celebrated by attending a Green Bay Packers game at Milwaukee County Stadium. And Richter took it all in.

Baseball teammate and neighborhood friend Sonny Hill was three years older than Richter and, like many of his age group in those days, worked as a newspaper delivery boy for Madison Newspapers, Inc., publishers of the *Capital Times* and the *Wisconsin State Journal*.

In those days, there were several key elements to having a paper route. The first was gathering and preparing the papers for delivery. The papers were usually delivered by Madison Newspapers, Inc. in a large bundle at a nearby street corner, in this case, the corner just outside the Hi-Lo Grocery Store. The papers were then unbundled and each was folded individually in preparation for delivery. There were a variety of ways to fold the paper; Richter employed the Tomahawk Fold method, but you had to be careful when you tossed them toward the front porches throughout the neighborhood: "Too tight and it could sail on you and go right through a window," Richter said.

The "administrative" part of the paper route involved the task of going house to house and collecting payment from those same customers.

"Sonny told me, 'Look, if you collect the money, I'll deliver the newspapers,'" Richter said. "Little did I realize that you had to collect every week. People were paying 25 and 30 cents a week. Heck, if they paid for the entire month, you were ecstatic.

"I quickly realized that the older and wiser Sonny was giving me the short end of the stick," Richter laughed.

He eventually would deliver and collect for both newspapers. Nearly every week, Richter and some of his Marquette Elementary School friends would hop on the bus and venture "downtown" to the offices of Madison Newspapers, then located just off the Capitol Square. After turning in his collection proceeds and retaining his modest share of income, Richter would venture around the corner to Wisconsin Felton, a local sporting goods store. Richter would walk the first floor of the store, admiring the new Wilson baseball gloves—on sale for $19.95—or the new baseballs, going for $3.95 each. Then, to top off the visit, he'd head downstairs to view the many shelves filled with shiny new wooden baseball bats.

While there, he'd listen in on the local sports stories told by Wisconsin Felton's Archie Morrow, Dutch Midland, and Lowell LaMore. And he'd do the same while visiting Badger Sporting Goods on State Street, where former Badger legend Johnny Kotz and John Roach and Dutch Leonard held court and covered most all of the sports topics of the day, and where hundreds and hundreds of new baseball bats filled the basement shelves.

For Richter, these were simple, uncomplicated days when you could hop on your bicycle and ride on an uncongested East Washington Avenue over to Central High School or Burr Jones Field, where UW baseball coach Dynie Mansfield and his assistants, Fritz Wegner and Jack Nowka, were holding youth baseball clinics. Sometimes, you'd stop by Breese Stevens and watch as groundskeeper Cliff Atkinson groomed the field. Other times, you'd stop by Mick's Pharmacy on East Johnson Street, because the word was that Mick's had the best baseball cards, and if you were looking for a Willie Mays or a Ted Williams, Mick's seemed to have them.

Richter remembers riding his bike to Wolff Kubly and Hirsig, a hardware store on the Capitol Square, where Badger stars John Coatta and Darrel Teteak were signing autographs.

When Pat was 12, the Richters moved from Rutledge Street to nearby Yahara Place. Their new home was a bit closer to the Lake Monona shoreline and across from a small, narrow park, which became Richter's home field for baseball, football, and other neighborhood games. Baseball continued to become Richter's favorite sport. At the park, which was about 40 yards wide, you learned to hit the ball up the middle. If you hit it to left, the ball went into the houses; to the right, and it went into the lake, and if you hit it in the lake it was your job to retrieve it.

While the park's layout was not conducive to a normal game of baseball, its long, narrow format was well-suited for football. On autumn afternoons, after a Badger or Packer game broadcast on the radio, there were usually enough neighborhood kids to put together a football game at the park. Richter recalls one of the coolest things about the games to be the many nicknames that were tossed around. "Fred the Midget." "Hugh the Beast." And Richter? He was known simply as "The Phantom."

Several other sporting activities filled Richter's younger years. Ice skating at the Tenney Park lagoon. Riding the toboggan slide at Olbrich Park. Boating and water-skiing behind the family's 10-horsepower Mercury-powered boat. Basketball games at neighbor Tom Rich's house or at the Lakewood School playground in Maple Bluff or, if you were lucky, in the school's gymnasium.

One of Richter's neighbors was Gary Messner, a star athlete at Madison East who went on to play football at Wisconsin, where he would become an All-Big Ten lineman and team captain in 1954. Messner, at offensive center, was perhaps best known for opening holes for Wisconsin's first Heisman Trophy winner, Alan Ameche.

And while most of Richter's sports world was his neighborhood, the big university down the road began to attract some of his interest. Richter recalls one of his first memories of Camp Randall was when Ohio State and their 1950 Heisman Trophy winner, Vic Janowicz, came to town. The Badgers held Janowicz to 11 yards on 11 carries en route to a 6–6 tie, lending credence to the defense's nickname of "The Hard Rocks." A young Pat Richter was impressed.

Messner helped to further strengthen the connection between Richter and the hometown Badgers. Occasionally, Messner would have some of his Badger teammates visit his house, just five houses from the Richters. He'd call Richter and other neighborhood friends and invite them over to meet some of the players— including the legendary Ameche—and get some autographs.

After completing sixth grade at Marquette School, Richter moved to East beginning seventh grade, where he began to build his loyalty to the Purgolders and continued his growing attachment to the Badgers. One of East High School's finest athletes, Dale Hackbart, was three years ahead of Richter and eventually moved on to play quarterback and linebacker for Wisconsin, and later, with the Green Bay Packers, Washington Redskins, and Minnesota Vikings of the National Football League.

As a freshman at East, Pat Richter now stood 6 feet 2 inches tall, weighed 185 pounds, and played tackle on the Purgolder freshman football team. He was moved to end as a sophomore, but despite the occasional punt he saw limited action on the varsity. It wasn't until his junior season at East that Pat Richter, future All-American tight end, began playing regularly for East's football team. That season, Richter caught two touchdown passes and kicked 11 extra points for East. His senior year, he scored four touchdowns and booted 15 extra points.

Basketball was much the same as football. Richter participated on the freshman and sophomore teams, improving steadily but not dramatically. It was dur-

Pat Richter (51) drives toward the basket in the 1958 State Championship game against Milwaukee North. East defeated North to win the state title. Photo courtesy of *The Wisconsin State Journal*.

ing his junior season at East that Richter experienced the highlight of his high school athletic career. Richter, now a starting center on the varsity team, scored only 89 points in Big Eight Conference play, but it was enough to help the Purgolders to a share the conference title with Madison West. In the postseason, Richter led his team in rebounds as they defeated West and then Milwaukee North to win the 1958 state championship at the UW Field House.

"He impressed scouts with the way he could take the ball off the defensive board and lead East's fast break," wrote *Wisconsin State Journal* sportswriter Tom Butler.

As a senior basketball player, Richter led the Big Eight Conference in scoring with 237 points and was named All-Conference as well as the Big Eight's Most Valuable Player. Unfortunately, East wasn't able to put together a postseason run like it did in 1958, losing to eventual state champion Milwaukee Lincoln 75–73 in a sectional game. In the season finale the next day, Richter scored a school-record 50 points in a consolation game against Cuba City.

At that point, baseball was still Richter's best sport. During his high school summers, Richter now played for the prestigious Monona Grove Lakers, a semi-pro baseball team managed by *Capital Times* sportswriter Lew Cornelius. The Lakers would come to be known as the who's who of amateur baseball in Madison, to include Hackbart, Bakken, former University of Iowa basketball coach Tom Davis, Rick Reichardt, Ron Steiner, Mike Cloutier, Dennis Sweeney, Tom Handford, and others.

Despite the annual plateful of summer baseball, Richter still found time for a summer job. Jon Ward lived three doors down from the Richters, and Ward's parents, Guy and Ruth Ward, owned a local drive-in called the Monona Drive In, better known as the Hungry Hungry. During his teen years, Richter and close friend John Moore worked for the Wards at the drive-in, earning $1.10 per hour. There, they donned the standard employee garb of white pants, T-shirt, and paper hat and dished out malts, cones, sundaes, floats, soft-serve ice cream, and the drive-in's specialty—curly fries. To this day, Richter proclaims that the Hungry Hungry, with its curly fries and all, could have been a prototype for a nationwide franchise. "It could have been McDonald's," Richter said.

After his junior year at East, Richter began receiving letters from college recruiters. Initially, he had a keen interest in attending the Air Force Academy, but eventually found out that his poor eyesight would prevent him from meeting the necessary requirements for admission.

As a senior at East, Richter earned All-City honors in football and basketball. And while the interest from recruiters continued to grow, Richter chose to limit his interest to basketball; the only college visit Richter scheduled was an official visit to the University of Kansas in the spring of 1959.

"I wasn't taken to, nor did I ask to go into their basketball facility," Richter recalled. "I went to a Kansas City Royals baseball game and thought, 'This is great. Where do I sign?' I think I was enamored about being away from home."

Whatever the motivation, Richter signed a letter of intent with Kansas and was to receive a basketball scholarship from the Jayhawks.

The news didn't sit well back home in Madison, where many Badger fans were disappointed that the local standout wouldn't be attending the UW. Among those who talked with Richter upon his return from Kansas was Gene Calhoun, who had "hired" Richter as a batboy for his Bowman Dairy teams and become a close friend and advisor.

Pat Richter (third from left) and his Madison East teammates celebrate their 1958 state championship. Photo courtesy of *The Wisconsin State Journal.*

"Gene told me that if I was really interested in playing baseball, the Big Eight isn't a very good baseball conference and Kansas really isn't a very good baseball school," Richter said. "He essentially told me that I'd be better off in the Big Ten."

Richter mulled it over and decided to call Kansas and tell them that he had changed his mind and would not be enrolling there. In the meantime, UW men's basketball coach John Erickson was called, and a meeting was set up at the Cathay House restaurant on East Washington Avenue. When Erickson sat down with Pat Richter and his father, Hugh, it wasn't a difficult sell. Erickson offered Richter a basketball scholarship to play for the Badgers, and Richter signed on the spot.

With his choice of colleges completed, Richter continued playing a full schedule of summer baseball with the Lakers and worked in the cooler section at Borden's Dairy. He also spent some leisure time hanging out on the Capitol Square like hundreds of other Madison area teenagers. During one of those summer nights, Richter ran into UW assistant football coach Fred Jacoby, who had come to the square to shop at Rundell's Clothing Store. Richter said hello to the coach, then asked if he thought UW basketball coach John Erickson would be upset if Richter chose to play football for the Badgers as well as basketball. Jacoby agreed to ask Erickson, who allegedly told the UW football staff that as long as Pat Richter was at Wisconsin, Erickson didn't care how many sports he played.

CHAPTER TWO
OFFICIALLY A BADGER

In September 1959, Pat Richter officially became a Badger when he entered his freshman year at the University of Wisconsin. He was receiving a partial scholarship—not a full scholarship—because his athletic scholarship was based on need. Pat's father, who now was a longtime employee at Gisholt, was making just enough money to prevent Pat from receiving a full scholarship.

Richter lived in Adams Hall, an older dormitory near the UW Crew House and the Lake Mendota shoreline. His roommate in Room 401 Richardson at Adams Hall was another student-athlete, 6 foot 5 inch basketball player Nick Brod from Huron, South Dakota. Madison restaurateur Fran Hoffman, owner of the Hoffman House, and his friend Joe Fedele, were frequent visitors to South Dakota, where they went pheasant hunting and became close friends with Nick Brod's parents. During one of the Brods' summertime visits to Madison, they introduced Nick to Pat Richter, and the two became freshman roommates at Adams Hall.

As a freshman football player, Pat Richter played tight end on offense and linebacker on defense. Pat O'Donahue, one of the members of the Badgers' legendary Hard Rocks defense in 1951, served as Richter's freshman coach. At the time, freshmen were not eligible to compete on varsity, so each Monday that followed a Saturday varsity game, the freshmen would play the varsity reserves in a scrimmage.

Richter remembers one Monday scrimmage in particular because it included a moment of uncharacteristic behavior—a day when Pat Richter lost his composure. On this particular afternoon, Richter was playing defensive line, across from fellow Badger tight end Butch Kellogg. On one play, as Kellogg broke across the line of scrimmage to block Richter, Kellogg's elbow came up and hit Richter, whose elbow subsequently came upward as well. Another elbow from Kellogg and then another from Richter.

"The next thing I know," Richter recalled, "I have my fist back ready to take a swing, and then I did. He had one of those single-bar face masks and I barely missed the bar and hit him in the face and he went down. The next day, I found out that he had a broken nose. I was lucky. If I would have hit his face mask, I would have broken my hand."

Dale Hackbart was the varsity quarterback for the 1959 Badgers. While perhaps not a national powerhouse, the team was coming off an impressive 7-1-1 campaign in 1958 and was ranked eighth in the country at the start of the season.

After nonconference victories over Stanford and Marquette, the 1959 Badgers lost 21–0 to Purdue, then won four straight conference games, including a 24–19 victory over second-ranked Northwestern. After losing 9–6 to unranked Illinois at home, the Badgers rallied to defeat Minnesota 11–7 and earn a trip to the 1960 Rose Bowl.

Unfortunately, the Badgers did not fare well in Pasadena, losing 44–8 to Washington on New Year's Day. "I still see guys on that team," Richter said. "You ask them what time it is, and they'll all say, 'It's 44–8.'"

Richter's freshman teammates included Merritt Norvell, Dion Kempthorne, Ron Carlson, Gary Kroner, and Ken Montgomery. Bob Franken, now an award-winning White House correspondent for CNN, was a member of that team. At the end of the season, teammate Dale Matthews and Richter would be voted team co-captains. Matthews later would marry Richter's sister Randi.

On campus, Richter took a brief look at pledging a fraternity, but decided to not follow through. The transition from high school to college was not a difficult one for Richter. Living close to home, Richter could exit and enter campus life quite smoothly and conveniently, and as such, there were plenty of visits "back home" to the Near East Side.

He also enjoyed visiting Gisholt Machine and Foundry, where his father had been employed since 1935. Those visits to the foundry led Richter to take an early interest in studying metallurgical engineering at Wisconsin, although during his freshman year, his schoolwork was limited to a variety of introductory courses.

As freshman football season wound down, basketball was next in line. Again, freshmen were not eligible to compete at the time, so much of Richter's freshman basketball season was spent scrimmaging his teammates and the varsity reserves. Two sprained ankle injuries hampered Richter's development that year. His freshman teammates included Tom Gwyn, Ken Siebel, John Stone, Lonny Ostrom, Ron Jackson, Gary Hobbs, Don Patterson, Nick Brod, and Tom Black. Richter described the group as close-knit. "We don't have a lot of contact with each other," he said, "but we're still close."

While football and basketball had freshman teams, baseball did not. So the spring of Richter's freshman year was spent on the football field in spring practice. In spring football, the freshman were merged with the returning upperclassmen, and the many spring practices culminated with an alumni game, where former Badger football players would compete with the current squad. Among the alums returning were likely to be some current professional players, which at times provided some interesting matchups.

"Since football was a two-way system back then, they put all of the tight ends on defense and had us play defensive line," Richter said. "I remember being an undersized defensive lineman trying to rush the passer against a guy named John Dittrich. He was a big, strong guy who had played guard for the Chicago Cardinals and for the Packers. I was a skinny, 6 foot 5 inch defensive lineman trying to rush the passer against this guy. He got his helmet underneath my chin, and to this day, I still have a double scar under my chin to remind me of that."

Much to his delight, that would prove to be Richter's only spring football practice during his collegiate career at Wisconsin. In subsequent years, Richter would spend the springtime playing a noncontact sport—Big Ten baseball for the Wisconsin Badgers.

There were no formal off-season weight training programs for any of the sports in which Richter participated, so much of his summertime was spent playing baseball and working for Grignano Construction in Madison. Once again, Richter was a member of the prestigious Monona Grove Lakers, with teammates Hackbart, Bakken, Ron Steiner, Dennis Howe, Rick Reichardt, Mike Rieder, Mike Sweeney, Dennis Sweeney, Mike Simon, John Braun, Al Schroeder, Tom Handford, and others, including Tom Davis, a talented infielder from Ridgeway, Wisconsin. Davis would later become one of the most successful college basketball coaches of his time, winning nearly 600 games at such schools as Boston College, Stanford, and Iowa. It was a baseball team that seldom lost, and one that advanced to the 1960 state amateur championship game at Milwaukee County Stadium.

Built in 1953, Milwaukee County Stadium was still a relatively new major league baseball park. Situated in the Menomonee Valley on Milwaukee's West Side, the park was home to the Milwaukee Braves, who had moved from Boston to Milwaukee in 1953. That first season, the Braves drew an astounding 1,826,927 fans—the National League record for single-season attendance. Led by future Hall of Famers Hank Aaron, Eddie Mathews, and Warren Spahn, the Braves thrilled the big crowds who came to County Stadium to see major league baseball in the beer city. Four years later, the Braves' right-hander Lew Burdette would win three games and help the Braves defeat the New York Yankees four games to two, and win the 1957 World Series.

The thrill of playing at Milwaukee County Stadium—site of the 1957 World Series—was not lost on Richter and his Monona Grove teammates, no matter how it played out.

"I remember playing right field and Walter 'Bunky' Holt, who played baseball and basketball for the Badgers, hit a line drive—a frozen rope—toward me in right field at County Stadium," Richter recalled with a grin. "I took one step in and it sailed right over my head." Despite Richter's defensive gaffe, the Lakers went on to win the state championship and advance to the National Baseball Congress championships in Wichita. Richter, however, stayed behind—it was time to begin practice in preparation for the start of his varsity college football career at the University of Wisconsin.

* * *

In late August, Richter would again report to the lakeshore dorms, where the football team would be quartered during training camp. On the day he arrived, he did not have an assigned room, so he wandered down the hall and poked his head into a room where he found upperclassmen Tom Wiesner and Hank Derleth.

"There were three beds and only two guys," Richter recalled. "So I said, 'Hey, do you mind if I stay here with you?' I think they were a little bit shocked, but they said it was OK. Turns out they were the cocaptains, and normally, the cocaptains would get a room to themselves. And if they did have a roommate, it certainly isn't typically an underclassman like me.

"I guess they must have figured that they could come home with me and get some extra food and a home-cooked meal," Richter said.

Football training camp went well for sophomore Richter, as he earned a starting spot on Coach Milt Bruhn's double-tight-end system. Richter's role was more as a receiving tight end, where Derleth's role at the other tight end position was primarily as a blocker.

In Wisconsin's season-opening 24–7 victory at Stanford, Richter set a school record with seven pass receptions for 75 yards. In the home opener the following week, the Badgers played host to in-state rival Marquette. For several years, the Warriors (later known as the Golden Eagles) and the Badgers met in an early season nonconference game at Camp Randall. Over the years, the two schools met 36 times, including every year since 1932. But this would be the last meeting, as Marquette dropped its football program after the 1960 season.

Richter continued to play a key role as a pass-receiving tight end for the Badgers, catching three passes for 62 yards in a 35–6 victory over Marquette,

Pat Richter and UW football coach Milt Bruhn. Photo courtesy of the UW Athletic Department.

whose roster included Milwaukee native Karl Kassulke; Kassulke would later transfer to Drake and then move on to the NFL, where he played 10 seasons for the Minnesota Vikings. Marquette's publicity director at the time was a young Bob Harlan, who later would become president of the Green Bay Packers and a good friend of Pat Richter.

The following week was the Big Ten opener for the Badgers. Richter matched his record-setting performance at Stanford with another seven pass receptions for 110 yards in a 24–13 victory over seventh-ranked Purdue on Dads' Day at Camp Randall Stadium. The Dads' Day celebration—later to become known as Parents' Day—included on-field introductions of the fathers of the players. Hugh Richter, however, was hospitalized with a gallbladder problem, and was unable to participate.

Second-ranked Iowa was next, and the Hawkeyes posed a difficult challenge, particularly on their home field at Iowa City. Wisconsin, down 21–7 in the fourth quarter, managed to rally and tie the game at 21–21, but the Hawkeyes scored on a deflected pass late in the fourth quarter to secure the win, 28–21. The nation's pollsters must have been impressed, as the victory vaulted Iowa into the number one ranking the following week. Richter was held to two catches for 15 yards in the loss.

The following week, in a 34–7 loss to ninth-ranked Ohio State, Richter caught five passes for 64 yards. He now had caught 24 passes on the season for

13

326 yards. As the Badgers entered their Homecoming game against Michigan on October 29, Richter needed just one more catch to tie Jerry Witt's school record for pass receptions in a season (25), and was within striking distance of breaking Dave Schreiner's record for most receiving yards in a season (386).

Curiously, the rivalry between the Badgers and the Wolverines was slow to develop over the years. In fact, this game would mark only the 25th time the two teams had met and the first time since 1947 that Michigan had played at Wisconsin. Incredibly, the Badgers had never defeated Michigan at Camp Randall Stadium.

Against Michigan, Richter's first pass reception came on the third play of the game—it was a long pass play on which Wolverine defender Benny McRae tackled Richter from behind just as he caught the ball. It turned out to be a 36-yard gain, but a big loss for the Badgers.

"He wrapped his arms around mine so when I hit the ground, I turned on my shoulder," Richter said. "When I went back to the huddle, it felt a little awkward. I put my hand inside my shoulder pads and ran it along the bone, and it just dropped off. Someone in the huddle asked 'What's wrong' and I just said, 'I broke my collarbone.'"

Richter turned, left the huddle, and walked toward the bench. He didn't stop there. He walked straight up the tunnel to the locker room and was taken to University Hospital.

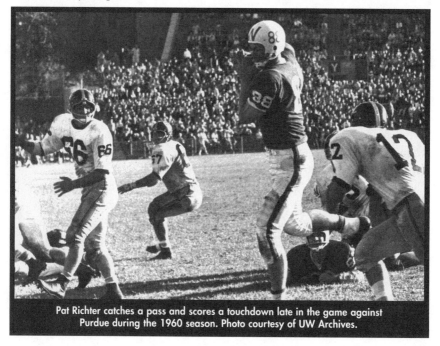

Pat Richter catches a pass and scores a touchdown late in the game against Purdue during the 1960 season. Photo courtesy of UW Archives.

Legendary columnist Roundy Coughlin of the *Wisconsin State Journal* wrote of the injury: "Then Pat Richter was hurt and was helped into the dressing room and the gloom in the Wisconsin section was thicker than free loaders at the opening of a new tavern."

The Badgers managed to defeat the Wolverines 16–13, but the injury ended Richter's season and put a halt to his record-setting receiving efforts. While he did tie the season reception record, he fell short of Schreiner's record for pass-receiving yards.

The game also became a milestone of another sort—the day marked the first date between Richter and Renee Sengstock, who, years later, would become his wife.

"I had noticed her walking on campus," Richter said. "She was walking with a girl named Barb Voss, who I knew was dating Brad Armstrong. Brad was from Janesville and was someone who we had played against in high school and who was on our freshman football team. I said to Brad that Barb knows this girl, so how about if she could make an informal introduction and tell her that I would see her sometime at the 'Pharm.' If she comes in, then I'll have a chance to say hello or whatever and at least she'll know who I am."

The Pharm, also known as Rennie's, was one of several drugstores owned by Rennebohm Drug Stores, Inc. in the Madison area. The Pharm, located in the heart of campus at 676 State Street, represented a gathering place for hundreds of UW students over the years. The "Ask Abe Archives" on the Wisconsin Alumni Association's Web site carries on the memories for alums who spent time at State and Lake during their college years: "The Pharm brings to mind heavily buttered grilled Danishes, famous chili, phosphate drinks, Bucky burgers, pink plastic dishes, speckled red counter stools, slippery Formica booths, and an entirely different era."

A drug store still exists at the location today, but it was long ago transformed from Rennebohm's to Walgreens. It no longer offers grill and soda fountain service, and while it is still a busy place, a visitor would scarcely guess that it was once considered the social hub of the lower campus.

While it didn't take Richter long to develop his plan to meet Renee, the implementation of that plan was not without a hitch. Barb Voss was slow in alerting Renee that Pat Richter wanted to meet her and had planned to introduce himself in the next day or so when he saw her at the Pharm.

A couple of days later, Richter spotted Renee Sengstock at the Pharm. Thinking that Renee was fully aware that Richter would be looking for her, he approached her and introduced himself. It became obvious, however, that Renee knew nothing about Pat Richter or about the planned encounter at the Pharm.

It was a rough, uncomfortable start for the big guy, but needless to say, he rallied. "We chatted a little bit and agreed to say hello again the next couple of nights," Richter said. "I had a 1949 Dodge and offered to give her and her friend a ride home, and she accepted. We talked about a date on that next Saturday."

That next Saturday was the Homecoming game against Michigan and Pat Richter's first date with his future wife. Unfortunately, that first date was cut short by Richter's injury. He spent the night at University Hospital, nursing a painful broken collarbone.

Before the game had ended, Renee made her way to the hospital where Richter was recuperating. "We just spent our first date sitting around and chatting in the hospital," Richter said. "I remember one moment, though, when I was lying down and they were asking me all the necessary questions about medical history and so forth. Renee happened to come by when they were at the point of asking me about my religion and I said, 'Lutheran.' Well, her eyes lit up because apparently up to this point, she hadn't met any Lutheran boys on campus!"

One of the doctors who assisted in treating Richter at University Hospital that night was Dr. Karsten, whose son, Adrian, is a former Northwestern football player and a sideline reporter for ESPN's football broadcast coverage team.

One week later, the Badger football team traveled to Northwestern, where they would lose 21–0, to the Wildcats. Sidelined for the remaining three games of the season, Richter did not travel with the team. Instead, on that first Saturday without his teammates, Pat and Renee went to the movie *Ben Hur*, starring Charlton Heston, on the couple's first "real" date.

Despite the season-ending injury, Richter was named second team All-Big Ten. After the Michigan victory, the 1960 Badger football team would lose all three of its final games to finish with a 4-5 overall record, 2-5 in the Big Ten. It was the school's first losing record since 1956, when the Badgers were 1-5-3 in Coach Milt Bruhn's first season as head coach. There's no doubt that it was a disappointing end to a disappointing season for Bruhn and his Badgers, who were coming off a 1959 Big Ten Championship and a berth in the 1960 Rose Bowl.

With the broken collarbone on the mend, Richter began looking ahead to the basketball season. As the weeks progressed, Richter started to run to get back in shape and joined the team in December. Despite being limited by a tender shoulder during the first part of the season, he managed to earn enough playing time to earn his first letter in basketball. Overall, the season was lackluster at best, as the team finished with a 7-17 record overall, 4-10 and eighth place in the Big Ten. For the year, Richter appeared in 13 games, sank 13 of 44 field goal attempts (.298), and 11 of 22 free throws for 37 points. He also had 55 rebounds.

There was one memorable basketball weekend for Richter that year. It came when the Badgers traveled to Iowa City to play Iowa in a Big Ten Conference game.

Prior to the varsity game, Iowa's freshmen played an intrasquad game. Richter and his teammates sat in the stands as a young and talented freshman named Connie Hawkins dazzled the crowd with his flamboyant style and his incredible talent.

"At halftime, he went out there with two basketballs, one in each hand," Richter said. "People were wondering what he was going to do. He started dribbling toward the basket, alternating the dribbles as he moved forward. As he got to the free throw line, he took off. He palmed the one ball in his right hand, then the other in his left—he's flying through the air with two basketballs, and he drops them in the basket one at a time. First the right-hand dunk and then the left-hand dunk. He just took off and flew through the air and dunked two basketballs. And we're all sitting there going 'Whew, thank God freshmen aren't eligible.'"

Richter would later develop a reputation for making excellent coaching hires; it's clear his ability to evaluate basketball talent wasn't too bad, either. Hawkins left Iowa that year and at age 19, went on to become the Most Valuable Player in the American Basketball League. He later played for the Harlem Globetrotters, in the American Basketball Association, and in the National Basketball Association.

"He was the greatest basketball player I'd ever seen," said Richter.

Richter's sophomore season in baseball was far from lackluster. In his first collegiate game, he had four hits against perennial national powerhouse Arizona State. Splitting time between first base and the outfield, Richter led the team in games played (29), runs scored (28), hits (43), doubles (13), triples (4), home runs (7), runs batted in (23), and batting average (.398). He finished the season with a 10-game hitting streak and was named to the second team All-Big Ten Conference. The Badgers, meanwhile, were quite competitive in most conference games, but finished in sixth place with a 5-9 record.

During his sophomore baseball season, Richter was notified that he had been selected to a 1961 preseason All-American football team by *Playboy* magazine. In order to accept the selection, each player had to agree to travel to Chicago for a team photo shoot and to participate in media functions surrounding the All-American selection. In order to go, Richter had to ask his baseball coach, Dynie Mansfield.

"Here you are, a kid finishing your sophomore year in college, and now you're supposed to go to Chicago to the Playboy Mansion and all this kind of stuff," Richter said. "It was almost like 'Please coach, can I go?' without looking too anxious."

Mansfield gave Richter permission to attend, along with his chaperone, assistant football coach Paul Shaw. It was Richter's first experience with an All-Star, elite group of football players. Syracuse star Ernie Davis was there, along with star receiver Gary Collins from the University of Maryland and other notables.

"There were a lot of really top-notch college athletes who you had heard or read about before," Richter said. "That was a big thrill."

The following spring, Richter was selected once again to the *Playboy* preseason All-American team. But this time, Mansfield didn't grant him permission to leave the baseball team for the weekend in Chicago, so Richter wasn't included.

Richter's performance for the baseball Badgers in 1961 presented him an opportunity to spend the summer in South Dakota competing in the Basin League. There, Richter and other college baseball players lived the life of minor league players, traveling from small town to small town during the day and playing a baseball game at night. For home games, the routine was simple. Arrive at the park for batting and fielding practice at 4:00 p.m., play the game at 7:00 p.m. Spend some time with your teammates at the local hangout. Late to bed. Late to rise. A few hours of free time to kill and then back to the park at 4:00 p.m. For road games, add in the long hours on the bus.

Richter and fellow Badger Ron Krohn lived upstairs in a small house in Watertown, South Dakota. The league, which was sanctioned by the NCAA, paid each player $300 per month. In exchange, the players had to participate in a youth baseball clinic every two weeks.

At the time, the Basin League was the premier summer baseball league for the top collegiate players. Many of the players would later sign professional baseball contracts, and a few would reach the major leagues. Bill Faul, who played for the University of Cincinnati and would later play for the Detroit Tigers, Chicago Cubs, and San Francisco Giants, played in the Basin League that summer.

In Rapid City, Richter took note that the team had recently planted some trees far, far away from home plate, marking the spots where Ohio State slugger and future major leaguer Frank Howard had hit prodigious home runs in Basin League action.

At Watertown, one of Richter's teammates was Eddie Watt, a pitcher from the University of Northern Iowa who played several seasons with the Baltimore Orioles. One of the assistant coaches for Richter's team was Art Hoch, whose son Scott would become a star on the professional golf tour. And future Boston and Houston manager Jimy Williams, then a collegiate star at Fresno State, played two years for Sturgis in the Basin League.

Richter competed well in the league and on one magical summer night, blasted three home runs in a game at Rapid City. But soon, it was back to Madison and time to prepare for the 1961 Badger football season.

* * *

While Pat Richter spent much of the summer of 1961 playing baseball in South Dakota, Badger football coach Milt Bruhn and his staff were spending time in Green Bay, Wisconsin, where the Badger football coaches shadowed Packer coach Vince Lombardi and his staff, particularly the offensive staff. Lombardi and the Packers were not yet a dynasty, but were clearly headed in that direction. In 1959, Lombardi's first season as head coach, the Packers finished at 7-5 and Lombardi was named NFL Coach of the Year. In 1960, the Packers won the Western Division of the NFL and advanced to the championship game, where they lost at Philadelphia, 17–13.

Lombardi and the Packers were quite accommodating to Bruhn and the Badger staff during their visits to Green Bay, sharing coaching strategies and the intricacies of the team's offensive system, including the vaunted Green Bay Packer sweep. Armed with the inside information from the up-and-coming Lombardi, Bruhn decided to install a new, pro-style offense for the 1961 Badgers.

It was a system that would work well for Pat Richter and returning quarterback Ron Miller, who had a soft passing touch and was known as a quarterback who had the innate ability to find an open receiver.

The Badgers opened at home with a 7–0 victory over Utah. Richter caught three passes for 23 yards and the game's only touchdown. He caught five passes for 60 yards in Wisconsin's next game, but it wasn't enough as the Badgers stumbled in their Big Ten opener at Camp Randall, losing 20–0 to 10th-ranked Michigan State. The following week, the Badgers collected a 6–3 victory at Indiana, and for the first time in nine career games at UW, Richter failed to catch a pass.

He got back on track the next week, catching eight passes for 138 yards in a 23–20 nonconference victory over visiting Oregon State and their star quarterback, Terry Baker, who would win the Heisman Trophy the following year. But in the following weeks, the Badgers were defeated by two highly ranked teams. Richter caught three passes for just 24 yards as fourth-ranked Iowa crushed the Badgers at Iowa City, 47–15. And despite Richter's six catches for 104 yards, sixth-ranked Ohio State edged out Wisconsin, 30–21, spoiling the Badger homecoming and dashing the team's slim hopes for a share of the conference title.

In the two weeks following the disappointing losses to Iowa and Ohio State, Richter and the Badgers put together two outstanding games. Against Northwestern, Richter caught seven passes for 156 yards and one touchdown in a 29–10 win over Northwestern. And in a 55–7 romp over Illinois, Richter tied the school record for most touchdown passes caught in a game (3) and set school records for most passes caught in a game (9) and most passing yards gained in a single game (170).

Against Illinois, Richter also broke the school record for most passing yards gained for a season, breaking the mark set by former Badger receiver Dave Schreiner. A two-time All-American from tiny Lancaster, Wisconsin, Schreiner had been a fan favorite when he played for the Badgers from 1940 to 1942. He once caught three touchdown passes in one quarter, which remains a school record. The 1942 Badgers—led by Schreiner, Pat Harder, Elroy Hirsch, and others—are still considered to be one of the finest teams in Wisconsin history. They finished with an 8-1-1 record, which included a victory over number-one-ranked Ohio State at Camp Randall, the first time in school history that Wisconsin had defeated a top-ranked team.

Sadly, Schreiner was killed in combat in World War II. His number 80 jersey was retired several years ago as a tribute to one of the school's fallen heroes.

The connection between Richter and Schreiner, two All-Americans who performed admirably not only on the field, but in the classroom and in their community, was duly noted by *Wisconsin State Journal* sports editor Monte McCormick.

"Most schools consider themselves lucky to have one boy the caliber of Schreiner and Richter representing them on the football field," wrote McCormick. "Wisconsin can count itself among the really lucky."

A few days after Richter surpassed Schreiner's school record, McCormick reprinted a letter Richter received from Mrs. H. E. Schreiner, the mother of the late Dave Schreiner:

Nov. 19, 1961
Dear Pat,

If Dave Schreiner were alive I'm sure he would have been the first one in the dressing room yesterday to congratulate you, not only on total yards to break his record but you're "fine" most all along the line. Since Dave could not say it, I am saying it for him.

And I want to tell you I've played with you at end through every game you've played. And I said that when you caught that pass in the Ohio State game, over your shoulder with two men on you, that you would never have to catch another pass for me. That was a beauty.

But I've thrilled to every pass since, and yesterday as you played I added and added till finally you had surpassed Dave's record, and I gloried in your success.

All good wishes to you and the team at Minnesota.
Sincerely,
Mrs. H. E. Schreiner

The Badgers' next game—their season finale—was on the road against archrival Minnesota. The mighty Gophers, after losing their season opener to Missouri, had won seven straight games to clinch the Big Ten title and a berth in the 1962 Rose Bowl. Heavy snowfall during the week leading up to the regular-season finale against the Badgers did little to hamper the field condition because Minnesota officials had covered the Memorial Stadium turf with a tarp and had warm air blowing underneath the tarp to keep the field in good condition.

The game didn't start well for the Badgers. On the first play, Gopher wide receiver Tom Hall could be seen waving his arms frantically toward quarterback Sandy Stephens because no one was covering him. A quick pass from Stephens to Hall, and suddenly the Gophers had scored an 80-yard touchdown on the first play from scrimmage.

But, despite the early seven-point deficit, the Badgers fought back to defeat the third-ranked Gophers 23–21. Richter again was outstanding, catching six passes for 142 yards and two touchdowns.

"I really think it served as a springboard for next year," Richter said. "There was good leadership on that team, a lot of excitement and enthusiasm when you beat a good team like that."

Apparently, the Badger fans shared that enthusiasm.

"We didn't go back to Madison right after the game," Richter recalled. "It was tradition for the team to stay overnight after the last game in Minnesota. We went to Murray's and a lot of other hot spots in Minneapolis. We ran into all kinds of fans and people from Madison who were excited about the win. Everybody was happy. It was a great end to the season."

Still, while the Badgers were celebrating their victory over Minnesota, their season was over. Minnesota would go on to the Rose Bowl and Wisconsin would go home the following day, where a sizeable crowd greeted the Badgers as their train rolled in the depot on West Washington Avenue.

"It gave the younger guys on the team a taste of what it's like to win a big game," Richter said.

Pat Richter had lived up to his preseason hype during the 1961 season. He led the nation in touchdown passes caught (8) and in pass-receiving yards (817). He was second in the nation in pass receptions with 47. At the time, he held every school pass-catching record and either held or tied Big Ten Conference records in passes caught in a conference season (36), yards gained (656), and touchdown passes caught (7).

He was named to the first team All-Big Ten team and the United Press International first-team All-American team.

As football ended, basketball started for Richter, who joined the team for practice on December 5. For the first several games, Richter was a part-time performer for the Badgers. One of those games was against defending national champion Cincinnati, which set a UW Field House record with a .607 field goal shoot-

Wisconsin's Pat Richter (88) reaches high to catch a pass at Camp Randall Stadium. Photo courtesy of UW Archives.

ing percentage in an 86–67 victory over UW. Still, the Badgers won four of their other five games as they headed east for an appearance in the prestigious ECAC Holiday Festival Tournament at New York City's Madison Square Garden.

On the New York City trip, Richter roomed with Gene Englund Jr., whose father, Gene, was an All-American center on Wisconsin's 1941 national championship basketball team. Richter, Englund, and their Badger teammates were awestruck by the big city, touring the many sights, including a trip to the Garment District and a Broadway play—*My Fair Lady*.

The Badgers opened the tournament against Providence, led by Ray Flynn, who later would become mayor of Boston, and John Thompson, the future Hall of Fame coach of Georgetown University. Early in the game, Richter found himself deep in the corner, where he caught a teammate's pass and quickly fired up a jump shot. "Thompson came flying at me so I shot the ball almost straight up in the air and it went in," Richter said. "I remember hearing our assistant coach Johnny Orr saying 'Oh no. Richter shot the ball—it went in!' Everybody was shocked."

The shock continued when Richter sank another long one from the same spot. And then another. "Then I did one of those things where, after your team scores a basket, you start down to the other end of the floor, quickly turn around and see if you can intercept their inbounds pass," Richter said. "I did that, and it worked, and I scored on a layup."

Richter had scored eight points in a very short period of time. "It was incredible," Richter said. "Our whole bench was laughing by this time. It was about three times my scoring average."

Richter ended with 14 points in the game as the Badgers defeated Flynn, Thompson, and the Friars 95–84. In the tournament's second round, the Badgers defeated the Dayton Flyers 105–93 to earn a berth in the Festival Championship and a rematch with defending national champion Cincinnati, which had easily defeated the Badgers weeks earlier at the UW Field House.

"We were riding high," Richter said. "The game was on national television. We had won our first two games in the tournament against some pretty good competition. But against Cincinnati, we got pummeled. We had run out of gas."

Indeed, the powerful Bearcats had put together a solid season to date and were ranked number two in the country. Led by Paul Hogue, Ron Bonham, and Tom Thacker, Cincinnati thumped the Badgers 101–71 to win the Festival championship. Later that year, Coach Ed Jucker and the Bearcats would go on to win

Pat Richter and UW basketball coach John Erickson.
Photo courtesy of the UW Athletic Department.

their second consecutive national championship. One of the assistant coaches on that team was John Powless, who later would join the Wisconsin staff as an assistant basketball coach and head tennis coach, and would be head basketball coach of the Badgers from 1969 to 1976.

Despite the defeat to Cincinnati, the Badgers left New York with a newfound confidence. They had a high-scoring, balanced attack, led by Ken Siebel, Mike O'Melia, Tom Gwyn, and Donny Hearden. "We had a nice team," Richter said. "We had a bunch of good, hard-working basketball players."

The month of January was good to the Badgers, as they reeled off six consecutive victories, five of which were in conference. But then came February, and with it came heartbreak for 20-year-old Pat Richter.

Late in the afternoon of February 1, Richter had just finished basketball practice. The Badgers were preparing for a road game two days later against Minnesota. Richter had made plans to stop after practice to pick up Renee, and the two of them were to join UW recruit and Madison East star Bill Maselter for dinner that night. Richter pulled up his car in front of the Victoria House to pick up Renee. There, standing in front of the house were Renee and Pat Richter's cousin, Pete Salg.

"He was looking sad," Richter recalled. "The only words I heard were 'Father died.' So I said to Pete, 'Your father died?' And he said, 'No, your father died.'"

Richter's first reaction was to get to his parents' Near East Side home as soon as possible. "I remember driving out there and blaming the job, the change in job that created the pressure and stress. That's about all you could hang your hat on at the time."

Big Pat Richter had worked at Gisholt since 1935 and had been a foreman at the foundry for many years. "As I got older, I realized that he was very well liked at the foundry," said Little Pat. "He was a good people person."

That personality and his other job skills led to a promotion in 1961, when Big Pat was named plant engineer. In his new position, he was now responsible for the plant operations, maintenance, and much more.

"He had not been college educated," Pat said of his father. "All of a sudden he went from wearing overalls and being with the guys at the foundry to wearing a shirt and a tie. I really think the pressure of that may have created some health issues."

Forty-five days short of his 43rd birthday, Big Pat would put in another full day of work at Gisholt, despite some nagging chest pains. "He waited until the end of the day and stopped by the nurse's office," Richter said. "He dropped right over in the nurse's office of a massive heart attack."

When he arrived at his parents' home on Yahara Place, Richter found his mother; his two sisters, Randi and Jane; and the family minister. Friends and neighbors, all of whom had just heard the news, were stopping by to offer their support.

"Gisholt was a like family at the time," Richter recalled. "It was really a close-knit, family-oriented place. His death was a shock, and a lot of people from the plant stopped by."

Among those who stopped was Richter's football coach at Wisconsin, Milt Bruhn. With him was Jack Hewitt, a businessman from the Neenah-Menasha area. "I think Milt was concerned that I might now end up going into professional baseball instead of going to school to get my degree," Richter said. "I think Milt had Jack along to say, 'If there is anything we can do to help, just let us know.' Back then, there probably was something that could be done within the rules."

Meanwhile, the Badger basketball team was continuing its preparation for the game at Minnesota, but Richter was no longer part of that preparation and would not be joining the team for its trip to Minneapolis. But before the team left at 2:00 p.m., they stopped by Frautschi Funeral Home to pay their respects to Big Pat and to offer their condolences to their teammate and his family.

"It was tough," Richter recalled of the team's visit to the funeral parlor. "It was very emotional."

Richter's teammates went on to defeat Minnesota. Coach John Erickson would later tell Richter that "they won this one for Hugh."

It was a milestone moment for Pat. "Things had been going so well for so long," he recalled. "Now, you're 20 years old and all of a sudden your dad dies. Back then, you're worried about all the financials and stuff, but we got through. My mother got a part-time job working at a podiatrist's office. She managed to provide pretty well for us. And I had always worked."

One month after the death of Pat Richter's father, the Wisconsin Badger basketball team provided its fans with one of the most exciting victories in school history. On the snowy Saturday afternoon of March 3, the Badgers stunned top-ranked Ohio State and snapped the Buckeyes 47-game winning streak with an 86–67 victory before a jam-packed capacity crowd at the UW Field House.

The Buckeyes were led by All-American center Jerry Lucas and forwards Jon Havlicek and Larry Siegfried. Among the reserves on that team was Bob Knight, who later would become infamous as head coach at Army, Indiana, and Texas Tech.

Sportswriter Mike Lucas interviewed Siebel and O'Melia for a February 2005 article in the *Capital Times*:

Asked for the first thing that comes to mind from that victory, O'Melia said, "The first thing was probably the fans. If I recall it was a pretty snowy day but the place was jammed. Not only that but when Lucas and Havlicek were introduced [to the crowd], they literally got standing ovations—which was just out of respect—and that kind of impressed me."

One of the most impressive elements of the game was Siebel's defense on Havlicek, the first-team All-American who converted just 3-of-15 field goal attempts. As a team, the Buckeyes were leading the country in field goal shooting percentage (.507). But the Badgers limited them to 24 field goals on 75 attempts (.320). "Havlicek, then, was not the offensive player that he would become with the Boston Celtics," recalled Siebel. "But he was a great defender, and tireless, he never stopped".

Ohio State's defense, meanwhile, centered on Lucas in the paint and an aggressive zone press. "We had practiced hard against the press the few days we had before the game," O'Melia remembered. "Out of the press, we got a dunk from Tom Gwyn. They tried it one more time and we beat it easily, so they called it off."

The Badgers were led in scoring by Don Hearden, a Kimberly sophomore who had 29 points. Siebel had 22.

"Everybody that played for us in that game just played their heart out," said Siebel, a three-time MVP for the Badgers. "It was like a dream. They talk about being in a zone and mentally we were clearly in a zone because no one thought, 'Oh, God, we're ahead by 10 points.' Or, 'Oh, God, we're ahead by 15.' We just kept playing . . . and we just dominated. That hadn't happened to them. When they got down, they never quit, but in the final two minutes there was just despair because they knew they were going to lose."

Richter, like Siebel, O'Melia, and others who were at the Field House that day, still has fond memories of that game. "Most people who were there said it was one of the best basketball games they'd ever seen," Richter said.

Richter played sparingly in the game, guarding Jerry Lucas in the post. "I was 6 foot 5 and he was 6 foot 8," Richter said. "It was like trying to look around a pole, he was so big."

Years later, Richter would needle Indiana basketball coach Bob Knight, who also played sparingly in that game as a reserve for the Buckeyes. "I used to kid Bobby about the game summary," he said. "At least I was on the board. He was zero, zero, zero, zero. I was zero, zero, zero, one. At least I had one foul."

The game marked a mini-reunion of sorts for Richter, Havlicek, and Lucas. The previous year, Richter and Badger quarterback Ron Miller were honored by the Columbus Touchdown Club as the top collegiate passing combination in 1961. "I got to spend some time with Lucas and Havlicek at the event and built up some nice friendships."

Wisconsin closed out its season the following weekend at Iowa, where Don Nelson, who had scored 30 points against the Badgers in their earlier meeting that season, poured in 35 points to defeat the Badgers 81–64. Nelson, who went on to play 14 seasons in the NBA and has served as a head coach for the Milwaukee Bucks, Golden State Warriors, and Dallas Mavericks, closed his collegiate career that day as Iowa's all-time leading scorer and was given a rousing ovation when he was taken out of the game with 51 seconds left—only to return to the game for a final dunk shot with four seconds to play.

Wisconsin finished with 17-7 record overall and 10-4 in the Big Ten. Richter averaged 2.3 points and 3.2 rebounds in 17 games for the Badgers, who finished in second place in the Big Ten.

"We had a good year," Richter said. "But back then, unless you won the championship, you didn't advance to the postseason tournament."

Richter did advance to the baseball season, where he quickly joined his teammates for indoor practice at the Camp Randall Memorial Sports Center, commonly known as the Shell. Built in the late 1950s, the Shell provided Wisconsin athletes with a state-of-the-art indoor practice facility that was among the best of its time. The Shell was originally built to partially offset the loss of the track that surrounded the football field inside Camp Randall Stadium. Searching for ways to increase seating capacity, the UW Board of Regents in 1957 voted to lower the field at Camp Randall by 10 feet, thus adding an additional 10,000 seats to the facility. Unfortunately, that move would eliminate the track, but the construction of the Shell nearby, with its indoor track, served as a suitable tradeoff for the loss of the Camp Randall track.

On a typical late winter afternoon, the Shell was utilized by the Badger baseball team, the men's and women's track teams, the freshman basketball team, and more. Additionally, the facility served as a classroom for a variety of physical education classes throughout the day.

Each spring, the Badger baseball team would leave the Shell and travel to a warm-weather area to open its season. This particular year, the Badgers would compete against Arizona State and other warm weather schools before returning to the cold and wet spring climate of Wisconsin and the indoor practice sessions at the Shell.

It was during his junior season that Richter was contacted by Elliott Maraniss, then a reporter for the *Capital Times*. Later in life, Maraniss would be enshrined in the Milwaukee Press Club Hall of Fame for his many accomplishments in a

45-year career in daily newspapers, including a Pulitzer Prize nomination. But journalism wasn't the nature of Maraniss's phone call to Richter. "He invited me to have lunch with Eddie Dancizsak, who was a scout for the Milwaukee Braves. It was an introductory meeting. We had lunch at the old Ivy Inn on University Avenue, and later on Eddie gave me six bats with my name on them. They were so much better than any other wood bats you could get," Richter said. "I never really did figure out the Maraniss connection. I think he just loved baseball and he was some sort of 'bird dog' for Eddie in the Madison area, scouting out local talent."

In 1962, the Badger baseball team split its conference games and headed into the final weekend of the season with a 5-5 record and out of contention. Their opponent that day was Michigan, whose roster included future major leaguer and ESPN broadcaster Dave Campbell. The Wolverines were battling Illinois for the conference title, and needed to win one of the two games against Wisconsin to win the league championship.

Before the game, Richter had received several phone calls from members of the Illinois team who had been teammates with Richter in Watertown, South Dakota, in the Basin League. "They were pleading with us to beat the Wolverines so they could win the title," Richter said.

Richter was as impressive on the baseball diamond as he was in football and basketball. Photo courtesy of the UW Athletic Department.

Richter didn't let his friends down, hitting a home run in game one to help the Badgers defeat the Wolverines 6–3. Still, if Michigan won the second game, it would still tie for the conference title.

In the second game, a mix-up on a long fly ball helped the Wolverines move ahead, 5–4, as the Badgers entered the bottom of the seventh inning.

The first two Badgers were easily retired, but Luke Lamboley gave life to the Badgers as he drilled a triple to right field. At that point, Michigan Coach Don Lund chose to bring in left-handed relief ace Fritz Fisher to face the right-handed-hitting Pat Richter.

An unusually large crowd of 1,200 at Guy Lowman Field—on an even more unusual 86-degree spring day—watched eagerly as Richter stepped into the batter's box. With the game and

Michigan's Big Ten Conference title hopes on the line, Richter came through for the Badgers and for his University of Illinois friends.

"The pitch came in to me and for some reason, it looked as big as a watermelon," Richter recalled. "It was one of the longest balls and one of the hardest balls that I ever hit. When I hit it, it was about four feet off the ground. When it cleared the centerfield fence, it was about seven feet off the ground.

"I remember coming around third base and heading for home and I looked over to see our coach, Dynie Mansfield, with his hat over his heart and he was slumped over on his knees," Richter said.

The home run gave the Badgers a 6–5 victory over the Wolverines and prevented them from sharing the Big Ten title with first-place Illinois. Richter was five for nine in the doubleheader with two home runs and a triple. Sun Prairie's Stan Wagner picked up both of the pitching victories with a 4-hitter in the opener and a seventh-inning appearance in game two. It was the first time since 1900 that a Wisconsin baseball team had swept a doubleheader from Michigan.

The significance of the doubleheader sweep over Michigan would become even more apparent in the upcoming weeks, as the Wolverines earned a postseason berth and went on to win the College World Series and the 1962 national championship.

Richter finished the season with a .313 batting average and led the team in games played (23), at bats (80), runs scored (15), hits (25), doubles (6), triples (2), home runs (7), and runs batted in (19). He set a school record with 10 straight games with two or more hits and 10 consecutive games scoring at least one run, and was named to second team All-Big Ten.

It had been an emotional year for Richter. The lowest point, of course, was the tragic loss of his father in early February.

On the playing fields, the dramatic baseball victory over Michigan capped a year in which Richter's three Badger teams all came up with big victories over national caliber opponents and Big Ten powerhouses.

In football, the Badgers defeated eventual Rose Bowl champion Minnesota Gophers in the final regular season game of the year.

In basketball, the Badgers defeated the number-one-ranked Ohio State Buckeyes.

And in baseball, the Badgers defeated the eventual national champion Michigan Wolverines in the final weekend series of the conference season.

"Junior year was very special athletically because of all the things that happened," Richter said.

CHAPTER THREE
A CORNER ON THE
CHAMPIONSHIP MARKET

The summer before his senior year at Wisconsin, Richter worked construction during the weekdays and spent a great deal of time honing his baseball skills with the Monona Grove Lakers, playing in the Madison City League on weeknights and in the Central Wisconsin League on the weekends. There was very little preparation for the upcoming football season. His workout regimen in advance of his senior year consisted of running and punting and very little weight lifting.

And while there was great anticipation for the football season and a great deal of optimism, there remained a key question mark for the 1962 Badgers: Who would be the team's starting quarterback? The Badgers had appealed to the Big Ten and the NCAA to gain one more year of eligibility for Ron Miller, the team's quarterback the previous two years. Miller had suffered an injury in his sophomore season and the hope was that the conference or the NCAA would rule him eligible to compete in 1962. But those appeals were swiftly denied, and the quarterback situation was suddenly as unclear as could be.

The preseason candidates were sophomore Harold Brandt, a left-handed thrower who had no varsity experience but had great potential; John Fabry, a returning senior from Green Bay who had played mostly on defense and very little at quarterback in previous years but had the ability to step in and take over the starting job; and Ron VanderKelen, another senior from Green Bay who had been around the program longer than any other player, but who also had played sparingly and had not been with the team in 1961. VanderKelen had initially been in the class that had recently graduated and in fact, was on the travel roster of the team that went to the 1960 Rose Bowl.

VanderKelen had left school for a year and decided to return for his final year of eligibility. "I think early on, Milt had identified him as the quarterback,"

Richter said. "Milt said to us that when it looks like the coaches are putting too much pressure on him, let us know and we'll back off."

Bruhn and his staff were enamored by VanderKelen's ability to scramble and gain yardage when the protection broke down, something that Miller didn't offer in previous seasons.

"Vandy was a different kind of quarterback," Richter said. "Miller had been more of a drop-back quarterback, whereas Vandy liked to run the ball a bit. He wasn't necessarily fast but he was shifty and could throw well on the run. So he bubbled to the top in the early practice to be the guy."

With VanderKelen taking over at quarterback, the rest of the team worked to blend in a group of talented sophomores with a strong corps of veterans. The team had an abundance of strong, talented lineman, including sophomores Al Piraino, Roger Jacobazzi, and juniors Ken Bowman, Dion Kempthorne, Roger Pillath, and Andy Wojdula. The Badgers were deep at tight end with Richter, Ron Carlson, and Ron Leafblad. Gary Kroner was a solid kicker and halfback. Versatile performers like Merritt Norvell, Lou Holland, Billy Smith, and Ron Smith provided the speed and quickness necessary to be a Big Ten contender. Ironically, the Badger cocaptains that year were the same two individuals who had served as cocaptains for the Madison East Purgolders just four years ago. Steve Underwood, the UW starter at offensive guard, and Richter, were designated by Bruhn to be the 1962 cocaptains.

The season opener was impressive, with the Badgers trouncing New Mexico State 69–13 at Camp Randall Stadium. Richter caught touchdown passes of 5 and 40 yards. More impressive, however, were blocks by Richter and teammate Ron Carlson that sprung Jim Nettles free on an 89-yard interception return that gave the Badgers a 7–0 lead in the first quarter.

The Badgers followed up with two more victories at home. The first was an easy 30–6 victory over Indiana. The previous season, in a game at Bloomington, the Hoosiers had held Richter to no pass receptions. This year, however, Richter caught five passes for 72 yards and one touchdown.

The Fighting Irish of Notre Dame followed the Hoosiers into Camp Randall Stadium the following week, with their All-American quarterback candidate Daryle Lamonica. The mighty Irish football program had been struggling of late. Head Coach Joe Kuharich's three-year record was 12-18 and the Irish had split their first two games of the 1962 season.

Still, when Notre Dame came to town, it was something special. Just ask the Madison Police Department.

On the Friday night before the game, a bar-time crowd gathered in the streets of campus and raised a ruckus, to say the least. Dean of Students LeRoy

Luberg told the local newspapers that "the great influx of Notre Dame men who had no place to stay, Wisconsin students with nothing to do, and the warm weather probably caused the near riot."

According to newspaper reports: "The mob began gathering shortly after the taverns closed at 12:45 a.m. when coeds in Allen Hall, corner of State and Frances Streets, waved undergarments through their windows. The throngs of men leaving the bars began cheering and blocking traffic. What started as a mild, impromptu pep rally for the Wisconsin-Notre Dame game soon turned to wilder sport."

One Notre Dame student was sleeping in the back seat of his car and awoke to find himself and the car in Lake Mendota. Fortunately, he was not injured, but the car had to be towed from the lake.

Meanwhile, the crowd proceeded toward another women's student residence, Lowell Hall. There, according to newspaper reports, they began to throw beer cans through windows and chant "We want panties!" That disturbance was quelled when Lowell Hall officials grabbed the fire hoses and used them to turn back the crowd. In all, 13 persons were arrested and 7 were injured.

On the football field the next day, Notre Dame fought hard, but fell to Wisconsin 17–8. Richter had two catches for 38 yards, including a touchdown. Back on campus that night, the weekend's disturbances continued, with 34 more arrests.

With the victory over Notre Dame came some positive attention from the national media. As the Badgers prepared to play host to Iowa in a key Big Ten Conference game, the Badgers had soared to number 10 in the latest Associated Press rankings.

Early on, the Hawkeyes and Badgers battled evenly, until Wisconsin broke the ice with their first score and a 7–0 lead. On the ensuing kickoff, Ron Frain's jarring tackle of Iowa's Willie Ray Smith forced a fumble, and Richter recovered the ball at the Iowa 14-yard line. The Badgers quickly scored and took control of the game. Said Iowa coach Jerry Burns: "They weren't sure of themselves, but they got momentum after that fumble."

The Badgers went on to easily defeat Iowa 42–14 to run their winning streak to four games. Richter was impressive in this game, catching six passes for 56 yards and one touchdown. The following week, the Badgers moved up to the number 5 ranking in the Associated Press poll.

Throughout the early-season games, Richter had battled a painful hip pointer. Then, when making a block during the victory over the Hawkeyes, Richter broke the ring finger on his right hand.

During practice the next week, Richter and the coaches kept the injury to themselves as they prepared for the team's first road game of the season against

Ohio State in Columbus.

"The biggest thing I was worried about was shaking hands at midfield for the coin flip," Richter said. "We were all thinking about that."

The Buckeyes, coached by the legendary Woody Hayes, were coming off a tremendous season in 1961, when they won the Big Ten championship and finished second in the nation in both wire service polls. Their success carried into the 1962 season, when the Buckeyes were ranked number 1 in the country until they lost to UCLA and Northwestern. The two losses did not make Hayes a happy man.

"All during the week leading up to our game he was harping on the officials about all the terrible pass interference calls that they'd been making," said Richter. "He knew we had a strong passing game, and he was obviously setting things up.

"They said it was very cold there during the week leading up to the game, and every day for practice, Woody was wearing a T-shirt," Richter said. "He told his players that Wisconsin was practicing in the cold, too."

Playing at Ohio State was always difficult. In fact, the last time a Wisconsin team had won at Columbus was in 1918. Still, among the 500 fans who provided an enthusiastic sendoff for the undefeated Badgers as they departed Madison's Truax Field, there was reason for hope and optimism. Perhaps this was going to be the year that would end the Columbus jinx.

Richter, his teammates, and the entire coaching staff knew this was going to be a tough game. "Before the game and the coin toss, we're ready for the pep talk," Richter recalled. "There was a rolled-up wrestling mat and Milt's just about ready to talk to the team and Art Lamboley, the equipment manager, he just kind of yelled, 'Milt, let me talk to the boys.' Well, Art gets up and pushes Milt aside, jumps up on this wrestling mat and begins to give us this pep talk. It was unbelievable," Richter said.

Fresh from their pep talk from their veteran equipment manager, the Badgers took the field for warm-ups, and minutes later, Richter went to midfield for the pregame coin toss, broken right ring finger and all. "I shook hands with one of their captains, Mike Ingram," he said. "I reached out real fast and grabbed his fingers before he could grab mine. He probably wondered what the heck kind of handshake that was."

Things didn't go well for the Badgers on that gray day in Columbus. The Buckeyes—still stinging from losing two of their last three games and tumbling from number 1 to unranked—edged out the Badgers 14–7, handing Wisconsin its first loss of the season. The Badger offense struggled for most of the game, due in part to a lackluster passing game. Richter did catch two passes for 41 yards, but was well covered most of the day.

Looking back, Richter recalled the comments made earlier in the week by Coach Hayes. "During that game there were some calls that in the normal course of events would have been called as pass interference," Richter said. "But Woody had sufficiently conditioned the refs."

Sports Editor Monte McCormick's game report in the *Wisconsin State Journal* concurred: "We don't think anyone will hear Coach Woody Hayes of Ohio State heap scorn on Big 10 officials after this game as he did a week ago," wrote McCormick. "There was one obvious pass interference against Richter and in this writer's opinion, there was another almost as obvious."

One week later, the Badgers were back on track as they easily defeated Michigan 34–12 at Camp Randall. The victory improved the UW record to 5-1 overall, 3-1 in the Big Ten, and it set the stage for one of the biggest games in years at Camp Randall Stadium. The upstart Northwestern Wildcats, undefeated and ranked number 1 in the country, were coming to town for Homecoming. The Wildcats, coached by Ara Parseghian, had won their first six games of the season, including impressive victories over Illinois, Minnesota, Ohio State, and Notre Dame. They boasted a vaunted passing attack with quarterback Tommy Myers and wide receiver Paul Flatley.

A sellout crowd of 65,501—the first capacity crowd since the 1959 season—watched the eighth-ranked Badgers defeat the top-ranked Wildcats 37–6.

One week later, the fourth-ranked Badgers traveled to Champaign and defeated Illinois 35-6 to improve their record to 8-1 overall, 6-1 in conference.

One Big Ten game remained on the schedule. Archrival Minnesota, ranked fifth in the country, was coming to Madison in a winner-take-all event: the winner of the game would win the conference championship and earn a berth in the 1963 Rose Bowl.

Another capacity crowd would fill Camp Randall for the Badger-Gopher matchup. The longest-running collegiate football rivalry needed little enhancement, but this year, the rivalry included two of the top-five-ranked teams in the country and some of the college game's most talented stars, including Richter, VanderKelen, and Minnesota's Bobby Bell and Carl Eller. And the Gophers were still a bit miffed that the Badgers had beaten them on their home turf in the final Big Ten game the year before.

The game was an intense defensive struggle between two very talented football teams. Wisconsin's Ron Leafblad had caught a touchdown pass, but late in the fourth quarter, Minnesota held a narrow 9-7 lead when the Badgers took over on their own 20-yard line for what appeared to be their final shot at putting together a drive that would give them the lead. But, based on Minnesota's outstanding defensive performance up to that point, the chances of driving 80 yards seemed slim.

VanderKelen started the drive with a 12-yard completion to Richter. Eller then sacked VanderKelen for a five-yard loss and after an incomplete pass, Vander-Kelen and Richter teamed up for an 18-yard completion to keep the drive alive.

After another completion to Richter for 12 yards, the Badgers had another first down and had moved into Minnesota territory at the 43-yard line. Less than two minutes remained in the game. The crowd was boisterous, but still concerned about the vaunted Minnesota defense.

On the next play, much to the dismay of the Wisconsin fans, Minnesota's Jack Perkovich intercepted VanderKelen's pass. The interception would put an end to the fourth-quarter drive and more than likely an end to the Badgers' dream of winning the Big Ten title and earning a berth in the 1963 Rose Bowl.

But as Minnesota began celebrating the apparent game-winning interception, the Badger fans took note of a penalty flag that lay on the ground next to VanderKelen in the Badger backfield. Officials had called a roughing the passer penalty on Bell, which nullified the interception, gave the ball back to Wisconsin, and moved the ball forward 15 yards.

Minnesota coach Murray Warmath was incensed. He went onto the playing field to protest the call, and in the process, grabbed field judge Joseph Schneider. And that led to another flag: 15 yards for unsportsmanlike conduct.

Sportswriter Tom Butler was covering the game for the *Wisconsin State Journal* and was seated in the press box next to Sid Hartman of the *Minneapolis Tribune*. "And after those penalties are called, I look next to me and Sid's gone," Butler said. "I looked down on the field and he's standing right there next to Warmath arguing with Robert Jones, the referee. And a few seconds later, he's back in the press box sitting next to me."

The Badgers now had the ball on the Minnesota 13-yard line. The crowd— energized by the turn of events—was loud. Three plays later, fullback Ralph Kurek scored on a 2-yard run and the Badgers had taken a 14–9 lead with just 97 seconds remaining.

The defending champion Gophers, angry and upset, didn't let up, nor did the handkerchief-throwing officials. On the ensuing kickoff, Wisconsin was whistled for a 15-yard unsportsmanlike conduct penalty and Minnesota took over at its own 41. A pass interference call on Wisconsin moved the ball to the UW 47. A second pass interference call moved the ball all the way to the Wisconsin 14-yard line. On the next play, Wisconsin's Jim Nettles intercepted Duane Blaska's pass and with 59 seconds left, Wisconsin took over.

The Badgers failed in their attempt to run out the clock. Richter was forced to punt from his own goal line in the closing seconds. His 51-yarder iced the victory, giving the Badgers the Big Ten title and a trip to Pasadena.

The Gophers and their fans were livid about the outcome of the game and were particularly upset with the officiating. Unruly Gopher fans chased down the officials as they left the field, and one fan had to be restrained by Minnesota football players after jumping an official near the locker room.

"I don't think that Wisconsin won," Minnesota guard Julian Hook told reporters afterward. "Tell me one thing they did all day to deserve a win. We deserved to win and I think we're the better team."

Again, Richter's contributions were not limited to passes caught and yardage gained. In a field-position battle with the Gophers, Richter's nine punts helped the Badgers tremendously. He had a 54-yard punt from the UW 6-yard line; a 43-yard punt from the UW end zone; a 45-yard punt after a high snap that forced him to sidestep an onrushing Gopher; and the game-ending 51-yard punt from his own goal line.

Richter had six catches for 82 yards against the Gophers. He finished the regular season with 38 catches for 531 yards and 5 touchdowns. He led the Big Ten in passes caught (33), passing yards gained (440), and touchdown passes caught (2). He also led the Big Ten in punting with a 39.5 average.

In the days and weeks that followed, Richter would travel the nation to accept accolades for his collegiate performances. They were many: first team Associated Press Big Ten; first team United Press International Big Ten; first team Big Ten

Pat Richter shakes hands with President John F. Kennedy at halftime of the Army-Navy Game in November, 1962. Photo courtesy of the UW Athletic Department.

Academic Team; first team Football Coaches Association/TV Guide All-American; first team Football Writers Association All-American; first team the *Sporting News* All-American; first team CBS-TV All-American; first team *New York Daily News* All-American; first team *Boston Record* All-American; and first team Fox-Movietone All-American.

He also was selected to the *Look* All-American team and traveled to New York City for the award festivities, including a December 2 appearance on the Ed Sullivan Show.

Ironically, one of the other players selected to the All-American team was childhood friend Dave Hoppmann. Richter and Hoppmann had gone to grade school together at Marquette Elementary and were both in the Class of 1959 at Madison East High School. While Richter went across town to attend the UW, Hoppmann went farther west and attended college at Iowa State, where he set numerous records as a single-wing tailback for the Cyclones.

"For the both of us to come to New York and be reunited on the All-American team was really kind of neat," Richter said.

While in New York, the All-Americans took a train to Philadelphia for the annual Army-Navy game, where Richter and his teammates—including Bobby Bell, Hal Bedsole, Terry Baker, and Jerry Stovall—met a special guest at halftime.

"President Kennedy was on the Army side of the field in the first half," Richter said. "They took all of us onto the field, and as he was switching to the Navy side at halftime, he stopped and shook all of our hands and spoke with each of us individually. He told me we had a great year at Wisconsin and talked about us heading to the Rose Bowl. I said something about [Senator] Gaylord Nelson. It was unique. I still have a picture of us shaking hands."

On December 1, Richter was selected by Denver in the 10th round of the American Football League draft. VanderKelen was selected in the 21st round by the New York Titans; Gary Kroner was selected in the 19th round, also by the Titans. And Ron Carlson was chosen in the 25th round by the Buffalo Bills.

Two days later, the Washington Redskins selected Richter in the first round of the National Football League draft. The last time a Badger had been selected in the first round was in 1955, when Heisman Trophy winner Alan Ameche was selected in the first round by the Baltimore Colts.

Four days after the NFL draft, Richter traveled to Washington, D.C., where he was honored as the national lineman of the year at the Silver Anniversary Banquet of the Washington Pigskin Club with nearly 1,200 in attendance.

"I think the banquets are hard on him," Richter's mother, Mary Alice, told United Press International at the time. "He never complains, but I hope it won't hurt his grades."

Mary Alice went on to tell UPI that her son had a great season despite injury. Most people knew about his nagging hip injury, but few knew about a broken right hand that he suffered in UW's loss to Iowa on October 20.

"He didn't tell me about it until about three or four weeks after it happened," she said. "I knew his hand looked bad, but I was more concerned over his bruised hip."

* * *

In the days leading up to the 1963 Rose Bowl, Badger fans were excited about their upcoming matchup with the University of Southern California, but there certainly wasn't the hype and attention that would be commonplace decades later.

"It was number 1 versus number 2, but it wasn't like what you'd see today," Richter said, whose Badgers were established as a three-point favorite in the game.

Years later, by the time Pat Richter became the UW's athletic director, the Rose Bowl payout would reach several million dollars. More than one million would be provided to the Big Ten representative for travel purposes. On December 13, 1962, the Big Ten Conference approved a Rose Bowl travel budget of $105,000 for the Wisconsin bowl travel party, including $61,000 for the team and $41,000 for the band. The travel party included nearly 200, including the team, coaches, and Athletic Department personnel. Additionally, 160 band members were scheduled to travel to Pasadena.

Rose Bowl travel packages were being offered for $288 per person by the Wisconsin Alumni Association. For an additional $22, WAA travelers could add a night in Las Vegas.

Wisconsin State Journal sportswriter Tom Butler would write of UW cocaptains Richter and Steve Underwood, both of whom graduated from Madison East, "The last time the Badgers won eight of nine games was in 1942, when the cocaptains were also high school teammates: Mark Hoskins and Dave Schreiner."

This would be Pat Richter's first Rose Bowl, and he, like his other Badger teammates, knew little about the trip ahead. "I remember being with Renee at a function here in Madison and talking with [Alumni Association director] Arlie Mucks," Richter said. "Arlie told me that there was a Big Ten dinner scheduled in Pasadena and that I was going to participate in a skit with a Hollywood starlet named Joi Lansing. Well, I sensed that it didn't go over too well with Renee, so I thought maybe it was time to give her a ring."

Richter purchased an engagement ring at Jason Johnson's East Side Jewelers on Atwood Avenue and soon, he proposed to Renee. "I put the ring in a popcorn box," Richter said. Renee accepted the proposal, and the wedding date was scheduled for June 8, 1963.

The Badgers had arrived in California on December 22 and were head-quartered at the Huntington-Sheraton in Pasadena. For the first several days in California, the pace was slow and the events were low-key. "We really didn't have any idea about the spectacle of the Rose Bowl, with the parade and everything," Richter said. "We hung around a lot at the hotel. We went to Disneyland. Again, even though it was number 1 versus number 2, it really didn't seem like there was that much hype."

Thirty-one years later, the coverage of Wisconsin's appearance in the Rose Bowl was ever-present, particularly with local news outlets in Madison. But the news of the day this December 26 in 1962 was the weather. Badger fans in Madison were dealing with a record low temperature of minus 22 degrees. In the sports sections, coverage of the Green Bay Packers, the Badger basketball team, and high school basketball continued to be the focus at holiday time.

The Madison West Regents, for instance, were busy preparing for their Big Eight Conference basketball game against Madison Central. Accompanying the *Wisconsin State Journal*'s advance story on the game was a team photo of the Regents, a photo that included Jim Doyle, future governor of Wisconsin. Doyle, the paper said, would be forced to miss the game due to a broken arm.

At the December 29 Big Ten Dinner at the Biltmore Hotel in downtown Los Angeles, it would turn out that Richter was not involved in the skit. Instead, teammate Steve Young from Mount Pleasant, Iowa, represented the Badgers during the program that night. Also appearing on the program that night with Lansing was Hollywood actor Dennis Morgan, a native of Prentice, Wisconsin.

Pat Richter (second from left) enjoys a card game with teammates Hal Brandt and Ron VanderKelen in the days leading up to the 1963 Rose Bowl.
Photo courtesy of the UW Athletic Department.

In the weeks prior to the trip, it was clear that Wisconsin football coach Milt Bruhn was determined to make his second visit to the Rose Bowl significantly more enjoyable than the first, when the Badgers were trounced by Washington 44–8 in the 1960 Rose Bowl.

In the wake of that loss, there had been some rumblings back home about the team's lack of focus during their preparation for the bowl game against the Huskies. Among the more vocal critics was *Milwaukee Journal* sports editor Oliver Kuechle, who implied that the Badgers treated the visit to Pasadena as a vacation.

"Our guys didn't play very well," Richter said of the 1960 game. "There was a lot of talk that this trip was going to be handled differently than last time. I think it was Milt who came up with the idea that we would seclude ourselves."

After a short stay at the Huntington-Sheraton in Pasadena, Richter said, the team boarded buses and headed to the hills. When they arrived at the Passionist Fathers Monastery in the Sierra Madre Mountains, they found the seclusion that Bruhn had sought.

"I don't want them standing around the lobby talking with well-wishers," Bruhn told reporters. "I want them in their rooms and off their feet."

Said Richter: "It was a beautiful place, but it was very secluded. We were assigned one person to a room. The rooms were very spartan and there wasn't much exciting reading material, to say the least. It was very stark.

"I think Milt just wanted to make sure that we didn't wander and that we took care of ourselves," Richter said.

On the afternoon of January 1, 1963, the Badgers left the seclusion of the Sierra Madre Mountains and traveled to the Rose Bowl to meet the Southern California Trojans. USC had a great receiver in Hal Bedsole, an outstanding fullback in Ben Wilson, and Willie Brown, the first in a long line of talented running backs to play for Coach John McKay at USC. The Trojans also had not one, but two star quarterbacks in Bill Nelson and Pete Beathard, both of whom went on to play several years in the NFL.

Their coach, John McKay, was in his third season at USC. Over upcoming seasons, McKay's teams would appear in eight Rose Bowls, win nine Pacific Ten titles, and four national championships. His win-loss record during 16 seasons at USC would be 127-40-8, making McKay the winningest coach in Trojan football history.

The stage was set for what was to become one of the greatest collegiate football games ever. But the show was delayed.

"We had gone through our pregame practice routine and returned to the locker room," Richter recalled. "And then we were called out onto the field. So we went out there and noticed that USC wasn't out there. There were still some bands playing and we were wondering what was going on. We stood there for a fairly lengthy period of time, maybe 10 minutes. Finally, USC comes out."

The delay, in Richter's opinion, hurt the Badgers. "You come running out of your locker room ready to go and all of a sudden, you have to stand there for 10 minutes and wait and you end up getting real flat."

The delay continued at midfield where referee Jimmy Cain was lining up the players for pictures and television camera shots. Richter said Cain, who must have noticed how anxious the Badgers were to move things along, told the group assembled at midfield that "if it wasn't for the press and the media, we wouldn't be here today."

"The whole thing was just stretched out too long," Richter said of the 15-minute delay. "And for some reason, USC had gotten different information than we did. And we start the game flat and aren't playing well at all."

The Badgers continued to feel like things weren't going their way throughout the first half. Fullback Ben Wilson was gaining big chunks of yardage, prompting the NBC broadcaster to repeatedly hail the USC star as "Mount Wilson," much to the dismay of Badgers fans watching back home in wintry Wisconsin. With the Trojans leading 14–7 early in the second quarter, Wisconsin's Ron Carlson recovered an apparent fumble for the Badgers on the USC 20-yard line. Unfortunately for the Badgers, the referees ruled that there was no fumble on the play, so instead of taking over with great field position and a chance to tie the game, the Badgers remained on defense, and USC scored shortly thereafter to take a commanding 21–7 second-quarter lead.

One of the Midwestern writers covering the game was Lloyd Larson, sports editor of the *Milwaukee Sentinel*. Larson was a former baseball and football player at the University of Wisconsin. He later became an accomplished basketball and football referee and officiated in Big Ten Conference games and in the 1951 Rose Bowl. Years later, Larson was inducted in the University of Wisconsin Athletic Hall of Fame.

Covering the Rose Bowl in 1963, Larson characterized that sequence for his *Milwaukee Sentinel* readers like this:

> Richter punts the ball out on SC's 24 . . . Then comes the worst break of the game . . . Bill Nelson, back to pass, is hit by Andy Wojdula and Carlson, fumbling the ball. Wisconsin recovers on SC's 20, but the referee rules the ball dead before the fumble . . . How could he? . . . That's really a rotten call.
>
> The value of that call to the Trojans is brought home moments later when Nelson hits Willie Brown on a 45-yard pass to Wiscon-

sin's 25 and sets up Ron Heiler's touchdown run on the next play.

As bad as that one was, there was still another tougher one to come before the end of the half . . . Two toughies, in fact . . . First, Holland apparently steps out of bounds by an eighth of an inch after taking Vandy's pass and running for what everybody in the stands thinks is a touchdown.

Then comes the superthriller that goes for naught . . . Vandy makes a sensational escape from would-be tacklers and fires a strike to Holland, who makes a dazzling diving catch in the end zone . . . But it's no dice . . . Wisconsin is called for clipping on the play and there goes the TD . . . With only second remaining at that . . . Such excitement.

The momentum continued to swing toward the Trojans throughout the third period. With the sun now set and darkness beginning to cover the stadium, Willie Brown returned the opening kickoff of the second half for 41 yards to the USC 43. On the next play, Beathard passed to Bedsole for a 57-yard touchdown and a 28–7 lead.

The Badgers responded with a 67-yard touchdown drive, but USC came back with a 67-yard touchdown drive of their own, as Bedsole scored on another touchdown pass for a 35–14 lead. In the waning moments of the third quarter, a pass interception put USC in great field position, and after Fred Hill caught a touchdown pass on the first play of the fourth quarter, Wisconsin trailed 42–14.

But then, Wisconsin rallied.

"When we were down 42–14, as is the case with human nature, they thought the game was over," Richter said. "They probably backed off a bit. We were motivated to try and make things respectable. I know my aunt and uncle had left the game, but as we started coming back, they turned around and came back to the stadium.

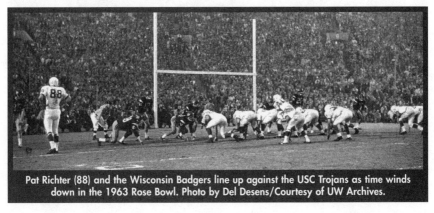

Pat Richter (88) and the Wisconsin Badgers line up against the USC Trojans as time winds down in the 1963 Rose Bowl. Photo by Del Desens/Courtesy of UW Archives.

"Psychologically, they were down and we started getting fired up. We were catching some crossing patterns. Ron would roll right and I'd come back to the left, and we got some momentum going and started to come back. And of course, it was tough for them to try and get their momentum again."

The shift in momentum began with an 80-yard touchdown drive. VanderKelen was on target, completing seven of nine passes on the drive. Lou Holland's 13-yard run trimmed the lead to 42–21, and if nothing else, lifted the spirits of Badger fans.

Next, the Badgers recovered a Ben Wilson fumble, and moments later, VanderKelen completed a 29-yard touchdown pass to Gary Kroner. Still, USC held a comfortable 42–28 lead.

After the Badgers stopped a Trojans' drive at the Wisconsin 32, the Badgers continued to move the ball at will, driving all the way to the USC four-yard line. However, with just over four minutes left in the game, Brown intercepted a VanderKelen pass to halt the Badger drive.

But the Badgers weren't done. On fourth down, the USC snap flew over the head of the punter and out of the end zone for a safety, trimming the USC lead to 42–30.

On the ensuing free kick, Ron "Pinto" Smith ran it back to the USC 43-yard line, and three plays later, Richter caught a 19-yard touchdown pass. With 1 minute, 19 seconds remaining in the game, Wisconsin trailed by less than a touchdown.

The Badgers tried an onside kick, but that failed, and USC took over with 1:06 remaining. On the next three plays, the Trojans lost 12 yards and were forced to punt on the last play of the game.

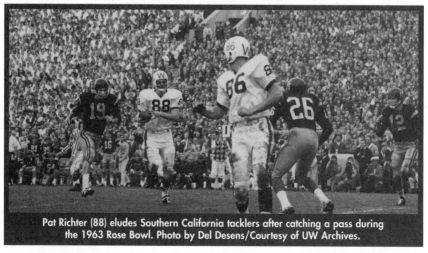

Pat Richter (88) eludes Southern California tacklers after catching a pass during the 1963 Rose Bowl. Photo by Del Desens/Courtesy of UW Archives.

"I was on the left-hand side," Richter said of the last play. "From my viewpoint, the guys on the right-hand side looked like they were going to block the kick. Years later, I talked with Elmars Ezerins about it. He was on the right side and he said that as he turned, the ball went right by his hip. It was that close."

Holland fielded the punt, but was tackled by the Trojans, and what could have been one of the greatest comeback victories in collegiate football history fell five points short.

The game produced a long list of Rose Bowl records. VanderKelen set records for passes attempted (48), passes completed (33), passing yards (401), and total yards (401). Richter, meanwhile, set records for passes caught (11) and pass receiving yards (163).

Back in Wisconsin, the home folks were proud of their team, regardless of the final outcome. Nearly 3,000 fans would greet the team upon its return home on January 3.

Roundy Coughlin, the legendary columnist for the *Wisconsin State Journal*, wasn't able to attend the game in California. He informed his readers in late December that doctors had confined him to watching the game from Madison after his foot was injured by a dropped bowling ball on December 17 and that he would watch the game from the home of Mr. and Mrs. Howard Bullis in Madison. Roundy was famous for his many unorthodox one-liners and not so famous for his ability to live by the rules of English grammar.

"The team played a beautiful game in the second half they stood out like Santa Claus on top of a chimney," wrote Coughlin. Referring to the many catches Richter made in the second-half comeback, he wrote: "Pat got everything but McKay's false teeth in case he has them.

"You'll never see another Wisconsin team play as good as Wisconsin did in that fourth quarter," Coughlin concluded. "Southern Cal was so dazed they didn't know if they were in the Rose Bowl or down in the valley picking strawberries."

The *State Journal*'s editorial writers took a more refined approach in their salute to the Badgers.

> They accomplished their task handsomely—they made Wisconsin proud—and they provided a valuable lesson for everyday life: Never quit trying while there is still a chance to reach your goal . . .
>
> Staring humiliation square in the face, they battled until they won everyone's admiration and respect . . .
>
> They played their hearts out and lost the game but they captured the hearts and praise of their fans.
>
> With the Green Bay Packers reigning as professional titlists, Wisconsin now has a corner on the championship market.

Over time, it became clear that the 1963 Rose Bowl was not just a moment that Badger fans cherished. It was a game that was a treat to watch for the millions of television viewers.

"Most people looked at it as an entertainment event instead of who won and who lost," said Richter. "Ron and I left the next day to go the Hula Bowl and we were guests on a local TV show there with a couple of USC players. And all the people could talk about was this great comeback by Wisconsin. At some point, the USC guys said, 'Hey, wait a minute. We won the game!'

"I think people looked at it as great entertainment and really enjoyed it," Richter said.

Authors David Wallechinsky and Amy Wallace, in their best-selling *Book of Lists*, placed the 1963 game on the list of the top ten sporting events of all time.

* * *

The echoes of that stirring afternoon in 1963 would follow Richter for the rest of his career.

In the mid-1970s, Richter was sitting in the Dallas airport waiting for an early morning flight. Across the way, he saw a familiar figure. "I look up and it's Woody Hayes," Richter said. "So I got up and was going to go over and say hello, and just as I did, he starts to grab his stuff because his plane must have been called. So as he's beginning to move on I say, 'Coach, Pat Richter.' And he says, 'Oh yeah. A couple of more minutes and you would have won that game!' And off he went."

Thirty-one years after the dramatic loss to USC, Richter returned to Pasadena, this time as Wisconsin's director of athletics, when the Badgers earned a berth in the 1994 Rose Bowl. "Barry [Alvarez] and I were in Pasadena at the Doubletree Hotel attending the Rose Bowl preparation meetings," Richter recalled. "We were sitting in the lounge and we look over and there's Tommy Lasorda. Barry said, 'Let's go over and say hello to Tommy.' So we go over there and Barry introduces himself. 'Tommy, I'm Barry Alvarez, coach at the University of Wisconsin.' 'Hey Barry, how you doing?' Then I introduced myself and he says, 'Oh hey, that was a great Rose Bowl.' Here's our coach sitting there and Tommy Lasorda's talking about the 1963 Rose Bowl!"

In the spring of 2005—more than 42 years later—Pat and Renee Richter are standing in a long line at the security checkpoint at an airport in Fort Myers, Florida. As the security agent reviews Renee's boarding pass and driver's license, he looks at her and says, "Richter . . . Richter . . . I remember a Richter in the Rose Bowl several years ago. You're not any relation to that guy are you?" Before Renee can answer, the security agent glances at the tall man standing behind her and says, "Hey, that *is* you. You're Pat Richter from the Rose Bowl!"

CHAPTER FOUR
A FASCINATING TIME

It had been a long football season for Pat Richter. Not only did the team play in the New Year's Day Rose Bowl, but Richter's appearance in the Hula Bowl extended the season. In addition, the many public appearances tied into the various All-America team awards were taking their toll.

It also delayed the start of his basketball season for the 1962–63 Badgers. By the time Richter joined the team and began to get in basketball shape, the season was well underway. He appeared in only eight games for the Badgers, averaging 3.3 points and 4.1 rebounds per game in limited playing time. The Badgers finished the season at 14-10 overall and 7-7 in the Big Ten, good for fifth place.

In the classroom, Richter had changed majors from metallurgical engineering to landscape architecture. If he stuck to his academic plan, he would have only eight credits remaining after his senior year and, if he played professional sports, would be able to easily return to UW to complete his degree.

After the shortened basketball season, it was once again time to turn his attention to baseball, with its indoor practices at the Shell, the warm-weather journey to Arizona to play some of the best teams in the country, and the return to a cold, rainy, and sometimes snowy Midwest for Big Ten Conference baseball.

During that time, Richter was mulling over his professional sports future. "During my senior year of baseball, there was some discussion about whether I was going to take a look at baseball," he said. "I had been drafted in the first round (seventh pick overall) by the Redskins. I was also drafted by the AFL team, the Denver Broncos. At that time, you could negotiate against both teams and had decent leverage. And baseball was hanging out there, too."

Redskins assistant coach Abe Gibron tried to help Richter in the decision-making process. Gibron, who later would become head coach of the Chicago

Bears, attended a Badger baseball game at Guy Lowman Field with Dale Hackbart, the former Madison East and UW star who was now playing for the Redskins in the NFL. "If I struck out or made an out, Abe would clap," Richter said. "When I'd get a base hit, he'd boo."

Richter had several conversations with Madison attorney Gene Calhoun, a longtime friend and advisor who years earlier had helped Richter with the decision to attend Wisconsin instead of Kansas. The more Richter talked to Calhoun, the more sense it seemed to make for Richter to sign with the Redskins. "As my thinking started to solidify, I kept thinking that baseball has an extensive minor league system," Richter said. "In football, you are either going to play at the highest level or move on to something else. There were a few guys who tried to play professional football and baseball; Tom Brown with the Packers was one of them. But it never really crossed my mind."

If there was any doubt about which sport to choose, the decision became crystal clear early in the baseball season his senior year. The Badgers played their home games at Guy Lowman Field, located on the far west side of campus, just off the shores of Lake Mendota. In early spring, when the north winds would flow briskly across the chilly lake, Guy Lowman could be a very cold place.

On this particular weekend, the team's Friday afternoon game against North Dakota was postponed due to cold, rainy, and snowy weather. It was rescheduled as part of a tripleheader the next day, again, at chilly Guy Lowman.

"We got there the next day and the snow had stopped, but the temperatures were just above freezing," Richter said. "We played two seven-inning games and one nine-inning game. It was just a long, long day . . . and so cold. That probably was one of the things that drove me to football."

Weeks later, Richter made it official, signing a two-year deal with the Redskins. He received a $15,000 signing bonus and a first-year salary of $15,000. In year two, he received an automatic salary increase to $17,500.

On the baseball field, Richter had a decent senior season for the Badgers, who finished 8-6 in the Big Ten Conference. For the season, Richter hit .339, led the team in runs batted in (32), and tied for the team lead in home runs (6) and hits (38) in 30 games. At the time, leading the Badgers in a hitting category was an impressive feat, considering that Richter's teammate, junior Rick Reichardt, was one of the most promising professional baseball prospects in the country. Reichardt won the Big Ten batting title that season (.429) and, after defending his conference batting title the next year (.472), went on to be one of major league's first "bonus babies," signing a $200,000 contract with Gene Autry's Los Angeles Angels in September 1964. At the time, it was the largest signing bonus in major league history.

In 82 career baseball games at Wisconsin, Richter finished with a .339 batting average, 20 home runs, and 74 runs batted in. In earning his third "W" letter in baseball in 1963, he became Wisconsin's first nine-time letter winner since 1927. There have not been any others since Pat Richter.

Several weeks later, Pat and Renee Richter were married on June 8 in an evening ceremony in downtown Madison at Bethel Lutheran Church's temporary location, which was at Christ Presbyterian Church, current site of the Concourse Hotel. Shortly thereafter, the two headed east, where Richter would play in a new college All-Star game in Buffalo, New York, called the All-American Game. It was a game that had been dedicated in honor of the late Ernie Davis, who starred as a running back at Syracuse and became the first black player to win the Heisman Trophy in 1961. Drafted in the first round by the Washington Redskins and traded to Cleveland, Davis died of leukemia the following year before playing a pro football game. His last football game was exactly one year earlier, the 1962 All-American Game in Buffalo.

Admittedly, Richter had done little to prepare for the game. "I decided I could use a rest after three years of football, basketball, and baseball," Richter told the *Washington Post.* "I didn't even try to get in shape until I reported here for the game. I'll do more as I get ready for the All-Star Game in Chicago and hope to be real ready when I report to the Redskins."

UW teammate Ron VanderKelen also had been selected to play in the game, and Wisconsin coach Milt Bruhn was the head coach of the east squad. Richter recalled one of Bruhn's more embarrassing coaching moments as the East team prepared for the game.

"We weren't doing very well in practice and he was mad and yelling at us," Richter said. "He brought us into a circle and said, 'Come on fellows, let's get out there and start doing things the way we're supposed to,' and rallied the troops, so to speak. And just at the peak of his speech, he slams the football down as a point of emphasis. Unfortunately, it bounces right back up and hits him in the groin. It doubled him over and he almost went all the way to the ground in pain."

Bruhn's East team lost the game 22–21, despite a 24-yard touchdown pass from VanderKelen to Richter. Prior to the game, the six East-West team coaches voted to give the first Ernie Davis Award to Richter as the player who displayed the most cooperation, leadership, and sportsmanship in practice drills.

While in New York, newlyweds Pat and Renee visited Niagara Falls, honeymoon capital of the world. They returned to Madison, where they stayed at Pat's mother's house on Madison's East Side. Weeks later, Pat and Renee would learn that Renee was pregnant and due to give birth in March.

The next stop on the Richter's 1963 summer tour was Chicago, site of the

Chicago Tribune All-Star Classic football game. The popular summer event was first played in 1934, when *Tribune* sports editor Arch Ward came up with the idea of a preseason game between the NFL champions and a team of college All-Stars to benefit the newspaper's charity fund. All of the games were played at historic Soldier Field in Chicago. In the early years of the game, the college players did pretty well against the pros. In later years, however, the NFL champions rarely lost. In fact, going into the 1963 game, the College All-Stars had won just twice since 1950.

But in 1963, college and pro football fans were paying close attention as the College All-Stars gathered for their pregame training camp at Northwestern University in Evanston.

After several days at Northwestern, the team moved to the Hilton Hotel on Michigan Avenue in downtown Chicago.

"At the time," Richter said, "the All-Star Game was a big deal. I think initially, the NFL needed something like that to help with their visibility. Later, the roles were reversed and it was good for the *Chicago Tribune.*"

The College All-Stars, coached by Otto Graham, were a confident bunch, with Richter, VanderKelen, Heisman Trophy winner Terry Baker of Oregon State, Minnesota's Bobby Bell, and LSU's Jerry Stovall, among others.

Confident or not, their opponent was formidable. As the defending world champions, the mighty Green Bay Packers were the NFL representative in the game. They posed quite a challenge, especially to someone like Richter or VanderKelen, who had watched closely as Vince Lombardi began shaping an NFL dynasty that would captivate the football fans of Wisconsin and the nation.

"We went to the field early and were sitting on the sideline benches," Richter said. "The buses came in on the other side and the Packers got off. Fuzzy. Max. Hornung. Starr. Taylor. Ron Kramer. They looked big and confident and we were in awe because these were the Packers. We had our eyes wide open just seeing these guys who were our football heroes."

If the All-Stars were in awe, they didn't show it. On a hot, muggy Chicago night, the two teams battled closely throughout much of the first quarter. Near the end of the quarter, Graham called a for a quick, five-yard pass to Richter. The play, known to Richter as the "Packer Pass," worked better than imagined.

"Ron [VanderKelen] had a hot hand," Richter said. "He hit me on a five-yard out, and as I turned upfield, Jesse Whittenton went to tackle me and he slipped off. I looked ahead and there was no one there and I went 73 yards for a touchdown. I wasn't the fastest guy around, and it was the longest touchdown I ever had."

The All-Stars continued to put pressure on the Packers, and shockingly, ended up defeating Green Bay 20–17. It was the last time the All-Stars were victorious in the game.

"It was quite an upset," Richter recalled. "It was a big deal."

Pat and Renee had made plans to go out after the game with former Badger John Fabry, who was a rookie free-agent quarterback on the Packer squad at the time. "I called him up after the game to see what time we were going to meet for dinner, he kind of quietly said, 'We can't go out tonight. We have to stay in.'

"Apparently, Lombardi wasn't too happy with the outcome of the game and basically told the team, 'Misters, you'll never, ever embarrass me again like that.'"

Several years later, the 1976 All-Star game was suspended and finally called off because of a heavy rainstorm late in the third quarter, with the Pittsburgh Steelers holding a 24–0 lead. That was the last game of the series.

Forty-two years after it started, the *Chicago Tribune* College All-Star Classic had ended, but not before the now-famous combination of VanderKelen to Richter had left another long-standing impression on football fans across the country.

* * *

Richter's next stop that summer was Carlisle, Pennsylvania, the training-camp home of the Washington Redskins.

Carlisle is a small, quaint town located in south central Pennsylvania, in the heart of what is known as the Cumberland Valley. Located 130 miles northwest of Washington, D.C., Carlisle was settled in 1775 and has a rich history. Dickinson College, a small liberal-arts college in Carlisle, was chartered only a few days after the end of the American Revolution in 1783; the first college in the new United States of America.

Carlisle was also famous as the home of legendary Olympian Jim Thorpe, who many claim was the greatest athlete ever. Thorpe, who was born in Oklahoma, moved to Carlisle in his youth. In the 1912 Olympic Games, he won both the pentathlon and decathlon events.

In 1963, the Redskins chose Carlisle and Dickenson College as the site of their team's training camp. It was a relationship that would continue each summer through 1994, and would start up again in 2004.

The head coach of the Redskins, Bill McPeak, had told Richter and College All-Star teammate Lonnie Sanders that they were not expected at training camp until Sunday, two days after their game in Chicago. Sanders drove from Chicago to Carlisle and reported to camp on Sunday as scheduled. Richter, however, arranged for a flight from Chicago to Harrisburg and arrived in Carlisle earlier than expected Saturday afternoon, just in time to watch the Redskins practice from the sidelines. The All-Star game had put Richter behind schedule, and he was anxious to start.

"We trained at Carlisle for a reason," Richter said. "It was a very quiet place."

Richter entered camp as one of the more notable rookies in the NFL that summer. The attention garnered from the 1963 Rose Bowl, his long list of post-season honors and his status as a number-one draft pick put Richter in the lime-light. His performance in the College All-Star game did nothing to diminish that. Twenty-four hours after playing a key role in defeating the world-champion Packers, Richter was reporting to camp.

"In the 1960s, NFL training camps were quite lengthy, usually about four or five weeks before the first exhibition game," Richter recalled. "There wasn't any pay in that day for the games themselves. Pretty much you made the team or you were out.

"Back then, there weren't any strength and conditioning programs at camp," Richter said. "You get up early and go to breakfast, maybe get a couple of minutes in your room, head over to practice, get taped up, get on the field. You always knew that with the two-a-day drills the grass was always wet for the morning practice. You spent a lot of time in training camp in the early morning dew and the wet grass, you'd spend a couple of hours in practice, then go back to the dorm, have lunch, maybe take a nap, and then do it all over again in the afternoon.

"You'd go back to practice for a couple of hours, maybe have time to go have a beer after practice, then go back to the dorm for dinner, then have a cou-ple of meetings, then maybe have a couple of hours after that before an eleven o'clock curfew. One of the better businesses in town was to rent fans or window air conditioners to all the players. That's pretty much your life. It was always a happy day when you went to one-a-day drills."

It was a veteran Redskins team in 1963. Norm Snead was the quarterback. Two years earlier, the Redskins traded first-round draft pick Ernie Davis to Cleveland for running back Bobby Mitchell, who became the first African American player in Redskins team history. Mitchell, after being switched to flanker, became a Redskins star over the next several seasons.

Former Badger Dale Hackbart was on the team as well. Hackbart had been drafted by the Green Bay Packers and played briefly for Green Bay in 1961 before being traded to the Redskins. His presence helped ease the transition for Richter.

The previous season, the Redskins had raised the hopes of their fans, start-ing the season with four victories and two ties in the team's first six games. Unfortunately, the Redskins lost seven of their last eight games and finished with a 5-7-2 record. The season before—McPeak's first—was even worse, as the Redskins struggled to a 1-12-1 record in 1961.

"The Redskins hadn't been very successful as of late and the pressure was starting to build a little bit," Richter said. "They were the nation's team. They really owned the entire southeastern coast of the United States. There were no other teams there. We played exhibition games in Tampa and Charlotte and Norfolk. They were pretty much all Redskin fans."

Richter's first professional football game was against the Cleveland Browns in Cleveland's Municipal Stadium. "I always thought it was perhaps the coldest stadium in the world," Richter said. "It had a baseball diamond with a dirt infield. It was interesting from a historical perspective, just like Yankee Stadium. The Browns had a good team back then. Frank Ryan was the quarterback and Jim Brown was in the backfield. I was playing tight end at the time with a single-bar facemask. Early in the game, Jim Houston thrust out with his forearm and got into my nose and eyes and mouth. After the play, he said, 'Sorry kid, I didn't mean to hit you in the face.' I sensed a bit of insincerity in his voice. That was my indoctrination into the NFL."

Richter caught his first professional touchdown pass that day, but the Redskins lost 37–14. The Redskins would win their next two games, but then lost 10 of their last 11 and finished with a dismal 3-11 record.

Richter caught 27 passes in his rookie season for 383 yards and 3 touchdowns. And despite the many losses, he enjoyed his new life as professional football player in the NFL, facing players that he had followed during his years as a high school and college football player.

"It was a daunting task to have to block down on guys like Gino Marchetti and Big Daddy Lipscomb, guys you had heard about for so long," Richter said. "Every time you played you were playing with people with reputations. The Giants had Andy Robustelli and Sam Huff and Rosey Brown. The Browns had Jim Brown and Leroy Kelly."

And as he learned about competing with the big guys, Richter also picked up on the inner workings of the NFL. "One of our first games, I was punting and the snap bounced its way back to me and I was able to get the punt off, but I got drilled after the kick," he recalled. "As I got up, I said to the ref, 'Hey, what about that?' He just shrugged his shoulders and said when the ball bounces back there, you're fair game.

"It was looser back then," Richter said. "Those kinds of things happened more than you'd see today. There were a lot of characters and history there."

The same could be said of Richter's new home away from home, Washington, D.C. Living in an apartment in Riverdale, Maryland, Pat and Renee were settling into their new home, taking in the many sights and sounds in the nation's capital. They visited Mount Vernon and Williamsburg. They even took a tour of the White House, thanks to John Gronouski, a Wisconsin native who had been appointed postmaster general by President John Kennedy.

"Washington is such a fascinating place with so much going on," Richter said. "You'd see a limousine with a flag and you'd wonder, is that the president? The vice president? The secretary of defense? You couldn't really grasp it all because we'd only been there the one year."

On the afternoon of November 22, Richter and the Redskins were practicing at Anacostia River Park. Somehow, Richter said, you could just sense that something was amiss.

"Cars were going slower and everything seemed to be slowing down," he said. "Then, someone ran down to the practice field and told us the president had been shot."

One year after shaking hands with Pat Richter and his fellow All-Americans at the 1962 Army-Navy football game, President John F. Kennedy, on a campaign trip in Dallas, had been shot and killed.

Forty-eight hours later, the Redskins were scheduled to play the Eagles at Philadelphia.

"There was a lot of discussion about whether the game should be played," Richter said. "But we finally got on the train to go to Philly. There was a special pregame ceremony for the president and the game went on as planned. Subsequently, there was a lot of criticism for [Commissioner Pete] Rozelle."

In a game that many thought should not have been played, the Redskins won 13–10, their third and final victory of the 14-game season. But it all seemed inconsequential, especially for those living in the nation's capital.

"A lot of things had happened while we were on the trip," Richter said. "Sunday was the day the President was lying in state at the capital. When we got off the train, there were thousands and thousands waiting to view the president. It was just a very eerie, surreal feeling."

Several days after the funeral, the Richters drove to Arlington National Cemetery to view the gravesite and its eternal flame. "You could see it as you went across the bridge," Richter said. "It was all part of this unbelievable scene. To be in that town at that time was exhilarating."

Prior to the Christmas holidays, the Richters returned to the Madison area, where they would rent a small home on Edgewood Avenue, just west of Camp Randall Stadium. The small home, ironically, was across the street from the home of Richter's UW baseball coach, Dynie Mansfield. Pat enrolled for the second semester at the UW.

While Richter was in school, Renee gave birth to the couple's first child, Scott, on March 16, 1964. Two months later, Pat graduated from UW with a Bachelor of Science degree in landscape architecture. In the months following graduation, Richter worked for the State of Wisconsin Park Planning Department and did some limited landscape design work on area parks and campgrounds.

* * *

Training camp came quickly for Richter and the Redskins, although, with the team's performance over the previous three seasons, one could argue that the sooner they could put the past behind them and get started on the new season, the better.

Washington Coach Bill McPeak was entering his fourth season with the Redskins. His first three were less than stellar; the Redskins were 1-12 in 1961; 5-7-2 in 1962; and 3-11 in 1963. His overall record was 9-30-2.

Still there wasn't nearly as much pressure as you'd expect with a win-loss record like that. "At that time, there was baseball in D.C.," Richter said. "Football was more of an entertainment thing. There wasn't a lot of pressure or expectations. The press wasn't riding them. They wrote a lot of it off on [owner] George Preston Marshall and his tight-fisted control of the team. The Jurgensen thing was perhaps a sign that things were about to change."

The "Jurgensen thing" was a stunning off-season trade prior to the 1964 season that had put new life and optimism into the Redskins and their fans. The Redskins sent quarterback Norm Snead to the Philadelphia Eagles for veteran quarterback Sonny Jurgensen.

Jurgensen had spent seven seasons with the Philadelphia Eagles, where he and receiver Tommy McDonald had teamed up to be one of the league's foremost passing combinations. The Redskins also added first-round draft pick Charley Taylor, a wide receiver from Arizona State, and tight end Jerry Smith, also from ASU.

"We had some good young players coming on the scene," Richter said. "There was a lot of optimism going into the season."

Jurgensen brought with him some impressive credentials as an NFL quarterback. He also brought with him a reputation as one of the league's off-the-field notables. And who would be the flamboyant veteran quarterback's new roommate at training camp in sleepy Carlisle and on NFL road trips? The mild-mannered tight end from Wisconsin, Pat Richter. "I think the intent was for me to calm him down and for him to get me a bit crazier," Richter said.

Richter not only enjoyed rooming with Jurgensen, he enjoyed playing receiver when the cagey veteran was at quarterback. "I remember that first year," Richter said. "Sonny had a sore arm, and on the first play of the game, he'd air one out and throw a long pass. After that, he wouldn't throw a long pass the rest of the day. He'd call all of his own plays. He'd pick grass and draw a play in the huddle. And he could put the ball in there anytime he wanted to. He reminded me of the way [Brett] Favre plays, although his arm was not as strong, but he was very accurate and threw an easy pass to catch."

Jurgensen's presence on offense clearly improved the Redskins' scoring punch. He passed for 24 touchdowns and earned a spot in the 1964 Pro Bowl. Unfortunately, Richter didn't catch many of them. Wide receivers Charley Taylor and Bobby Mitchell were Jurgensen's main targets, and Richter, playing behind Pres Carpenter at the tight end position, was limited to just four passes for 48 yards and no touchdowns. In addition, he finished 13th in the league in punting with a 41.2 yard average.

The Redskins stumbled out of the blocks, losing five of their first six games. They put together a mid-season run, winning five of six, then lost their last two games and finished at 6-8 for another losing season.

Still, the Richters continued to enjoy their life in the nation's capital and, instead of heading back to Wisconsin in the off-season, they chose to stay in D.C. After the 1964 season, Richter accepted a part-time position with Thurman Donovan and Associates, a landscape architecture firm in Silver Spring, Maryland. He still enjoyed that business and wanted to learn more about it. Meanwhile, he and the Redskins had come to terms on a new contract for his third year in the NFL. Faced with what appeared to be a sound financial picture, the Richters put $5,000 down on a $25,000 home in Silver Spring. "After the closing, we went back to our apartment and said to ourselves, 'What did we just do?' We felt sick to our stomachs to sink that much money into a house."

The buyers' remorse didn't last long. The value of the house, like others in the D.C. area, grew significantly over the years. "Washington was really starting to take off," Richter said.

Richter and his teammates would often make guest appearances on behalf of the team, particularly during the off-season. One time, Richter was asked to represent the Redskins and give an award at the residence of Eunice and Sargent Shriver. Eunice Shriver was John F. Kennedy's sister. "I met them both and they asked where Renee was, and I told them she was at home. They said, call her and invite her out here. So I went into the kitchen to use their phone on the wall and there were all these handwritten numbers on the wall: Jackie, Bobby, Teddy. They were all there!"

It wasn't his first brush with the famous family. Of course, he had met the late John Kennedy in the fall of 1962 at the Army-Navy game. He had met Ethel and Ted Kennedy—along with Gerald Ford—when they attended a Redskins postgame party. And Bobby Kennedy would occasionally stop by the Redskins practice.

"It was a fascinating time," Richter said.

* * *

With just four catches to his credit in the entire 1964 season, Richter headed into camp determined to play a bigger role in the Redskins offense in 1965. He was frustrated with his low production. So too were his Redskin coaches. And a published report in the July 25 edition of the *Washington Post* was direct, if not blunt:

> The 6 foot 5, 230-pound former All-American from Wisconsin has all the physical requisites to be a fine pro football player, but he has not been doing the job.
>
> Richter is capable of being one of the finest ends in the league. He has big hands and the ability to catch a football. He is not slow, but surprisingly fast moving from his stance at the scrimmage line.
>
> Coach Bill McPeak has set up special drills for Richter, using the linebackers to hold and maul the third-year tight end.
>
> Richter's personality may be working against him. He is an easy going young man who refuses to be riled up in any circumstance. He is putty in the hands of the in-fighting linebackers and this McPeak would like to change.

In addition to the extra work, McPeak and the coaching staff chose to move Richter to the outside and play him at the left end position. The move worked well, as Richter caught 16 passes for 189 and two touchdowns in 11 games for the 1965 Redskins. His punting improved as well: his 43.6 average ranked fourth in the league. The numbers would have been better had not Richter suffered a ruptured kidney in an exhibition game and a broken collarbone during the regular season.

Sonny Jurgensen, though, did not have a great season in 1965. He did throw 15 touchdowns, but also had 16 interceptions, and only one NFL team scored fewer points than the Redskins scored that year. Once again, the Redskins started slow, losing their first five games and finished with a 6-8 record.

In the three years Richter had been with McPeak and the Redskins, they had compiled a 15-27 record. To no one's surprise, the team's overall performance and its seeming lack of improvement over the past five years under McPeak led to the firing of the head coach.

The new Redskins coach was Otto Graham, a five-time Pro Bowl quarterback for the Cleveland Browns who led his team to seven championships in 10 seasons. A proven winner on the football field, Graham had no head coaching experience in the National Football League. But he did coach the 1963 College All-Stars who—led by Pat Richter and Ron VanderKelen—defeated the defending world champion Green Bay Packers.

"I thought it would be a good move for me," Richter said.

There was some question whether the move would be right for Jurgensen. "Sonny had always called his own plays and Otto wasn't like that," Richter said. "Also, the lifestyles were quite different. We used to kid that Otto was a milkshake guy and Sonny preferred Scotch. It was the method and the system more than anything else. And while optimism was building with Otto as the new coach, the fact is that Otto didn't have a lot of head coaching experience."

As the team reported to training camp at Carlisle in summer of 1966, it soon became clear that camp would have a different flavor than in previous years. The team was subject to bed checks at 11 p.m., and if you were found not to be in your room after that time, you'd be fined $100 for each hour that you failed to report to the head coach upon your return.

Jurgensen and Richter were still training camp roommates. And the fourth-year receiver and punter continued to be an interested observer of the 10th-year quarterback's antics.

"One night, they came in to check on Sonny at eleven and he was in the room," Richter said. "He later left, and about twelve thirty or one the coaches came back and checked again. I could hear them come into the room and poke around Sonny's bed. He finally came in around two thirty or three and I told him he better go down and tell Otto that he's back. He did that, and Otto asked him where he had been. Sonny told him he was at the bowling alley. Otto said, 'A bowling alley, Sonny?' Yes, Sonny insisted. 'And I have a witness.' And he reached around the corner and brought forth Duey Graham, Otto's teenage son. That was the last time Otto's teenage son was at training camp," Richter said.

As the Redskins broke camp, there was continued optimism in Redskin land. Graham was a highly successful quarterback who fans hoped could bring a winning tradition, or even a winning season, to the nation's capital. But there was no major shift in the fortunes of the Redskins, who continued their inconsistent ways and finished 7-7 and in fifth place in the NFL Eastern Division.

The coaching change from McPeak to Graham did not have the impact that Redskins fans had hoped. "It was a strained relationship because it was different lifestyles, different experiences," said Richter. "Otto was a real gentleman, and an outstanding athlete. But I think he was uncomfortable in the professional coaching ranks. As the seasons wore on and things became more problematic, there was a lot of negative press and media. It got to the point where the team was kind of doing goofy things as well.

"Otto had a tendency to get excited and when he did, he'd bang his clipboard with his open hand," Richter recalled. "One time, one of the guys who was injured and not practicing suggested that we have a pool to see how many times

Otto hits his clipboard in practice. So everybody threw in five bucks and picked a number. It ranged from 15 or 20 times to over a hundred."

Graham was banging the clipboard repeatedly, especially early in the practice, Richter said. The winner of the pool had selected 93, and a prize was presented in the locker room amid some hearty laughter and a lot of back-slapping and good fun. "Just after that," Richter said, "Otto came into the room and we all kind of quieted down. The irony, and in some respects it's somewhat sad, is that Otto was quoted in the paper the next day that this was perhaps the most enthusiastic practice that he'd had with the Redskins. And of course, of lot of it was artificially stimulated by the clipboard pool."

It was during the Graham years, Richter said, that he noticed that Edward Bennett Williams, president of the Redskins and a famous criminal attorney, began to take a more visible role in the ownership and the operation of the Redskins. It was Williams, Richter recalled, who introduced him to one of the country's greatest sports figures, former New York Yankee star Joe DiMaggio.

"We were playing at San Francisco and in our room with the door opened, and Edward Bennett Williams walks by," Richter said. "I didn't really notice who he was with at the time, but we said hello and he came in and who should follow him in the room but Joe DiMaggio. The two of them sat down and we were shooting the breeze for about 30 minutes or so."

Richter was fascinated. "Williams was a dynamic person with a tremendous mind," Richter said. "He was a very interesting guy. DiMaggio seemed like he was very shy and reserved. I asked him what motivated him, especially during his long hitting streak. He said he went to the ballpark every day with something in mind that would motivate him. He said he went there thinking that on that particular day, there was a youngster or adult or someone who was coming to the ballpark for the first and only time in their life and having a chance to see Joe DiMaggio. And he said 'I didn't want them leaving the park disappointed. That motivated me to do the best I could possibly do and drove me every time I went to the park.'"

Richter's relationship with Redskins ownership led to another chance meeting of a lifetime. Richter and some of his teammates were attending the funeral of one of the minority owners of the team, attorney Leo DeOrsey. "I happened to be sitting in one of the front rows and shortly after we sat down, the seven original U.S. astronauts came in and sat right in front of us. That was a big deal," Richter said.

There were several other celebrity sightings that added to the aura of living in the nation's capital. "We'd go to the Redskins office at the corner of Connecticut and 16th to pick up our paychecks," Richter said. "You'd park your car, and if you happened to be walking on Connecticut at the right time, around noon, this limo would pull up alongside and the door would pop open and it would be [FBI director] J. Edgar Hoover. Whenever he was in town, he'd have lunch at the Mayflower, where he had a regular table back in the corner.

"That was the way it was in Washington," Richter said. "It was a fascinating place to be, especially at such a young age."

During Graham's first two seasons, Richter's playing time diminished and his numbers dwindled. In 1966, he caught seven passes for 100 yards and no touchdowns. The Redskins muddled their way to a 7-7 record. Perhaps the season highlight was a late-season victory over the New York Giants, a game that included an interesting grudge match between veteran Redskins linebacker Sam Huff and New York Giants coach Allie Sherman. Huff, it seems, still hadn't forgiven Sherman for trading him from the Giants to the Redskins. "It comes to the final moments and we're ahead 69–41," Richter said. "The Giants have the ball and Don Heinrichs, trying to stop the clock, throws the ball out of bounds but it was fourth down and now it's our ball on their 20. So Sam goes up to coach and says, 'Let's kick a field goal.' So we did, and that made the score 72–41. Sam just wanted to stick it to Allie just one last time."

The following season was another disappointing one for the Redskins and for Pat Richter. The 1967 Redskins, in Graham's second season, finished 5-6-3. Remarkably, the former Badger tight end caught just one pass in 14 games.

In Graham's third season, however, Richter's numbers changed dramatically. Graham made the decision to move Richter to the outside receiver position, and more importantly, make him a starting receiver and give Richter significantly more playing time.

It turned out to be his best year as a professional receiver, as he caught 42 passes for 533 yards and nine touchdowns.

It didn't turn out to be one of Otto Graham's best seasons, though. The team's defense struggled all year and ranked near the bottom in points allowed. Following the team's disappointing 5-9 season, Graham was fired and the search for the Redskins' new coach began in earnest.

* * *

In *The Redskin Book*, published by the *Washington Post*, Ken Denlinger writes that Redskins majority owner Edward Bennett Williams had once tried to hire Green Bay Packer Coach Vince Lombardi.

"Before Williams hired Graham in 1966, he had tried to lure Vince Lombardi. But Lombardi wanted something Williams could not provide then—equity in the team. So Lombardi went on to win two more NFL titles, and the first two Super Bowls, before retiring as Packer coach in February of 1968.

"Lombardi remained general manager of the Packers" Denlinger continues. "Less than nine months later, however, during a breakfast meeting with Williams before a Redskins-Packers game in RFK Stadium, Lombardi admitted that he missed coaching."

Eventually, Denlinger writes, Lombardi would agree to a package that gave him five percent ownership in the team and the title of executive vice president and coach, at a salary of $110,000.

Pat Richter, a Wisconsin native, had met Lombardi only once, when Lombardi was the main speaker at Madison Pen and Mike Club banquet in 1963. "Being from Wisconsin, the announcement kind of stunned you a bit," Richter said. "He brought instant credibility and instant respect."

He also brought with him a reputation for being a strict disciplinarian and a hard-driving taskmaster.

"There was a lot of uncertainty and a lot of anticipation," Richter said. "What was it going to be like?"

Training camp continued to be held at tiny Dickinson College in Carlisle, where Richter and Jurgensen continued to be roommates. "We had a good-sized room that overlooked the front area of the dorm," Richter said. "The theory was that maybe he could keep a better eye on Sonny if he was in the front. But Sonny never gave him any trouble. He had tremendous respect for Vince. He really didn't test him at all."

Upon arrival at training camp, the team's first meeting was scheduled in the evening. "We had gotten word that Lombardi time meant that if the meeting was at 7:00 p.m., then you needed to be there at 6:45," Richter said. "Our first meeting was at 7:00, and we're all there at 10 minutes to 7:00. Everybody seems to be there waiting and waiting."

At five minutes before seven, one of the team's rookie receivers entered the room. "Lombardi looked at him with penetrating eyes and said, 'Young man, do you know that all of these gentlemen here are waiting for you?' He could have crawled under a nickel. He was five minutes early for the meeting, but according to Lombardi time, was about five minutes too late. That kind of set the tempo."

Entering his seventh training camp as a professional football player, Richter had plenty of practice experience; three years with McPeak and three more with Graham. Before long, Richter noticed a distinct difference in the new coach's practice regimen.

"Lombardi was very efficient," Richter said. "We had practices for about an hour and a half. We worked hard and got our work done. Wherever you were out on that field, you had the feeling that he could see you. Whether you were in front of him or walking away from him, you didn't want to make any faces or do something goofy because you always had the feeling that he was all-knowing.

"He was a robust character," Richter said. "He'd have a V-neck, short-sleeved T-shirt, with those khaki coaching pants that Red Blake probably wore. But he was very efficient. He could make hair stand on your back when he'd holler at you. He'd bellow at you. He had a tendency to take off his hat and rap it against your chest, or once in a while he'd take the whistle off and bounce it off your pads."

Richter also noticed Lombardi's apparent ability to know when he had pushed enough and when to back off.

"I'd heard a story about [former Badger] Ken Bowman in Green Bay," Richter said. "He used to get after Bowman pretty good. This particular day Bowman was mad about something that Lombardi said and he's in the locker room afterward throwing his pads and stuff around and cussing and saying 'I'm not going to take this,' and saying a few things about Lombardi. And just then he felt this arm reach out from behind him and whisper to him, 'We had a great practice today, Kenny, didn't we?' And it was Lombardi. He knew he had him out there and he reeled him back. He had a great ability to do that."

Lombardi's training camp had another distinct difference from previous years—the training room. "Heretofore, people were always in there," Richter said. "When Lombardi was coach, for the large part, it was void. You didn't want to be seen there because he looked at that with disdain, unless it was a serious injury."

It didn't take long for Richter to be tested. It came during an exercise called the hamburger drill, in which two blocking bags are placed about three feet apart and an offensive blocker is pitted against a defensive player. The offensive lineman tries to make room for the running back to find a hole between the two bags.

On this day, Richter, with the old single-bar receiver's face mask, was the offensive lineman in the hamburger drill. He was up against a linebacker named Tom Roussel. "I fired out and he came toward me with his forearm and caught me in the nose," Richter said. "I could tell he pretty well smacked it and broke it. I went back and felt it and thought, 'Well, I know Lombardi's watching and I want to make sure he knows I can play hurt.' So I went through a couple more blocks. I just fired out and threw caution to the wind. I actually made a couple of good blocks.

"It probably wasn't the smartest thing to do because I could have hurt it even more," Richter said. "After practice, I went to Carlisle Hospital and had my nose packed with about a hundred yards of gauze. But somehow, it got back to me that someone overheard Lombardi say that it took a lot of guts for the kid to do that with a broken nose.

"Someone took a picture of me," Richter laughed. "It was just a face shot with all the blood and the gauze. I sent it home to the family with a note that said, 'Having a great time.'"

With the broken nose, Richter was unable to participate in practice the next day. Standing on the sidelines at practice, he began to jog on the track surrounding the field. That's when Lombardi called him over. "I wasn't sure what was going to happen," Richter said. "But he just told me to take it easy.

"A few days later I went back to practice and had a bird cage for a face mask," Richter said. "And one of the first days back was picture day. Lombardi said to me, 'Oh, that nose looks beautiful!' Howard Cosell was standing there and asked what he meant and Lombardi said, 'The kid broke his nose a couple of weeks ago and hell, if he stays long enough, he's likely to break it three or four more times.'"

At the time, Richter had become the team's player representative. It was a turbulent time for player-owner relations, and Richter came into camp concerned about the way Lombardi would view him in this potentially adversarial role.

"He and I had a decent relationship," Richter said. "He made it very clear that I had a certain job to do, but that he was the coach and he didn't want that to interfere or create a conflict so that it affected the team camaraderie and togetherness. It was a good relationship. I didn't have to deal with him frequently, but we were going into a year that the contract was expiring the following summer [after the 1969 season], and he understood that."

Richter continued to be impressed with the efficiency of the team's training camp. He was also starting to be impressed by the coach's personality and values.

"He was a very religious person," Richter said. "He had real values. Your family, your church, and football. Football was third in the order. That was a contrast to other coaches. And he was very patriotic."

On one occasion during training camp, Lombardi's wife, Marie, mentioned to the priest and that their wedding anniversary was coming up, and asked if he would say a few words about that. Coach Lombardi wasn't happy with that. "He thought she was telling the priest how to handle his own business," Richter said. "And when they got to the service, he sat on one side of the room and she sat on another."

With each passing day, each passing week, Lombardi continued to make a positive impression on Richter.

"He was always trying to instill that positive attitude," Richter said of Lombardi. "He would almost daily try to keep you motivated. He'd talk about winning, about having a positive attitude, and about professionalism. He would talk about accomplishing things together that we couldn't do as individuals.

"One of the real great lessons learned was his attitude about professionalism," Richter said. "He talked to us not about being football players per se, but about being at the top of our profession. You're expected to do the job. You have a situation in front of you. You have a book that you've read. You understand what you're supposed to do and if everybody does what they're supposed to do, we'll be successful and the organization will go on to great rewards. However, if there is someone among us who has a sloppy, careless attitude, doesn't do their job, doesn't perform the way they're supposed to, the organization will not be successful, the enterprise will not be successful, and you won't see those rewards. What he was driving at was not so much athletics. He was just teaching all of us the value of making sure that you did the best job you could all of the time, regardless of the profession."

Richter said Lombardi often reminded his players that when you left the Redskins and left professional football, you'd find yourself in another occupation and when people came to you for advice in your chosen field, you needed to be at your best.

"You have to give them the appropriate advice and you can't take the day off," Richter said. "You can't turn it on and off like a water faucet because what happens are things that are much more important than an athletic contest or game. You lose lives. You lose financial stability. What he was driving at is that you have to build those foundations, because whatever you did then would have to carry you through later when the results of your actions were more significant.

"He would talk about that all of the time," Richter said. "He was just constantly reinforcing that. He had a tremendously positive attitude."

The schedule makers were not kind to Lombardi and his 1969 Redskins team. Five of the team's first seven games were on the road, including the season opener at New Orleans.

"Everybody was excited to start the season," Richter recalled. "Back then, you only had 14 games so when you won a game, it was a big deal, especially the first game of the year with a new coach."

The Redskins played well and defeated the Saints 26–20. In the locker room after the game, Richter said there was great excitement and cheer among the players. "We're all in there celebrating," Richter said. "Monday was an off day and then everyone came in Tuesday to watch film of Sunday's game. Of course, if you did something well, you're hoping the coach is going to single you out with a compliment."

Lombardi began the film session and things erupted. "All of a sudden, he goes on a tirade," Richter said. "Everybody is shell-shocked. He's criticizing every play and we're thinking, 'What's going to happen when we lose?'"

One week later, after a 27–23 loss to Cleveland, they found out. "No one wanted to be in the front of the room," Richter said. "No one wanted to be noticed at all. But he was just the opposite of the week before. He was low-key and soft-spoken. It was reverse psychology and that's very difficult to pull off with professional athletes.

"He knew you felt bad about losing the game so he didn't need to get your attention," Richter said. "When you won, your mistakes tend to be overlooked and if gone uncorrected, would cause you to lose another game. When we lost, he knew he didn't have to snap you to it.

"He really understood that we were working to win every game," Richter said. "We were going to lose some, but if we're going to lose, then we're going to get some value out of it. If, in fact, we lose, there is something to be gained from a loss."

On those first Sundays in the 1969 season, Lombardi and the Redskins fared well, overcoming that difficult early season schedule, and they were 4-2-1 through the first seven games. "The thing that was amazing was that Lombardi put everything he had into the games," Richter said. "We'd go on the road and if it was a 20-minute bus ride to the airport, he'd fall asleep going from the stadium to the airport. He was totally spent. He put everything into the game. And then he'd come back the next week."

As the weeks passed, the team grew more comfortable with the new coach and the Lombardi way of life became the Redskins' routine.

"Monday was our day off." Richter said. "Tuesday, we'd watch film. If you made a mistake in the game, you had to sweat it from Sunday all the way to Tuesday. You'd hope he'd go past it, but he wouldn't. Then you'd get through it and get your ass chewed and go on. Wednesday, he's forgotten about last week and is more comfortable with what's coming up. Thursday, he's really into it. Friday, again, everything is set and in the system."

Saturday was a light day of practice and when the team was at home, Lombardi often let his players bring their children to practice. "On this particular day, I took my oldest boy, Scott, who was 5 at the time, and Brad, 3. On the way to practice, I was telling them, 'Now when we get there, be very polite. When we see Mr. Lombardi, it's 'Mr. Lombardi.' Yes sir. No sir. If you don't do that, dad could end up in Buffalo!'

"We went into the locker room and there are lots of kids running around," Richter said. "I went into the training room for a brief time to get taped, and when I got back to the locker room, things had gotten real quiet. One of the guys motioned me over and said, 'You should've heard what your kid just said.' Apparently, Lombardi was going around the room patting all the kids on the head saying 'How are you, young man' and so forth. Hello, Coach Lombardi. Hello, Mr. Lombardi. All the kids are very polite.

"Then he comes to Scott and pats him on the head and Scott says, 'Hi ya, Vince! How's it going?'"

Fortunately, the coach had a sense of humor. "I'm told the players were absolutely stunned," Richter said, "But Lombardi had that toothy grin and kind of got a kick out of it."

The Redskins finished that season with a 7-5-2 record, good for second place in the NFL's Capital Division, 3 games behind the division champion Dallas Cowboys. It was Washington's first winning season since 1955. "There was a lot of excitement and enthusiasm because everybody thought that Lombardi had the ability to bring this to the level of success people thought they could have," Richter said.

While there was little doubt that Richter was enjoying playing for Lombardi and was thrilled with the team's first winning season since 1955, he was clearly disappointed in his diminished role on the team. Among Lombardi's personnel moves was the acquisition of one of his former players in Green Bay, flanker Bob Long. Lombardi then moved Redskins flanker Jerry Smith to tight end, and Richter was the odd man out. In 11 games, he failed to catch a pass in his role as a backup tight end.

* * *

Pat Richter always seemed to recognize a good thing when he saw it. And when he was in Washington, D.C. in the late summer of 1969, he knew he was part of something special.

His coach with the Washington Redskins was the legendary Vince Lombardi. At the time, the Redskins shared the facility with Major League Baseball's Washington Senators, whose manager was Ted Williams.

"Looking back," said Richter, "you had Lombardi on one side of the hall and Ted Williams on the other, which is just amazing."

During that time, the Senators' batting practice catcher was George Susce, a veteran baseball player and coach whom Richter had met several years ago during a workout with the Milwaukee Braves. Late one afternoon, as Richter was headed back to the Redskins' locker room after practice, he ran into Susce, who had seen Richter play baseball and was aware of his ability to hit the ball. Susce invited Richter to put down his football helmet and join the Senators for batting practice.

"I told George that I haven't swung a bat in a long time and besides, if Lombardi sees me, he'll kill me," Richter said "I ended up going down there and Don Zimmer is throwing batting practice. I stepped into the cage. I still have my football cleats on and my football shorts. I started to get used to hitting the ball and hit some line drives and eventually hit a few out of the park. I batted for about 10 minutes and that was it. When I got done, George says, 'Let's go talk to Ted.' George takes me over and introduces me to Ted Williams, and Williams is asking me about where my hands are when I hit the ball. Then he starts asking me about my hips: Where are my hips when I make contact with the ball? We spent about 15 minutes just talking about hitting."

For several years, the story about taking batting practice with the Washington Senators and spending 15 minutes talking about hitting with Ted Williams was a story that Richter seldom told. "It was just a story to tell and there was never really anybody to collaborate it for me," Richter said. But it was a moment that would come back to him later in his career.

Thirty years later, Pat Richter is in Milwaukee attending ceremonies honoring the 1999 inductees into the Wisconsin Sports Hall of Fame. Among the inductees that night is Kenosha native Ray Berres, a former major-league catcher who spent two decades in the American League as a pitching coach with the Chicago White Sox. Richter approaches Ray Berres to offer his congratulations. Berres greets Richter and says: "I know you, I was there that day." Richter isn't sure what Berres is talking about.

"Then he said, 'I was there the day you took batting practice in Washington D.C.,'" Richter recalls. "He said he was a coach with the White Sox and he was sitting in the third base dugout and watched the whole thing. I said, 'Hey, I finally have a witness.'"

On the night of July 9, 2002, Pat Richter is in attendance at the Major League All-Star Game at Milwaukee's Miller Park. Prior to the game, Richter sees Zimmer, now a coach with the New York Yankees, standing near the batting cage. Richter hands his business card to *Milwaukee Journal-Sentinel* sportswriter Dale Hofmann and asks Hofmann to deliver it to Zimmer.

"He gave him the card and Zimmer turned around, waddled over, and we had a great conversation," Richter said. "We hadn't seen each other since that day he pitched batting practice to me over 30 years ago. He said 'I wish I had a hundred dollars for every time I had told that story about you taking batting practice.'"

CHAPTER FIVE
THE GREATNESS
OF A LOSS

While the nation's capital was thrilled with the resurgence of the Redskins under their legendary new coach, a cloud hovered over the league. The players association and the owners were preparing for their upcoming negotiations, which would prove to be heated and lengthy.

The landscape of professional football was changing rapidly. The NFL's long-standing effort to hold back the upstart American Football League had failed, and the two parties sat down and worked out a proposed merger. In October 1966, the U.S. Congress approved the AFL-NFL merger, passing legislation exempting the agreement itself from antitrust action.

The league also began to look at expansion opportunities, and on December 15, 1966, New Orleans was awarded an NFL franchise to begin play in 1967.

"I remember a tongue-in-cheek comment I heard at a banquet," Richter recalled. "Senator Everett Dirksen was speaking about how the merger took place. It was humorous. He was talking about how to get things passed, and he talked about how this bill was tacked on to another bill. He talked to his friend, Russell Long, and said, 'Russell, how would you like to have a team in New Orleans?' . . . That's probably how it happened."

Another significant change was the establishment of a postseason championship game between the champions of the two leagues. On January 15, 1967, Lombardi's Green Bay Packers defeated Kansas City in Super Bowl I, the first meeting of the AFL-NFL champions.

Meanwhile, NFL commissioner Pete Rozelle continued to advance the league's television package—and the league's television revenue.

In early 1970, the league announced a bold new television package. Under the new four-year contracts, CBS would televise all NFC games and NBC would broadcast all AFC games (except Monday night games). The two networks would divide televising the Super Bowl and AFC-NFC Pro Bowl games.

Also in 1970, the NFL announced a new prime-time programming agreement with ABC for *Monday Night Football* in which the network would televise 13 NFL regular-season Monday night games in 1970, 1971, and 1972.

Later that year, Baltimore, Cleveland, and Pittsburgh agreed to join the AFL teams to form the 13-team American Football Conference of the NFL. The NFL also agreed on a playoff format that would include one wild-card team per conference; the second-place team with the best record.

"Heretofore there had not been a great deal of strength in the players association and the players were beginning to see the things that were happening with the NFL with the television packages and exposure." Richter. said. "Rozelle had done a great job marketing the league, so the feeling was that this was the right time to move things along."

Shortly after the merger of the two leagues, the two players associations met to discuss plans for a merger of their own. John Mackey of the Baltimore Colts was president of the NFL Players Association, and future U.S. congressman Jack Kemp, the Buffalo Bills quarterback, was president of the AFL Players Association. Mackey was selected to preside over the merged Players Association.

The merged groups formed an executive committee. Joining Richter on the committee were Ken Bowman, Ernie Wright, Tom Keating, Nick Buoniconti, Kermit Alexander, and Mackey. One of its first assignments was to select an executive director, someone who could serve as their counterpart to Commissioner Rozelle in the negotiations.

In recent months, the players group had been working with a Minneapolis law firm and, on occasion, with UW Law School professor Nathan Feinsinger. "That's when Ed Garvey's name bubbled up," said Richter, who knew Garvey from their days on the Madison campus.

Garvey's background was not in the world of sports, but he did appear to be battle-ready nonetheless. After earning an undergraduate degree from the University of Wisconsin, he served as President of the U.S. National Student Association and was involved in the civil rights movement in the early '60s. He entered the U.S. Army as a first lieutenant, served two years of active duty, and then returned to Wisconsin and graduated from the UW Law School in 1969.

Following his graduation from law school, Garvey took a position as an associate with Lindquist & Vennum, an activist labor law firm in Minneapolis. Shortly thereafter, Richter and the players group extended an offer, and Garvey became the first Executive Director of the National Football League Players Association (NFLPA). Years later, Garvey would practice law in Madison and become a mainstay in Wisconsin politics.

The NFL owners, meanwhile, were represented by Rankin Smith of the Atlanta Falcons, Ralph Wilson of the Buffalo Bills, Art Modell of the Cleveland Browns, Wellington Mara of the New York Giants, Tex Schramm of the Dallas Cowboys, as well as commissioner Rozelle.

"Publicly, most of the information that got out indicated that Rozelle was really in the background and wasn't actively involved in the meetings," Richter said. "I know this; he was at every meeting I ever attended. At one point, we offered, tongue-in-cheek, to pay half his salary. We said if he's the commissioner of the whole league, including the players, then we should pay half his salary and share the governance. He was actively involved. The owners declined our offer."

It didn't appear that the negotiations were going to move along at a brisk pace. "It dragged on," Richter said. "We had made a proposal to share in the percentage of income. At the time, the TV package was something like $14.8 million for three years and we were told that pro football was peaked out on the television side of things. They told us that it was maybe as good as it was going to get, and that we were kind of at this peak and we're starting to slide down the backside of this hill.

"So we proposed to take a percentage, if it goes down, we get less. If it gets better, then we share the revenue. 'No, no, no,' they said, 'That won't fly.'"

As the negotiations stalled and the start of training camp neared, the talk of a work slowdown or lockout continued. Richter and the executive committee weren't sure that the slowdown would work, especially with the increasing number of high-paid players now in the league.

"It was not publicly and politically the right thing to do to stay out of camp when you're making so much money," Richter said. "That was always going to be an issue and problematic as to whether we could get the support of the big-name players to really back everybody and stay out of camp.

"It was very difficult to find replacements at that time because there wasn't another league," Richter said. "But the feeling was that if some players went in, you'd start to lose traction and lose the ability to have any power and strength."

The negotiations continued throughout the summer. "The issue for us was whether there was enough clout to bargain effectively, whether you could get the support of everybody."

Richter wasn't the only lawyer-to-be in the players group. Bowman was well on his way toward earning a law degree from UW. And Buoniconti, a graduate of Notre Dame, had recently earned a law degree from Suffolk University. Led by the feisty Garvey, they proved to be an effective—if somewhat irritating—negotiating team. "The three of us were always taking lengthy notes on everything that was said," Richter said. "Somebody would say something a couple of days later and we'd say, 'Wait a minute. A couple of days ago, you said this.' They didn't like that. We had our stuff together."

As training camps were scheduled to begin, the players association asked its members not to report to camp. Some called it an informal lockout. Others simply called it a strike.

"We didn't like the word 'strike' so we called it a withholding of services," Richter said. "Regardless, players weren't going to camp."

Throughout the league, many players were practicing on their own with their teammates in an informal manner. And as the Redskins gathered for their workouts at Georgetown University in Washington, some troubling news about their coach began to circulate rapidly: Coach Lombardi's colon cancer, discovered four months earlier, had worsened.

Richter was often tied up with negotiating sessions in New York City and unable to join his teammates in Washington. But he does remember one particular day when he was able to be there.

"We were practicing at one end of the field and we were doing the drills Lombardi used to have us go through," Richter said. "As we were going through the drills and calisthenics, there was a dark limousine that pulled onto the field about a hundred yards away. A person got out and it was Leroy Washington, Lombardi's driver. He opened the door and this figure got out of the back seat of the car. He was very thin and frail. You could just make out the very shell of a person. It obviously was Lombardi. He had lost so much weight. He stood there for a moment. We continued to do what we were doing. He got back in the car and left. That was the last time we saw him."

The negotiations continued. The first week of exhibition games passed. "The feeling was that if we don't get into training camp that week," Richter said, "then we were going to face a cancelled season. We felt that as it moved along, we had to put a deal together because we probably weren't going to be able to hold everyone together much longer.

"Ultimately, Mackey and Rozelle went offshore," Richter said. "Within a couple of days, the signals were there to put a deal together. We went up to New York in late July and we met at LaGuardia Airport and subsequently in downtown New York City at the NFL offices . . . and that's when we got it together."

On August 3, 1970, the Players Negotiating Committee and the NFL Players Association announced a four-year agreement guaranteeing approximately $4,535,000 annually to player pension and insurance benefits. The owners also agreed to contribute $250,000 annually to improve or implement items such as disability payments, widows' benefits, maternity benefits, and dental benefits. The agreement also provided for increased preseason game and per diem payments, averaging approximately $2.6 million annually.

The informal lockout had ended. The players reported to training camps and the exhibition games took place as scheduled.

Less than one month later, on September 4, 1970, Vince Lombardi died of cancer.

The Redskins were in Tampa for an exhibition game and flew to New York for the funeral at Saint Patrick's Cathedral. Among the mourners was Howard Cosell, who handed Richter a tape of the radio show Cosell had recorded with Lombardi in which the Redskins coach talked about Richter and the broken nose and the young receiver's perseverance that so pleased the coach. "I thought you might want this," Cosell told Richter.

Several weeks after the funeral, Pat Richter had a brief conversation with Marie Lombardi, who mentioned that afternoon practice at Georgetown, when Vince Lombardi had watched from afar as his team conducted their unofficial workout.

"She said he had started to break down and cry and got back in the car," Richter said. "She felt that, as he described it to her, with us going through the drills that he had taught us, at that time, he realized that he had had an impact on that team to the point that we were now disciplined to do the things we needed to do without him being there, not taking the easy way out. He felt he had taught us something.

"Subsequently, after he passed away, his assistant came to Jurgensen and me. She had a piece of paper and said 'You might find this interesting. Coach Lombardi had written this down on his desk pad after his first operation.' Things didn't look good, apparently. That's when he wrote down: 'The greatness of a loss is not so much determined by what is lost, but by what is left.'

"You think about it," Richter said. "It's a very profound statement. The greatness of a loss of a Lombardi is not the loss itself but the greatness of what he left behind, his greatness as a human being, as a coach, as a parent, with his family and church, and as a patriot. What he wrote down could apply to any difficult situation in life."

* * *

A few short weeks after the burial of the former head coach, the Washington Redskins embarked upon the 1970 season with former Green Bay Packer assistant Bill Austin as the team's new head coach.

As expected, it wasn't a great season. A five-game losing streak at mid-season led to the team's 6-8 finish. It wasn't a great year for Richter, either. He caught just two passes for 30 yards, again playing a backup role at tight end.

Off the field, Richter continued receiving encouragement from teammate Vince Promuto, who had gone back to school to earn a law degree. Richter had started taking law classes at American University in 1967, where he was a part-time student in the fall and a full-time student in the spring. Later, he would complete his work in Madison and earn his law degree from the University of Wisconsin in 1971.

Following the 1970 season, the Redskins decided to seek out another big-name coach and hired George Allen. In five previous seasons as head coach of the Los Angeles Rams, Allen had twice led the Rams to the playoffs and had compiled an impressive 49-17 record.

Richter was now entering his eighth year in the NFL. Allen was his fifth head coach. And, with each coaching change, there was a transition, an adjustment peri-

Richter's role as player representative began to eclipse his spotlight on the field. Photo courtesy of the Washington Redskins.

od, and a learning process; a time of getting to know the new coach and a new way of doing things.

"George was an interesting character," Richter said. "He'd do just about anything to win. I remember calling Sonny and asking him 'What's George Allen like?' And he said, 'Every time I sit down with George I have a feeling that he's got his hands in my pocket.' And that was a good description because George would try anything. That year, we tried the Universal weights as well as free weights. We had someone who came in to test your eyes to see how fast your eyes moved side to side because the theory was your eyes move in a series of snapshots, not a continuous motion.

"He had a reputation of getting older players, giving up some of the future for winning now," Richter said. "That was vastly different from the Lombardi philosophy of using draft choices and improving the team through trades."

Richter also found Allen to be dedicated to building a strong defense. Offense came second with Allen, Richter said. "I remember getting to Carlisle and picking up the information about the new system. The defensive material was bound and almost looked almost like the *Encyclopedia Britannica*. The offense had a three-ring binder; the defense had a huge burgundy and gold manual."

Richter noticed several other significant changes. The 90-minute practices of Lombardi had now changed into three-hour practice sessions with Allen. Plus, for the first time, Richter was looking at the possibility of being cut by the team.

Pat Richter took part in graduation ceremonies in June, 1971, receiving his law degree from the University of Wisconsin. Photo courtesy of *The Capital Times*.

"I wasn't getting much playing time and started to think about getting cut early so that I could catch on with someone else," Richter said. "Recognizing that with the negotiations and such, word had gone around that 'You guys won't get much playing time.' The question was, what was my career going to be beyond that? The feeling was that being a punter and a wide receiver, I could play some-place and that there were other opportunities out there."

Richter approached his position coach, former Green Bay Packer Boyd Dowler. "I said, 'Boyd, if I'm not going to play, I'd just as soon go on waivers.'"

Shortly thereafter, Richter's wish was granted. He was released by the Red-skins, placed on waivers, and was claimed by the Dallas Cowboys.

Richter flew to Dallas to meet his new team. Tom Landry was the head coach. Ray Renfro, who had been with the Redskins when Otto Graham was head coach, was Richter's position coach. Gil Brandt the head of personnel. Richter knew the team's owner, Tex Schramm. The two had sat across the negotiating table in the recent labor dispute between the players association and the owners.

"I remember going through a lot of meetings when I first got there," Richter said. "I was amazed at how organized they were, at how first-class they were. It was impressive."

While in camp, Richter stayed at a Dallas hotel and roomed with Don Tal-bert, brother of one of Richter's teammates with Washington, Diron Talbert.

Pat Richter's stay with the Dallas Cowboys didn't last long. He was signed and subsequently released by the Cowboys prior to the start of the 1971 NFL season. Photo courtesy of the Dallas Cowboys.

In training camp, Richter was compet-ing for a position as a pass-catching tight end. The team's current tight ends were injured: Billy Truax had a leg injury and Mike Ditka had a broken arm. He also was competing for the punter position held by Ron Widby.

"It was a different environment for me," Richter said. "Their system was very compli-cated. The variations were mind-boggling. It was a completely different dynamic."

The team's last exhibition game was played in Baltimore. "On the flight home, I recall sitting in an aisle seat and Tex Schramm came down the aisle and saw me sitting there and did a double take," Richter said. "It was almost like he didn't know I was there. Tex had been the manager of the NFL's committee at the bargaining table . . . It was almost like, 'What the hell are you doing here?' The next Monday was the final cut day before the regular season and that's when they let me go. It may have been for a lot of different reasons, but it was ironic that Tex had noticed I was there."

Richter tried to network with as many of his NFL contacts as possible. He still thought there were opportunities out there, but none surfaced. Suddenly, after eight years in the National Football League, Pat Richter's playing career had come to an abrupt halt.

"Some of it had to do with finding the right spot and some of it had to do with our players association affiliation," Richter said. "At that time, it was a more contentious relationship with the beginning of the union, so I think there was some reluctance at the time to pick up players with the union-affiliated background."

The Dallas Cowboys went on to win the Super Bowl that year. Pat Richter, his eight-year NFL career now ended, began his new journey, traveling a road that would take him from legal work to the corporate world and to athletic administration at his alma mater.

CHAPTER SIX
GOING HOME

Pat Richter returned to Madison, where he began working with a local law firm, Aberg, Bell, Blake, and Metzner. During the early days on the job, the NFL season was still going and Richter continued his efforts to make contacts throughout the league in hopes of a roster spot opening up somewhere. But once again, there were no opportunities to be had.

As the months passed, Richter settled in with the firm and began to pick up clients along the way. In January 1972, he was approached by two local business-men, Bob O'Malley and Don Hovde. The pair represented a group of downtown Madison business leaders called the Central Madison Committee. They were looking for someone to represent the downtown interests and work for them independently of the Chamber of Commerce. They wanted to talk with Richter about this new opportunity.

Richter met with them over breakfast to learn more about it. "It sounded interesting and unique," Richter said. "It was something where I could use my contacts and experience with people in Madison. So we talked it over and I thought about it. I was off and on about it, so I decided to call P. Goff Beach, president of Oscar Mayer at the time."

Beach had been president of the Mendota Gridiron Club, a football boost-er club, when Richter was at the UW. He met with Richter, who asked the Oscar Mayer president what he thought about Richter's new opportunity.

"I asked him what the position would do with regard to future opportuni-ties in Madison," Richter recalled. "He said that from Oscar Mayer's perspective, down the road, it likely wouldn't be a fit [for a prospective employee], but it prob-ably could lead into a business, banking, or development opportunity."

Following that discussion, Richter made his decision. He said he felt the opportunity might prove to be somewhat limiting and as such, made the decision to stay with the law firm. He contacted O'Malley and Hovde, thanked them for presenting the opportunity, and told them he was going to continue practicing law.

Within a day, Beach placed a phone call to Richter. "He said, 'Hell, if you're looking around, why don't you come out and talk with us?' I had already told the law firm that I was going to stay there. A couple of my neighbors were with Oscar Mayer. My grandfather had worked for the company. In my own mind, maybe it was time for a little bit of structure. Maybe something with a little bit of time discipline would be good."

It didn't take long for Richter to make that decision. In March 1972, he accepted the company's employment offer. At Oscar Mayer, he was placed in the Pre-Management Training Program (PMTP). It was a six-month program that provided PMTP trainees with exposure to all the facets of the business. The plan, Richter said, was to go through the program, then eventually take over the position that managed the program.

By fall, Richter was in charge of the program and began getting involved in the company's college recruiting efforts. That lasted until January 1974, when Richter took a position with the company as personnel manager at its Nashville plant.

"Prior to that, in the fall of 1973 we had started to make some trips to Nashville for preliminary discussions regarding the labor contract there," Richter said. "It was strictly a manufacturing plant. The intent was to sit in on the contract discussions."

Richter and his family enjoyed their time in Nashville. They lived in Hendersonville, calling it "one of the best places we've ever been." But their time in Nashville was short —just 16 months—before the Richters moved back to Madison, where Pat was to take over the reins as plant personnel manager at Oscar Mayer's plant in Madison.

His contract-negotiating skills—honed during his stay in Nashville—were put to the test in Madison, Oscar Mayer's largest plant with more than 3,000 employees. There, he dealt with some key figures in the labor movement nationwide.

"It was interesting to see the dynamics in the process—what went on in public in front of everybody on the negotiating teams and what was happening in the back room," Richter said. "They called it the turkey dance. A lot of stuff was just for show. It was a good learning process to see how all of it took place."

The Madison plant presented an interesting combination of the plant and corporate headquarters at the same location. "It was a great experience dealing with a lot of people in a large plant environment," Richter said. "We had all the things going on in there that went on in the outside world—confrontations, legal issues, drugs."

Two years later, Richter's duties were increased when he became manager of corporate personnel. The new job put Richter at the executive management level within the corporate structure at Oscar Mayer. In that capacity, he was responsible for overseeing and directing all of the hiring, job search, and other employment functions for the entire company.

In 1981, Richter was watching his son's team play a youth hockey game at Hartmeyer Ice Arena in Madison when a fellow employee, Dick Belsito, hurried in with some startling news: Oscar Mayer had been purchased by General Foods.

"That was a shock," Richter said. "At the time, we were told that the General Foods people at the high level were pretty good about not coming in and making a lot of changes," Richter said. "Typically, they weren't going to come in and mess it up."

At first, the change in ownership had little effect on Richter. Eventually, some of the General Foods executives came to Madison and became part of the Oscar Mayer staff, but generally speaking, there still were no major changes.

One of Oscar Mayer's top executives had recently made a move out east to General Foods headquarters, and in 1984, Richter was asked to do the same. He was offered the position of manager of human resource planning and employment at the General Foods corporate office in Rye Brook, New York.

"I felt that it was an opportunity to be one of the first Oscar Mayer guys to go out there," Richter said. "And it was a promotion."

In his new role, Richter had responsibility for the human resource plans for the corporation, the recruitment function, and hiring search firms to make placements.

With the Redskins, Richter had been a keen observer of the manner in which different coaches employed different styles to create their desired work environment. It prepared him well for corporate life.

"It was interesting to see the cultural differences between General Foods and Oscar Mayer," Richter said. "General Foods did a lot of communicating by writing, whereas Oscar Mayer was more of a hallway communication. It was just an entirely different way to operate."

After several years back in Madison, the move east at this time was a bit more difficult for the Richter family. Housing costs were significantly higher than in the Midwest. The mortgage on their new house in Connecticut, Richter said, was more than the total value of all the houses they had lived in previously. Richter's commute to work would be more than 35 minutes—on a good day.

Richter served as a one-man advance party, moving boxes in and unpacking and getting things somewhat settled prior to arrival of the rest of the family.

"We had left a nice home in Madison and spent nearly twice as much on a home out there," Richter said. "I remember the night they arrived. It was dark and late. One of Renee's first comments was, 'We won't have here in 10 years what we had in Madison yesterday.'"

Richter had viewed the move as a career opportunity that he couldn't pass up. And, while the initial adjustment was difficult, the Richters made the most of their time in Connecticut.

"We bought a dog to help with the move," Richter said. "And that helped us. We did a lot of traveling, some of it with the youth hockey. We really did more than we might have if we thought we were going to be there a long time."

Still, the signs of a difficult transition remained. While Richter started his new job in April, his family chose to remain in their familiar Madison home until September, when they moved east. The following summer, the family went back to Madison and stayed at a family friend's vacant house in their old neighborhood.

And it didn't take long for Richter to clarify his thoughts regarding his next career move. "Shortly after we got there, in my own mind, I thought, even if I had my boss's job, which is the top job, that's not really where we wanted to be. And so we communicated that through Jim McVey, who was president at the time, that at some point, we'd like to come back to Madison, sooner rather than later, but under the right circumstances, not just give everything up and come back, but to look for something good that might become available. That was our mind-set."

Richter served as manager of human resources planning at General Foods headquarters for about a year. During his second year there, he was named the company's director of personnel for the beverage division in White Plains, New York. And then, in the spring of 1986, Oscar Mayer called and offered Richter the opportunity to return to Madison as director of personnel at Oscar Mayer. The Richters were coming home.

* * *

From the standpoint of Pat and Renee Richter, it was beginning to look as if they had drawn up a game plan and executed it flawlessly. While in Connecticut, they had said to each other that if they had a chance to return to Madison, they would like to do so, and they'd like to do so sooner rather than later. But, it had to be under the right circumstances.

And that's just the way it worked out. Pat was getting comfortable in his new role at Oscar Mayer, a key corporate-management position as director of personnel. Oldest son Scott was at the College of William & Mary, where he had just graduated. Son Brad was back in Madison going to school and playing hockey. Son Barry had finished at Fairfield Prep and was planning to attend Culver Academy and join a long list of hockey stars who had attended school there, including Madison's Gary Suter. And son Tim was settling in at Edgewood Grade School and was active in the Wisconsin Youth Symphony orchestra.

"The experience at General Foods was positive," Richter said. "But everyone seemed to be pleased to come back."

Across town at the UW Athletic Department, there was sad news. Head football coach Dave McClain collapsed and died of a heart attack in the spring of 1986. McClain had served as head coach of the Badgers from 1978 to 1985 and led his teams to bowl games in 1981, 1982, and 1984.

One of his top assistants, Jim Hilles, had been named interim coach for the upcoming 1986 season, but things didn't work out too well. In the team's 1986 opener at Hawaii, the Badgers were embarrassed by the host Rainbow Warriors and lost 28–7. After a nonconference victory over Northern Illinois in the home opener, Wisconsin lost four straight games. As the losses mounted, so too did the pressure on Hilles, who was hoping to rid himself of the interim label and earn a long-term contract as head coach of the Badgers. However, after another four-game losing streak to close the season, athletic director Elroy Hirsch announced plans to search for a new football coach.

In the end, Hirsch and the UW Athletic Board chose Tulsa's Don Morton to replace Hilles as the UW's new head football coach beginning with the 1987 season. One of the brightest young coaching prospects at the time, Morton had achieved incredible success at North Dakota State—his coaching success there landed him in the school's Hall of Fame—and more recently, at Tulsa.

Early in 1987, with the hiring of the school's new football coach completed, Hirsch announced his plans to retire as athletic director. The candidates were many, including two then-current UW administrators, associate athletic director Otto Breitenbach, and deputy athletic director Ralph Neale. Other experienced and well-qualified candidates with local ties showed interest, including former Badger and NFL veteran Jim Bakken, who had previous experience as athletic director at Saint Louis University, and Bob Brennan, a former UW track coach who had achieved great success in leading the Greater Madison Chamber of Commerce.

Pat Richter, however, was not a candidate.

"At the time, I was approached and asked if I had any interest," Richter said. "But I really wasn't interested in it. I was thinking more along the lines that the company had brought me back to Madison and I had an obligation to them. Without getting any farther into it than that, I dismissed it out of hand at that point in time."

Among those talking with Richter was veteran *Wisconsin State Journal* sportswriter Tom Butler, who had known Richter since he first covered his games in the 1958 state boys basketball tournament. Butler grew up on Madison's East Side and, like Richter, graduated from Madison East and from the University of Wisconsin. "Pat had a legal background and a business background," Butler said. "On top of that, he was a great athlete. There was nobody better prepared to be athletic director than Pat Richter. Before they named Ade Sponberg, I talked to Pat and tried to get him interested, but he didn't want it. I thought he would have been the right choice back then."

The UW Athletic Board, led by chairman Barney Webb, announced on May 7, 1987, that four candidates were being considered finalists: James Jones, associate athletic director at the Ohio State University; Carl Miller, athletic director at Pacific University; Don Purvis, athletic director at Ball State; and Ade Sponberg, athletic director at North Dakota State.

Despite what appeared to be a strong pool of local candidates, none of the four finalists had any previous connection with the UW. On May 15, 1987, the UW announced that Sponberg had been offered the job as the school's next athletic director.

"Following Elroy with someone like Ade was difficult," Richter said. "Ade was a fine man but he didn't have the knowledge or the contacts or the understanding of what it would be like to be with the Badgers."

Richter recalls sitting next to the new athletic director at the annual W Club banquet in 1987 and Sponberg was wearing a green jacket. "I just suggested that at this kind of thing, maybe he should be wearing the red one. He said it was at the cleaners. So I said, 'Well, you have to plan a little bit better than that and make sure you have that red jacket. It's very important that you wear the colors at functions like this.'"

Late in 1987, the UW Board of Regents announced the selection of Donna Shalala as the next UW–Madison chancellor, replacing Irv Shain, who had retired. When Shalala took office on January 1, 1988, she became the first woman to head a Big Ten school. She also would become a key ingredient in the future success of the University of Wisconsin Athletic Department.

Shalala had come to Wisconsin from tiny Hunter College in New York City. She was fiercely competitive, having played tennis as a youngster growing up in Cleveland, where she won an Ohio state tennis title. She also played Little League baseball on a team managed by the future owner of the New York Yankees, George Steinbrenner.

It didn't take long for people in Madison to notice that Shalala was an intelligent, perceptive, and dynamic leader. And she rarely wasted any time before attacking the challenges she faced.

One of those challenges would be the faltering fortunes of the football team. In Morton's first season—concluded just before Shalala's arrival—the team won two of its first three games, but lost seven of the last eight and finished 3-8. Worse yet, the attendance numbers had started a downward slide. In Morton's first season, the average attendance had dropped from 68,052 in 1986 to 59,256 in 1987; a decline of nearly 13 percent. It was the first time since 1970 that the Badgers had averaged fewer than 60,000 fans per game.

The following season, things kept getting worse, as the 1988 football Badgers lost their first nine games before defeating Minnesota for the only victory of the season. The 1-10 record was the worst record since 1968, when the Badgers were winless in 10 games.

Again, attendance continued to decline. The per-game average attendance dropped to 49,297; a 17 percent drop.

"I went around the state and talked to a lot of alums," Shalala said. "Mostly, they were pretty polite, but they were so disappointed about UW athletics. And it wasn't just the men's program. It was the women's program as well.

"There was just a great deal of disappointment that we had lost our glory," Shalala said. "On campus, everybody said that it was all because we had increased our academics. That was actually the coaches' view, too. I went off to Michigan before I came to watch a game with [Michigan president] Harold Shapiro. They had just as good academics and yet seemed to be able to put together a good athletic program."

Shalala also conducted some formal survey research to assist in her decision-making. "The people in our survey said two things," Shalala said. "First, they were very proud of the university but it was too liberal and their kids weren't being very well treated—they said all we cared about were graduate students.

"And number two, they were devastated that the athletic program had gone to such depths," Shalala said. "And those were the two things that I decided to work on first."

One of her other key personnel moves was to hire longtime Badger activist Arlie Mucks, who was finishing his term as executive director of the Wisconsin Alumni Association. As Gayle Langer replaced Mucks at the WAA, Shalala hired Mucks to provide the new chancellor with assistance in addressing the ever-growing issues in the Athletic Department.

"That really happened because there was going to be a transition," Shalala said of Mucks. "He was going to be stepping down and I felt a responsibility to Gayle to find something for Arlie to do, and I liked him so much and he was so useful when I traveled around the state because he knew everybody. He was my best source in terms of identifying people. He was actually quite quiet, but whenever I asked him a question, he knew the answer and he knew who I should call. He was immensely important through this whole process and people don't give him proper credit."

Led by Mucks into fertile football booster territories, Shalala continually thrilled longtime observers of UW athletics when she publicly proclaimed that excellence in athletics can coexist with excellence in academics.

One of Shalala's other key advisors on campus during this time was Roger Formisano, a professor in the UW School of Business. Formisano, born in North Bergen, New Jersey, and raised in Portsmouth, New Hampshire, earned an undergraduate degree from the University of New Hampshire and a PhD from the University of North Carolina at Chapel Hill. After three years on the Business School faculty at the University of Maryland, Formisano accepted a position in the School of Business at the University of Wisconsin, where he became friends with another newcomer to the Madison campus, football coach Dave McClain. As the friendship grew, so did Formisano's knowledge of the football program and his involvement with it. Formisano was among the UW faculty who assisted in the football recruiting efforts, meeting with recruits who had an interest in the school of business. But when Don Morton arrived as coach, Formisano and the others who had been participating in the recruiting process were not invited to return.

In spring 1988, Formisano was returning to Madison from Washington, D.C., and by chance, was seated on the airplane next to Donna Shalala. The chancellor was new to her position at UW–Madison and had several questions about the school, the community, and more. But the conversation always seemed to return to the topic of Wisconsin athletics.

"To get a three-hour meeting with Donna Shalala is impossible," Formisano said. "But on a plane ride, that's as good as it gets."

About a month later, Formisano's phone rang. It was Shalala, who gave Formisano a new assignment. "She said she was appointing me to serve on the Athletic Board," he said. 'You're a finance guy and they're really in the hole. I'm going to make you chairman of that finance group and I want you to report back to me and tell me what the heck is going on over there. Tell me what we need to do to fix it.'"

In August, Shalala announced that she was naming Formisano, as well as Bobbi Wolfe and Susan Lubar, to the UW Athletic Board. "I spent the first three months with Ade trying to understand the finances of the Athletic Department," Formisano said. "And basically, I was appalled at what I saw."

It was late in 1988 when Formisano presented Shalala with a set of three recommendations for consideration. First, he said, Sponberg was a very nice guy, but Formisano and others questioned whether he was capable of doing what was necessary to turn things around. Second, Formisano said, there were a variety of significant changes that needed to be made to organize and update the manner in which the financial operation was conducted in the Athletic Department. And third, Formisano said, was the need to take a close look at firing the football coach. "She got very upset about this," Formisano said. "I just said to her that you need to think about the football program. Football is the engine that drives the finances of this organization and at some point in time, if things don't improve on the field and in the stands, you're going to have to think about the coach and whether or not he can get the job done.

"She said something to the effect that 'I'm not going to be known as someone who's going to get rid of football coaches.' I think she misread my recommendation. My recommendation was that you need to pay attention to this; you need to think about how this might happen in case things don't work out."

Formisano knew he wasn't alone in his recommendations, particularly the third one. "I must tell you that at that time there was a cabal on the Athletic Board—Tom Prosser, Andy Wojdula, myself—who already were thinking there's no way that Don Morton can lead this football program. We got the wrong guy for the job and we have to start thinking about making changes. We sort of nudged her in that direction."

In October 1988, the boys' hockey team from Culver (IN) Military Academy was in Madison for a game against a local opponent. Pat Richter's son, Barry, was a senior on that Culver team and had declared his intention to attend the University of Wisconsin to play hockey for the Badgers.

Following the Culver hockey match that night, Pat and Renee Richter hosted parents and friends for a postgame gathering at their residence in Maple Bluff. Among the guests was Formisano, whose college friend was the head coach of the Culver hockey team. With continued discussion going on behind the scenes about the need for a new athletic director, Formisano put Richter on the spot about a job opening that didn't exist, but one that would become available one year later.

"I was the last person to leave that night," Formisano said. "Pat and I stood outside on his lawn and I asked him straight up, 'Are you interested in being athletic director?' And he hedged enough on his answer to let me know that he was interested. From that moment on, in my mind, he was the guy to get. There was no question."

In March 1989, Shalala added another player to the team when she borrowed Al Fish from state government to try his hand at helping the UW Athletic Department steady the listing financial ship. Fish had worked for the state's Legislative Audit Bureau, which had recently completed a critical audit of UW

Athletics. He also had worked with two governors and the state's Department of Health and Social Services. His presence would provide immediate assistance to Shalala and Formisano, and later, to the next athletic director, Pat Richter.

Fish clearly understood what Shalala wanted to accomplish. "Donna quickly realized that athletics was a big access point for turning statewide attention in a positive way back to UW–Madison," Fish said. "She also had another theory that the state as a whole, outside of Dane County, still hadn't forgiven Madison for the Vietnam War protests. And having great sports teams would help get over that as well. She wanted to be embraced statewide and have the institution embraced statewide. So in order to reach all these big goals both for herself and for the institution, we needed to make these changes. I think by the summer of '89, she had not only decided that we're going to make a bunch of changes and the process to make those changes was underway, but she had already targeted Pat Richter as someone who had the credibility to come into a really difficult situation and immediately create some space, some goodwill, the promise of the future."

CHAPTER SEVEN
THE OOH, AAH
FACTOR

The 1989 football season, Morton's third year, wasn't much better than the two previous seasons. The Badgers struggled again, finishing with a 2-9 record. At the last home game, the announced attendance was 29,776, although those in attendance at Camp Randall Stadium on that snowy day would tell you that in the second half, less than 10,000 fans remained as Michigan State trounced the Badgers 31–3. Attendance had hit rock bottom. The per-game attendance of 41,734 in 1989 was the lowest since 1945.

As the losses mounted and the attendance dwindled, Shalala took action, forming an ad hoc task force of alumni, Athletic Board members, former players, and athletic donors. She instructed the group to closely scrutinize the condition of the UW Athletic Department and get back to her with a solid set of recommendations.

Shalala selected Pat Richter to chair the group.

"Looking back, I suppose that was Donna's way of getting me intertwined into the system," Richter said. "It was probably done for a reason."

Not so, said Shalala: "I was advised that he was the most prominent among the graduates," she said. "It never occurred to me that he might be available to be athletic director."

Very quietly, the committee met in November in the Milwaukee area. "We all talked about what we each thought was the problem," Richter said. "But it all boiled down to one thing, and that was football. Attendance had suffered so much. We just felt that if football was healthy, that would solve much of the problem."

Media reports indicated something a bit stronger coming from the committee, something greater than a change in football coaches. Newspaper reports

quoted an unidentified member of the task force as saying the group would recommend a housecleaning of the department's administration.

The group met with Shalala and presented her with the results of their
work. "She indicated that because of the relationships Ade had with Don, she
was thinking that something had to change in football but she wasn't sure Ade
was prepared to make that change," Richter said. "So ultimately, she decided she
had to make a change with both the football coach and the athletic director.

"Normally in the organizational structure you would have the football
coach reporting to the athletic director who hired him, and the athletic director
reporting to the chancellor who hired that person," Richter said. "In this case,
the football coach had been hired, then the athletic director, and then the chancellor after that. Nobody was responsible for hiring anybody below them. It was
an odd situation."

According to newspaper reports at the time, Shalala first outlined her
intention to fire Sponberg at their regular weekly meeting on October 23, 1989.

"I talked to him about the fact that we had a financial disaster on our
hands," Shalala recalled of the meeting. "He struck me as being a really nice guy
and totally over his head, with no real ties to Wisconsin or to our boosters, our
supporters, and our former athletes. I knew more than he did about the public's
attitude of what was going on."

They met again on October 30, and shortly thereafter, representatives of
both sides worked out the details.

On November 13, 1989, Shalala held a press conference to announce the
firing of athletic director Ade Sponberg. "A mutually agreed upon decision is an
indication I lacked confidence that he could continue in the position, knowing
what I know was in front of us and knowing what large jobs needed to be done,"
Shalala told reporters.

"The tendency at this university," Shalala said, "is just to hang on, to take
intermediate steps to solve a problem, not to bite the bullet, not to make the tough
decision. The Athletic Department is too important for that. The student-athletes
are too important. Not just important to the university but to the whole state."

The search for the new athletic director would be watched closely. Some,
like the *Wisconsin State Journal*'s editorial writers, didn't like the way things were
handled last time, and they offered their advice:

Last time around, the Athletic Board rushed to act before a new chancellor was hired and did its best to freeze out former athletic director Elroy
Hirsch as well as two campus experts, law professor Frank Remington
and history professor Diane Lindstrom, both former faculty representa-

tives to the Big Ten Conference. When Maryland and Michigan set up study committees to scrutinize their athletic programs, Remington was chair of those committees. At home, he was persona non grata... Whether the academically pure crowd likes it or not, college athletics is here to stay. Smart universities leverage that fact. The naïve wish it away.

Many Badger fans were still upset that the qualified candidates with local ties were not given much consideration when Sponberg was hired. Former Michigan athletic director Don Canham was among those asked about the preferred profile of a candidate for athletic director at the University of Wisconsin.

Shalala, at the advice of former athletic director Elroy Hirsch, invited Canham to visit Madison in 1989 and conduct an informal audit of the Athletic Department. "She wanted confirmation that Ade couldn't do the job," said Formisano. "And I think she also just wanted another set of eyes to look at things."

Shalala and Formisano, who would soon be named chair of the UW Athletic Board by Shalala, were at Shalala's university-owned residence, the Olin House, waiting for Canham's arrival. "She said, 'What do you think we need in an athletic director?' I said, 'Donna, what we need is someone with an ooh, aah factor.' She said, 'What do you mean by that?' I said that when you announce who the athletic director is (in my mind, whether officially or not, we had already decided that Ade was not the guy) I don't want you to have to stand up there with a resume and explain why he's a good guy for the University of Wisconsin. I want you to name his name and I want to hear the whole state go, 'Ooh, aah. That's a great choice.' And I want them to know right away, that's who we've got."

Canham spent two days on the Madison campus. Among those he talked with were members of the local media, including Butler. "He met with Mike Lucas and I and a few others in the W Club Room and each of us said that someone had to go out and get Pat Richter," Butler recalled. "I think he agreed with that."

Canham then met with Shalala and Formisano to discuss his findings. "We have this meeting and she asked him the same question," Formisano said. "And his answer was this: 'You need somebody with strong Wisconsin ties, somebody who can pull this thing together, get donations up, get the people excited, get them ready to buy football tickets again. You need somebody who is a known entity from a Wisconsin point of view.' She looked at me and said, 'The ooh, aah factor!'"

In the local newspaper, Canham repeated his verdict for local sports fans: "You need a man or woman who is familiar with the scene," Canham told reporters. "You need someone who knows the situation, knows Wisconsin, knows the Big Ten, and starts out running. You don't want to hire someone who doesn't know where Wausau is."

And in a more informal tone, *Wisconsin State Journal* sports editor Bill Brophy wrote that the University and its Athletic Department could ill afford another hiring mistake: "Bucky Badger isn't healthy enough to overcome the black eye that a bad hire would give him."

As word of the vacancy spread, a variety of names surfaced as potential candidates, including Bart Starr, Stu Voigt, Ron VanderKelen, Andy Wojdula, Willie Davis, Jim Bakken, and Mike Reinfeldt. Publicly, Pat Richter remained a noncandidate. "I'm really not the person I think we need," he told reporters. "I think we need someone who has enthusiasm, a person whom you see on camera and you think of a winning tradition."

To no one's surprise, Chancellor Donna Shalala conducted her due diligence in the matter, and she was doing it behind the scenes. She continued to consult with Formisano and other Athletic Board members, with law professor Frank Remington, and with Canham. She consulted with alumni, with coaches, and with donors. If she needed any assistance in identifying the department's true needs, she received it from a *Wisconsin State Journal* editorial: "What is desperately needed now is an athletic director who can put excitement back into football and fans back into Camp Randall's empty seats."

Shalala's visits with Canham—the former Michigan athletic director—were particularly insightful for the new chancellor. "His take was that we needed a much more businesslike approach, which was kind of the way he did things at Michigan," Shalala said. "He said that if I could find a businessman to run the Athletic Department with ties to Wisconsin, then that would be the ideal situation.

"And immediately a light bulb went off in my head, although he did not come out and specifically recommend Pat Richter," Shalala said.

But at the moment, the athletic director vacancy was not foremost on the chancellor's mind. There was other work that needed to be done. She had decided that she needed to fire football coach Don Morton, whose three-year record was 6-27. There were some, including then governor Tommy Thompson and UW System president Buzz Shaw, who were concerned that the firing might upset some state legislators and others at the state Capitol.

"I thought everybody around me was going to die," Shalala said of her plan to fire the coach. "The governor said, 'Don't do it. The boys downtown think there'll be blood on the streets and you can't find someone better.' Buzz also transmitted a message to me that said he'd support me in whatever I decided to do, but that the general consensus is that I shouldn't do it."

Seeking some advice and counsel on the matter, Shalala paid another visit to one of her newfound friends in Madison, former UW athletic director Hirsch. "I went to Elroy and said, 'Who are the boys downtown?' I had no idea who the boys downtown were. Elroy said, 'Don't worry about the boys downtown. You do whatever you think is right and I'll take care of the boys downtown.'

"I heard that after that, Elroy went around town and said, 'I like this girl. I think she's going to be great for the university.'"

On November 28, 1989, only 15 days after the firing of Ade Sponberg, Chancellor Shalala announced the firing of football coach Don Morton.

"I said when I arrived at Wisconsin that we would strive for excellence in everything we do," Shalala told reporters. "That includes the football program. The truth is," she continued, "we want a football program as good as this university. The football program sends a message, not by whether we win all our games and the Rose Bowl, but whether we have a competitive program."

Shalala didn't think she'd have any difficulty hiring a good football coach. But again, she did her homework, contacting UW alum Chuck Neinas, who was president of the College Football Association.

"After the governor and others said we couldn't recruit a coach," Shalala called. "I called Chuck and said, 'Call around the country and see if we can recruit a coach.' And he called back with a list, and among those on the list was Barry Alvarez.

"He said two things to me," Shalala recalled of Neinas. "First, he said, you're going to have to get into the process yourself and help the new person recruit and change the culture. And second, you're going to have to pay market salaries. And that's when we came up with the idea of writing to all the high school coaches. I wrote to every high school in this state and said, 'Trust us, we're going to hire a great coach for Wisconsin.'"

Back at the corporate office, Pat Richter continued to grow in his management role at Oscar Mayer. He had been promoted to Vice President of Personnel and had no interest in the vacant athletic director position. "There was a lot of discussion about me looking at the job, but frankly, I really wasn't that interested," Richter said.

Richter had suggested to Shalala that former UW hockey coach Bob Johnson would be a strong candidate for the position. "I started focusing on some people who I thought would be good for the job and I focused on Bob, who was with USA Hockey at the time," Richter said. "I pursued him and tried to determine his interest in the job. I happened to be going to Denver for a hockey game so I made plans to have a conversation with him there."

Meanwhile, at Oscar Mayer, the winds of change had arrived, and suddenly, Pat Richter was beginning to feel increasingly uncomfortable. During Richter's term of duty at General Foods headquarters, the company had been purchased by Philip Morris. Recently, Philip Morris had acquired Kraft Foods. The transaction, merging General Foods with Kraft Foods in late 1989, created the largest food company in North America.

"Top management at Philip Morris had always been quite protective of Oscar Mayer," Richter said. "They felt it was a well-run business and could not be as easily picked up by just anybody. So they kind of protected Oscar Mayer from the incursion of people who wanted to come and say, 'Let's do it this way.' When Kraft came in—obviously they were a very strong marketing company. There were occasions of friction and bumping heads as to how to do things in the food business.

"The dynamics of the meat business were somewhat unique," Richter said. "It's a very low-margin business. The culture was pretty much unique to Oscar Mayer. As that cross-fertilization began, that's when, as you move forward, things began to shift a bit. At that point, I was vice president of personnel, and you could start to see some of the functions changing. Some of the things we were doing in Madison were now going to be done in Chicago. You could see that shift taking place. You could see that Oscar Mayer's independence was starting to change.

"You could see, understandably, that wherever they could save money and find synergies, that was their intent," Richter said. "You could see over a period of time that more things were headed for Chicago. And the feeling was that that's where I'd end up. Oscar Mayer might not have a top-level human resources officer. They're likely to end up in Chicago."

With that backdrop, Richter headed to Denver to watch his son, Barry, play hockey and to have a conversation with Bob Johnson to gauge his interest in the athletic director job at Wisconsin. "When I went back to Denver, it seemed like so many things had changed with the company," Richter said. "It was no longer a corporation at Oscar Mayer, it was more of a business unit. And I started to think that it was possible that if you moved along in the organization, the next step was Chicago. And that's not where we wanted to be. So we began to think that maybe this athletic director thing was something to think about.

"The chance of being the top person at Oscar Mayer was not practical and not in the cards," Richter said. "So that was what was going through my mind and even though initially as a family we were not interested in becoming that public, the thought of being able run your own organization was intriguing. Here was a chance where, coming in, you could do some of the things you couldn't do at Oscar Mayer. You could come in here and have ultimate responsibility for marketing, promotions, communications, fundraising, and human resources. All the functions you have in a company.

"And so, although there was some initial reluctance," Richter said, "it was clear that this was a chance to run my own organization and that's the way we looked at it. Here was a chance to be the CEO and hire the people and have a chance to take something in a difficult situation and improve it.

"That's the process that ran through our minds," Richter said. "We wanted to stay in Madison with an opportunity to run our own organization and be part of something that we had a close affinity to and a close relationship with over many years. Maybe we should start to take a look at it and begin some conversations with some people about it."

Suddenly, Richter was in somewhat of an awkward situation. He called Johnson to explain. "I said, 'I feel bad about this,'" Richter said. "'I'm not sure if you were interested in this or not, but whereas before I really was not interested and was pushing you and wanting you to apply, things have changed with the company and now I think I'm going to get into the mix.' He accepted that. I'm not sure he really had an interest. He never really said he did."

In 1990, Bob Johnson was named head coach of the Pittsburgh Penguins. In his first season with the team, he led the Penguins to a Stanley Cup championship. On November 26, 1991, Bob Johnson died of brain cancer.

Richter recalls talking with Bob's wife, Martha, after Bob had passed away. "I mentioned to Martha that given what we had gone through early in our tenure with cutting sports and other stuff, and given that Bob had gone on to Pittsburgh and won the Stanley Cup, the life that he had—not knowing at the time—was probably a lot more fun and he probably had a lot more enjoyment in the middle of hockey and all the things that happened after that time. It was probably much more satisfying than what he would have had to deal with here early on."

Although he now had an expressed interest in the job, Richter still had some reservations worth considering. "It certainly wasn't, in my mind, a slam dunk," he said. "Were we, as a family, and was I, as a person, interested in doing that? Because by nature, I'm not necessarily considered a party person, a glad-hander, or whatever.

"It wasn't easy," Richter continued. "Giving up your privacy was the first thing on our mind. We didn't really care to be as public as this job would be. At that point, Barry had already decided to come to Wisconsin. He was in school. All the different ramifications were there. On the plus side, this was a chance to run your own operation in the place where you want to be—in Madison.

"I was on another hockey trip when I sat down and wrote a letter to Renee about all the different aspects of the job—which she still has—outlining the upside and downside and more or less asking permission to take a shot at it," Richter said. "That was really the final piece in place for us to move forward and throw our hat in the ring."

From Shalala's view, Renee Richter was the key. "I think in the end, Pat desperately wanted to do it, and I think Renee realized how much he really wanted to do it. And even though she knew their lives would change forever, she wanted the best for him."

"If I hadn't gotten Pat Richter, I don't know what I would have done," Shalala said. "I did not have a number two. He had told me twice that he wasn't going to take the job. I just decided he wasn't going to say no."

And when he finally said yes? "I almost fell off my chair," Shalala said. "I think I came as close to crying as I ever did while at Wisconsin."

Once Richter decided to pursue the job, things moved quickly. Richter interviewed with a UW Athletic Board committee. "At that point, I'm not sure what Donna had said to them," Richter said of the one-hour meeting. "It seemed like a routine interview. It seemed like it was a fait accompli at that point. Unless something really jumped out at the committee, I think this was the way it was going to be."

With the committee's approval, the announcement of Richter's hire was imminent. "It became the worst-kept secret," Richter said.

On the afternoon of December 15, 1989, Richter and Shalala entered the UW Field House, met the press, and announced the hiring of Pat Richter as athletic director:

> Today we begin a new era in Wisconsin athletics with the naming of Pat Richter as UW athletic director.
>
> I know this is a popular choice. It also is a great choice for Wisconsin.
>
> I can think of no one better suited for this job.
>
> Pat Richter is one of Wisconsin's greatest sports heroes, a UW Law School graduate, a successful businessman with strong leadership qualities, and a man of complete integrity. He is a wonderful role model for all of our student-athletes.
>
> The combination of his athletic and academic background and his years as one of the top executives at one of our area's major corporations make him ideally suited to lead our athletic program into the 1990s.
>
> I'm going to put him to work quickly. I've already assigned him four tasks.
>
> His first assignment, and an immediate one, will be to hire the best football coach that he can find.
>
> Second, he will review the organization of the Athletic Department, and assemble a strong management team.
>
> Third, he will review the Athletic Department's academic programs. We have agreed that we will make the investment necessary to give our student-athletes the best academic support systems in the country.
>
> Fourth, I have asked him to begin a concerted effort to reconnect the Athletic Department with the university.

Pat Richter, with Chancellor Donna Shalala at his side, spoke to reporters
upon being named Athletic Director on December 15, 1989, at the
UW Field House. Photo courtesy of the UW Athletic Department.

The people of Wisconsin have high expectations of us; so do our gifted coaches and the young women and men who proudly identify themselves as student-athletes.

Over the last two months, we have made it painfully clear that nothing will deter us from fulfilling our goals—and our dreams for Wisconsin.

Richter received a five-year contract with a rolling horizon clause, which meant the university would renew the contract for an additional year so that the contract remained a five-year term. His annual salary was $135,000, and he was to receive use of a leased car and memberhsips in both a country club and in the prestigious Madison Club.

Following the press conference, Richter joined a Big Ten Conference phone call in which information about Penn State's entry into the Big Ten was the topic of discussion. "I remember Doug Weaver, athletic director at Michigan State was chair of the athletic directors group, and Bo Schembechler asked if he knew anything about the Penn State announcement. Weaver said he didn't and Bo kind of went off. Apparently, that was the first indication that the athletic directors had heard anything about it. I had been tipped off by Shalala a couple of weeks earlier that it was going to happen sometime. That turned out to be my first order of business, so to speak."

Looking back, Shalala recalled with great pride her decision to hire Richter.

"We hired him because he had such great credibility and leadership abilities that no one else had. We hired him not to manage UW Athletics, but to lead it.

"The reaction I had when I first met Pat Richter was, 'What a graceful man.' I think he was such a natural for this job. He had the golden touch."

CHAPTER EIGHT
HOW'S THAT?

On a cold December night in 1989, Heisman Trophy finalist Major Harris had started strong, mixing his great passing ability with the run during a 96-yard first-quarter touchdown drive and leading his West Virginia Mountaineers to a quick 7–0 advantage over Clemson in front of nearly 83,000 fans in the 1989 Gator Bowl in Jacksonville, Florida. By all accounts, this would be a great night for Harris, his Mountaineer teammates, and their veteran head coach, Don Nehlen.

But it didn't turn out that way. Indeed, Clemson quickly shifted the momentum and eventually notched a convincing 27–7 victory over West Virginia, a loss that left the Mountaineers and Nehlen extremely disappointed.

Nehlen, in fact, was so disheartened that he decided to change some important travel plans that had been previously arranged. In the days prior to the Gator Bowl, Nehlen had been in continued conversation with Wisconsin's newly named athletic director, Pat Richter, about the head coaching vacancy there. Richter had narrowed his field of candidates to Nehlen and Notre Dame assistant coach Barry Alvarez, whose team was scheduled to play in the Orange Bowl on January 1 in Miami.

Richter and Nehlen had several telephone conversations, but the two had yet to meet in person. As such, Richter made arrangements for Nehlen to come to Madison immediately following the Gator Bowl to discuss the head coaching vacancy. Then, shortly thereafter, Richter would fly to Miami to for a second visit with Alvarez in the wake of Notre Dame's Orange Bowl appearance.

"I was looking at Don Nehlen, a very successful current head coach, or Barry Alvarez, assistant head coach from good lineage in terms of programs and players, very confident and all, but had never been a head coach," Richter said. "Those were my options."

There had been other options, developed shortly after Richter's hiring back in December. He had asked former Badger coach John Jardine for assistance in identifying potential candidates for the job. "We had quickly pulled together the files of applicants for the football job," Richter said. "Then we called John, who was helpful in identifying some of the things to look for. He advised us to look for someone who has a staff in mind, someone who has other coaches lined up and ready to come with him. John said that was a strong indication of confidence."

Richter reviewed the letters and resumes, made several phone calls, and began to set up interviews with the candidates.

"I thought I'd talk to those not in bowl games, talk to assistants, talk to others who were in practice for bowl games before they left for the bowl site," Richter said. He talked with Jim Donnan, an assistant coach at Oklahoma who would later become head coach at Georgia; Jim Colletto, an assistant coach at Ohio State who later would become head coach at Purdue; Doug Graber, a former UW assistant who weeks later would be named head coach at Rutgers; Lloyd Carr, who later would become head coach at Michigan; and Jim Harkema, head coach at Eastern Michigan.

A number of interviews were conducted at an airport hotel in Chicago; others were held on college campuses. In the end, it came down to the two of them: Nehlen and Alvarez.

Alvarez had been the defensive coordinator for Notre Dame's impressive national championship team in 1988 and continued to be one of the hottest head-coaching prospects during the 1989 season, when the Irish and their tenacious defense were flirting with a second consecutive national championship. Alvarez, who had played at Nebraska, was an assistant coach at Iowa from 1979 to 1986. There, he helped head coach Hayden Fry turn around the Hawkeye football program.

Alvarez was well aware of the possible opening at Wisconsin. In fact, on the November day that Shalala announced the firing of Don Morton, she also announced that until a new athletic director was named, Formisano would coordinate the search for a new football coach. Upon arriving home that same night, Formisano had two telephone messages from coaches interested in the job. One of the messages was from Barry Alvarez.

Alvarez had recently interviewed at Pittsburgh but had taken his name out of consideration for that job. He briefly had considered the Rutgers opening, but did not apply. In fact, he had told his boss at Notre Dame, head coach Lou Holtz, that there was just one job out there that interested him.

"I told Lou that if I didn't get the Wisconsin job, I was coming back to coach with him at Notre Dame," Alvarez said. "When you are in those situations, you sit back and take a look at what are the possibilities. This was one that I had really set my sights on because I knew the area. I had recruited the Midwest. I knew the Big Ten very well and I knew it would be a good fit for me. I kept my eye on it. One of the guys I had coached with, Chuck Heater, had coached here and he really gave me a good background about Wisconsin and what the issues would be coming in. The high school coaches had lost confidence. The empty stadium. The academics. I really had a good pulse for what was needed here."

Following his meetings with Colletto and with Carr, Richter flew to Notre Dame, where the Irish were practicing prior to traveling to Miami for the Orange Bowl. Alvarez had made arrangements to meet Richter at the South Bend airport. "Pat told the story to [former UW teammate] Merritt Norvell, who relayed it to me several years later. Pat was scared to death that I was going to be 5 foot 6 and look like Danny DeVito," Alvarez said. "He said that's all he could think of getting off the airplane. Pat said later, 'What a relief to get off the plane and look at you standing there!'"

Alvarez and Richter visited at the Alvarez home near South Bend. "We just sat there and talked; we visited for a long time," Alvarez said. "I thought we connected. I felt very comfortable. I had a sense that he was very interested. You never know in an interview but I felt good when it was over. I was prepared for it. I knew the issues and felt that some of the things he was looking for, I could bring to the table."

During this time, Formisano and Richter stayed in contact in an effort to move the process along at brisk pace. "My sense was that Pat wanted a young guy with fire in his belly, someone with mountains to climb and who knew how to climb them," Formisano said. "He came back from that trip to South Bend and he basically said, 'I found my football coach.' He said he'd never seen anybody so organized. He had practice plans. He had an organizational chart. He had charts on the coaches he was going to hire. Pat said, 'This guy is ready to be a head coach.' He said, 'Look who he's been with: Nebraska, Iowa, and Notre Dame.'

"Barry impressed the hell out of Pat as a manager. Being in the business world, I think Pat really respected this organizational ability, this ability to see structure and get things done as a real plus," Formisano said. "It wasn't just some sort of innate ability. He had a plan and he executed that plan. When Pat came back from that trip, basically, the search was over."

Alvarez and Richter stayed in constant telephone contact throughout those days leading up to Notre Dame's Orange Bowl game against Colorado. "Pat had been calling me every day, keeping in contact," Alvarez recalled. "So I called him a couple of days before the game and I can remember telling Pat that if you're going to hire me, you need to do it before the game because we'll get more publicity than the school could ever afford and it will really help us in recruiting. He said, 'I'll have to go to the board with it.' He said, 'We won't be able to release anything on it,' and I said, 'Don't worry, we can leak it!'"

Richter, meanwhile, was still looking at Nehlen. He was well aware that Nehlen had a very nice financial package at West Virginia and that he was in the midst of a very successful career with the Mountaineers. He knew it might be difficult to steal him away from West Virginia. Still, the two had continued with their plans to meet, with Richter planning to call Nehlen the day after the Gator Bowl and arrange for a quick visit.

"We were going to fly out and pick him up and bring him back to Madison to look around," Richter said. "They lost the game and when I called him, he was down, felt bad about losing the game, and he said, 'Gee, maybe it's because of the game, I just feel down today. Maybe I could think about it for a day or so and decide what to do.'

"Once Don indicated that he had some questions and just didn't feel right about visiting, I felt that that of frame of mind was not what we were looking for," Richter said. "He certainly had an emotional attachment to West Virginia and we needed someone who was ready to come in here cranked up, dive into recruiting. He'd been so successful . . . did he really want to get into that game again? And he had a good financial package so it was understandable. When he gave me that indication, I just felt that we should stop pursuing him."

Wasting no time, Richter called Formisano and told him he was going to make his run at Alvarez.

"I think it was the day before their game that I called," Richter said. "I got Barry on the line and asked him how he'd like to be the next head football coach at the University of Wisconsin. He accepted. I said we'd fly down the next day."

On December 31, Formisano announced to the Madison media that Richter had offered the job to Alvarez and was on his way to Florida to meet with the new UW coach.

Richter arrived at Notre Dame's team hotel while the game was still in progress. He had told Alvarez that he'd wait at the hotel for his arrival after the game and the two would meet to go over the many issues at hand, including the travel arrangements for a press conference in Madison. Richter had slipped a note under Alvarez's door, alerting him to his room number and asking Alvarez to give him a call when he got back to his hotel room.

While Nehlen was pondering his team's disappointing performance in the Gator Bowl, Alvarez and the Fighting Irish were enjoying a different type of bowl experience. Colorado came in ranked first in both the Associated Press and United Press International polls with its perfect 11-0 record. Notre Dame came in ranked fourth in both polls with an 11-1 record. The Irish completely shut down the high-scoring Colorado Buffaloes en route to a 21–6 victory and, eventually, a number two ranking in the country. The architect of the stellar defensive performance was Alvarez, the team's defensive coordinator.

On the national television broadcast that night, the announcers made several references to Alvarez taking the Wisconsin job. "We got a good kick out of it on the broadcast," Richter said. "And the fact that Notre Dame did such a fine job defensively on Colorado, that just kind of built up the interest and we got some good publicity. I remember Bill Walsh was involved in the broadcast and I never really felt like he gave Barry the credit that night. Unbeknown to most, Bill had called me on behalf of Jim Colletto and Jim wasn't the successful candidate, so I think on that broadcast, Bill wasn't necessarily giving Barry the kudos that he might have gotten otherwise, because Notre Dame really stuffed 'em."

With the game now over, Richter waited at the team hotel, and waited and waited. "It really took a long time," Richter said. "I started thinking, 'Geez, he did such a great job and there are a number of jobs open at the time.' I'm thinking to myself, the longer the wait goes on, did somebody grab him right off the field before he got back to the room and now we don't have a guy?"

Finally, the phone rang. On the other end, and the soon-to-be Badger coach said to his new boss, "Well, how's that?"

The two went to Notre Dame's postgame party at the hotel, where Alvarez gave Richter a gift. "He gave me a little Saint Christopher medal that Notre Dame had given to the players and coaches before each game," Richter said. "I held on to that medal and kept in my desk for years and subsequently after our victory over Michigan State to qualify for the 1994 Rose Bowl, I gave it back to Barry and said, 'Here, this is yours.' I actually had it made into a little trophy that said "How's that?" and we put the medal into it."

Said Alvarez: "Over the years, that was kind of our saying. We'd kind of laugh. That was our deal . . . How's that!"

* * *

On February 1, 1990, Pat Richter climbed the two flights of stairs inside the tunnel in the southeast corner of Camp Randall Stadium and walked into the second-floor office that previously had been occupied by Elroy Hirsch and, more recently, by Ade Sponberg, and officially began his new career as athletic director at the University of Wisconsin. After a 45-day whirlwind that saw Richter accept his new job and promptly hire a new football coach, Richter settled into his new home away from home.

The thick, red shag carpeting in the office was well worn. The dark wood paneling—circa 1950s—was on all four walls, not just in Richter's office, but throughout the facility. The red push-button phone on the athletic director's desk did not have a hold button, nor did it ring at the receptionist's desk.

"It was probably the first reality check," Richter said. "And all of a sudden you begin to get a good understanding of the environment. It looked like a lot of things had been patched together and you started to notice those things a little more closely and you realize that a lot of needs had not been met to that point. I really hadn't been to the Athletic Department offices since I was a student-athlete.

"The program itself, aside from football and basketball, was treading water," Richter recalled. "Hockey was fairly successful, and the rest of the programs were pretty solid but had been beaten down because football had not been healthy, and that left a pervasive attitude throughout the department."

Clearly, there was a lot of work to be done. Between the time Alvarez was hired and the time he joined the UW full time, Richter attended the state football coaches meetings in Stevens Point in an effort to keep everybody's mind on the Wisconsin football program as it was hiring its coach.

"We needed to generate some enthusiasm," Richter recalled. "There were lots of service club presentations. We went just about anywhere that we could go to spread the word."

Richter and Chancellor Shalala also put significant time into supporting the efforts of Alvarez's new football staff. Their support was well received by the football staff and by the recruits.

"They ended up with a pretty good class," Richter said. "That's when they said they have to build a fence around Wisconsin and keep the Wisconsin kids here. Get the bodies from Wisconsin and the feet from somewhere else.

"I remember one of the state's top recruits was Jim Flanigan, who Barry had been recruiting at Notre Dame," Richter said. "Flanigan actually kind of helped us in that regard. He was committed to Notre Dame, but was willing to say Alvarez was going to be a good coach."

When he wasn't on the road promoting UW Athletics, he was looking under the hood of the department. "For a good period of time there we were trying to get used to what's going on around here," Richter said. "We were trying to understand the people, understand the finances, the concept of revenue sharing, and all of the dynamics of how we were operating," Richter said. "We were doing the budgets in a very rudimentary fashion on a 20-column ledger sheet. There wasn't much of a technological understanding of the inner working of the department that we could readily access. That quickly appeared to be an area that we had to get into right away. At Oscar Mayer, you were used to getting monthly tab runs, actuals versus budget, and so forth. None of that was here, just numbers."

Richter decided to utilize some of his business background to attack the problems. At Oscar Mayer and at General Foods, Richter often had participated in strategic planning sessions. Those sessions had proven to be effective tools in Richter's corporate world experience, so he decided to bring the concept into play in the athletic environment. But before the planning proceeded, Richter and the department were dealt a huge setback.

"We really just started to scratch the surface on the planning process when the state informed us that the deficit in the Athletic Department was not $1.4 million, it was $2.1 million," Richter said. "Apparently, there was a miscalculation along the way and some assumptions that were built in didn't occur. That seemed to trigger an awful lot of angst downtown with the legislature. We had been going through a process of trying to meet everybody down there. Then all of a sudden, when this came up, we were like a pawn before the Joint Finance Committee. For them it was kind of a fun thing to do. Everybody likes to get involved in athletics."

The news that the deficit had jumped by nearly 50 percent was devastating. From a political standpoint, the department's credibility with the state legislature, the media, and the public was damaged. In addition, the department took a hit on campus when the Legislature chose to impose a parking surcharge on the entire campus, with the funds directed toward athletics. Financially, it was a boon to the department's finances, but politically, it created resentment in other UW departments and clearly hindered the Athletic Department's efforts to better connect to campus. "In many respects, we were dealing with that negative for years," Richter said.

With faculty and staff upset about the new surcharge, the department also inherited some ill will from student government. A $10 per semester student fee for all UW students—not just those interested in intercollegiate athletics—was put in place in 1989. And while the student fee helped the department financially, it was not without its burden. "Early on, that created more desire on the part of students to be part of the process," Richter said. "They wanted input into what was going on. We had to go to a lot of student meetings and now they were taking another kick at the cat."

"We now had the legislature, the university, student government, and the UW System hovering over us, wanting to make sure this was right from a system standpoint. There wasn't any instant fix where we were going to raise a lot of money overnight."

With a $2.1 million deficit and considerable oversight and second-guessing from the legislature, UW faculty and staff, student government, and others, Richter and the department dug in their heels and tried to build some trust with their many different constituencies.

Cheryl Marra, who Richter hired only five months after his arrival on the job, remembers those challenging early times, the changing financial numbers and the subsequent fallout. "Every time we'd go back to the athletic board, we'd have a new number," Marra said. "That Athletic Board didn't trust us for two seconds because we didn't know how bad it was—we had no idea. Everyone was resentful because of the parking surcharge. We had the student fee. It was such a period of mistrust. I remember that during those first two or three years, trying to get anybody around here to trust us was ridiculous. We probably spent two or three years just trying to get people to trust us."

Still, despite much resistance, Richter led his team forward, ever so slowly.

"Basically it was all about building constituencies and relationships," Richter recalled. "We knew that football is the big stick and if that's healthy, everything else is healthy, not only financially but mentally as well. So we worked hard with Barry and his staff to build satellite booster club operations in Wausau, Chicago and places like that to build a bigger broader base. There was a lot of outreach going on."

Meanwhile, the department's planning process had been short-circuited. "In those early days, we were meeting in the morning about what was happening in the afternoon. It was all about putting out fires. It was tactical and not strategic.

"Our strategic planning was pushed aside as we started to dig deeper and deeper into the financial situation," Richter said. "There was a time when we talked about all of us taking a week off without pay just to help the numbers."

There would be additional bad news. In 1989, a complaint against the University of Wisconsin Athletic Department had been filed with the United States Office of Civil Rights (OCR). The complaint alleged that the department was not in compliance with Title IX, the 1972 federal legislation that mandates equal educational opportunities for women in federally-funded programs. "Educational opportunities" includes athletics, and ever since Title IX became law, publicly-funded schools had been struggling with the challenge of providing more athletic programming for girls and women without taking opportunity away from boys and men.

One way to address the OCR concerns would be to add an additional women's sport, but with the huge deficit and the cost of adding a new program, that was not a viable option.

Another possibility was to eliminate some existing men's programs. As the discussions continued, the unpleasant option of cutting sports continued to move forward.

"We said, 'Look, we've lost all this money. We need to cut back our programs,'" Richter said. "We have facility issues. Support services issues. Maybe by having a somewhat smaller program we can help ourselves financially and get back on track and help ourselves gender-equity wise."

Richter wanted to know more about the complaint filed with the Office of Civil Rights. His initial frustration with that office would turn into an ongoing consternation that would last for several years.

"I asked at the time where the OCR complaint was," he said. "I assumed they had come on site, investigated, and then shared their findings. I was told, 'No, that's not how it works. They verbalize it over the phone and we respond.' There was never anything in writing. It was an archaic process and it didn't make any sense. But that's the way it was."

Richter met with the OCR in Chicago. "We sat in there and they talked about the problems," Richter said. "We said 'Here's what we're doing and here's what we are planning to do.'"

One of the issues raised in the complaint was the amount of department money allotted to recruiting. More money was targeted for recruiting in men's sports than women's sports.

The other issue was the mere fact that the number of male student-athletes was significantly greater than the number of female athletes at Wisconsin.

"The recruiting part was difficult because some programs recruit in different ways, some recruit closer to home than others," Richter said. "But the numbers, trying to get them better in line with the campus numbers was a bit more difficult. They wanted us to get to 50/50, which would match the numbers overall on campus. At the time, we were about 58 percent men, 42 percent women."

"There just wasn't a windfall anywhere," Richter recalled. "We were getting money from the conference's shared revenue plan. We began to increase our marketing efforts in the hopes of increasing our tickets sales. Our first slogan was that Badger football was 'A Whole New Animal.' We were making an effort to try and get more students involved. We're now getting into our summer programs and golf outings and outreach to generate enthusiasm for the upcoming fall. We were going everywhere, speaking everywhere."

But with a $2.1 million deficit and the federal government's demand to increase opportunities for women, there would be no quick and easy solutions. Instead, the situation would continue to require slow, steady movement.

And while external outreach efforts increased, there was also an internal message that needed to be communicated. "I'll never forget a conversation Pat and I had about people here accepting mediocrity," Marra said. "We agreed that one of our challenges was to overcome the sense that mediocrity seemed to be acceptable here. From the campus, from the athletic board—it permeated down to the coaching staff. For Pat, who was used to achieving everything at the highest level, and from where I had come at a successful Division III program, mediocrity was not what you settled for. You went after the best."

*   *   *

In December 1989, the attention of the Badger community had been focused on the firings of Ade Sponberg and Don Morton, the hiring of Pat Richter, and the search for the new football coach. Meanwhile, it was business as usual for the many other coaches and teams in the UW Athletic Department. One of those was the Badger hockey team, in its second season under Coach Jeff Sauer. Just two weeks after the announcement of Richter's hiring in the spring of 1990, the University of Wisconsin hockey program embarked on an innovative scheduling experiment that took the team to Milwaukee's Bradley Center for the inaugural Bank One Badger Hockey Showdown. The brainchild of then associate athletic director Joel Maturi, the tournament proved to be a huge success, particularly in the early years. The event became a gathering place for UW alumni in the greater Milwaukee area who rarely caught a glimpse of the school's national powerhouse hockey program. Secondly, with no football bowl games on the horizon, the Showdown became a holiday road trip for many badger fans.

The Badgers defeated Notre Dame and Boston College to win the first Showdown, and the championship would prove to be a precursor for the rest of the season. Wisconsin went on to take first place in the Western Collegiate Hockey Association and win the McNaughton Cup. And on April 1, 1990, the Badgers defeated Colgate 7–3 to win the NCAA championship at Detroit.

The team's 36-9-1 record was the second best in team history. The NCAA championship was the fifth in team history and the third in nine years for the Badgers, who had won the championships in 1981 and 1983.

Weeks later, the team, which included Pat's son, freshman Barry Richter, would be invited to the White House to meet President George H. W. Bush. A framed photo of that meeting would hang on the wall in Pat Richter's office during his remaining years as athletic director.

"The hockey championship really did a lot for morale," Richter said. "It added a great deal and gave us a boost. It was a signal to us that the program was still strong."

CHAPTER NINE
MOVING FORWARD

The recruiting scramble of early 1990 had proved somewhat successful for Coach Barry Alvarez and his new staff. Despite getting a late start on the recruiting trail, they had signed what appeared to be a good class of high school recruits. Along the way, they received help from the Chancellor Donna Shalala and the school's new athletic director, Pat Richter.

"The thing you saw about Donna right away was how involved she wanted to be," Alvarez said. "Most chancellors would stay at arm's length, but whatever it was—meet a recruit, call a recruit, talk to the parents—however you wanted her to be involved, she was going to be involved, which I really liked.

"And Pat was right in the middle of it, too. We'd bring recruits in, and we wanted the Chancellor and the athletic director to be there, and both of them were there. We'd have a recruiting weekend, and they'd be there."

In addition to the recruiting trail, Richter and Alvarez and his staff were in full swing on the summer circuit, with golf outings, speaking engagements, and high school camps and clinics. "We're going everywhere, speaking everywhere," Richter said.

As football training camp opened in August, there was guarded optimism. The program's fortunes had slipped so far that just about anything would be an improvement. Among the returning veterans were senior defensive lineman Donald Davey and junior defensive back Troy Vincent.

Recognizing the need to promote its product and seek out new customers, the department had entered into an agreement with veteran advertising and marketing professional John Robertson, who developed a marketing plan for the 1990 season that would try to take advantage of the excitement generated by the team's new coaching staff. The team's slogan touted the 1990 Badgers as

"A Whole New Animal." Robertson's efforts, first started during the Morton years, would be the beginnings of a marketing program that would expand greatly during the Pat Richter years.

The Badgers opened their 1990 football season with three straight nonconference games at home. The first, against California of the Pac-10, was a 28–12 loss before 45,980 fans at Camp Randall Stadium. "They were in the same situation we were in," Richter said of the California football program. "Just before the first half, one of their guys intercepts a pass and returns it 100 yards for a touchdown. It was so fragile for us then. Barry had gotten them mentally where they were, even though he wasn't sure if the physical part was there. Instead of going into halftime with a 10-point lead, you're down by four points. That really hurt."

The following week, the Badgers recorded their first victory under Alvarez, defeating Ball State 24–7 before 44,698 fans. Sadly for Richter, Alvarez, and the rest of the new regime Badgers, it would be the team's only victory of the season.

"People were saying it looked like the same old animal," Richter joked. "But if you understood the game, you knew it really was different—and better."

The Badgers drew nearly 65,000 for the Big Ten home opening 41–3 loss to Michigan, and nearly 68,000 for a 21–3 Homecoming loss to Illinois. And while the football team's 1-10 record was a disappointment, there was indeed a newfound glimmer of optimism and hope, as evidenced by the attendance increase. Badger fans, after three consecutive years of walking away, were beginning to return to Camp Randall Stadium.

For the season, the team averaged 51,027 per game, an attendance increase of nearly 9,300 per game. General public season tickets, which had dipped to 21,254 in 1989, increased to 24,672, and student season tickets, at a paltry 4,117 in 1989, increased to 5,977.

Still, there was a long way to go, not only on the playing field, but off the field as well.

"What stands out that first year for me is financial crisis after financial crisis after financial crisis," said former Athletic Board member and chair Jim Hoyt. "The numbers kept changing. We'd be about ready for a meeting and suddenly there'd be a phone call saying 'Oops, the deficit isn't really what we thought it was. It's something else.' Nobody had a firm grasp on it."

Those changing financial numbers made for several uncomfortable moments for Richter and his staff. There were meetings with the Board of Regents and its Business and Finance Committee, meetings with the UW–Madison vice chancellor for budget and finance John Torphy, meetings with the UW Athletic Board and its Finance Committee, and meetings with the State Legislature's Joint Finance Committee.

"It felt like the wolves were circling around the program," Hoyt said. "It was usually Pat and Al [Fish] going to answer their questions, and in most cases, they were pretty hostile. In some cases, they were grandstanding to, in my opinion, embarrass the department and to make public how miserably this place had been run."

Hoyt recalled one meeting before the state legislature's Joint Finance Committee, a meeting in which Hoyt caught a glimpse of the new athletic director's impact, and the manner in which Richter's stature would lead the way for the UW Athletic Department.

"We were getting ready for a meeting that was about the athletic budget and whether they thought we were doing enough to cut costs," Hoyt said. "And before the meeting begins, the members of the Joint Finance Committee came down from their desks to the table where we were seated to get Pat's autograph. And I sort of smiled and said, 'This is not all bad.' There probably aren't many witnesses who testify before this committee who the members are so enthralled by that they come around to get his autograph beforehand. I know some members of the Athletic Board, when I explained that, they thought that was terrible. But Pat had credibility and respect and recognition that, for his position of leadership in the department, nobody could match. The questions in that particular meeting became less hostile and much more supportive. In part it was because the department had put together this plan—it was a primitive plan, but it was a business plan to show how they were going to reverse the finances. And, because Pat had the credibility that he did, people were willing to say, 'OK. Give it a try. Go for it.'"

While Richter encountered some edginess in his appearances before the many different oversight groups, the reaction elsewhere continued to be positive. In most cases, wherever Richter went during those early years, he was met with encouragement and enthusiasm. "The support he got from people in the community was tremendous," said Renee Richter. "People would come up to him and say 'Good luck. We're behind you.' It gave him such strength and hope in the days when he was just trying to get the ship back on course. He was just trying to get parts of the ship headed in the right direction and the rest would follow. And everybody was just tremendous."

* * *

In the spring of 1991, Richter contacted Bob Drane, a friend and former coworker at Oscar Mayer, whose marketing and strategic planning expertise had impressed Richter during his days in the food business. Richter asked Drane to help the Athletic Department leadership develop a strategic plan.

"Bob took us through some planning exercises and went through some of the basics," Richter said. "He told us, 'Let's think out over the next 10 years. What are the things you like to have accomplished in that time?' We put all kinds of things up there and narrowed it down. We wanted fiscal integrity and credibility. We wanted to be financially solvent and have good financial underpinnings. We wanted to be competitive athletically. We wanted a good solid academic record. We wanted to comply with the rules. We wanted to be gender equitable. Those were the things we identified as what we wanted to be part of our program."

Incredibly, the team was quite specific with some of its goals. "We said that we'd like to go to three bowl games over that time, including one Rose Bowl, and wanted to go the quarterfinals in men's basketball," Richter said. "Those were the yardsticks we set. Out of that flowed the strategic planning process and in that process that forced us to take a look at what are the things that basically will bring us to this point. We had financial goals. What are the short term actions that will get us there? Competitiveness—what are the things we need to do there? Academics—how can we get more resources there? How can we better provide a well-rounded experience for our student athletes? How do we get closer to gender equity and comply with federal law? And what are the things we need to do to make sure we have a strong compliance program?"

The group's work from those planning sessions with Bob Drane—the easel tearsheets with all of the goals scribbled on them—were saved for posterity. From time to time, Richter would pull them out to share with this staff and other interested parties. "We wanted to save them as sort of a time capsule," Cheryl Marra said of the written goals from 1991. "We wanted to look back and see how we did."

* * *

By this time, there was another new face seen in and around the UW Athletic Department. It was Rick Telander, a senior writer for *Sports Illustrated* and the author of *Heaven Is a Playground* and *The Hundred-Yard Lie.* Telander was interested in writing a book about the trials and tribulations of managing a Division 1-A athletic program. Telandar was a former defensive back at Northwestern, and as such, was quite familiar with teams in the Big Ten Conference. Additionally, he was a regular on the *Sportswriters Show,* a sports talk show on cable television throughout the country. The producer of the show was Madison native and UW graduate John Roach Jr., who had kept Telander abreast of the Wisconsin sports scene and encouraged Telander in his book-writing initiative.

"The only thing that was out in the public was that we had a new football coach and we were in debt," Richter said. "He wanted to write about big-time football; how do you survive? We weren't sure that we wanted somebody poking around and peeking under the tent, so to speak."

Unlike the television exposure that Wisconsin teams would receive years later, the Badgers were rarely seen on national television, and this lack of exposure was an ongoing recruiting issue for Alvarez and his staff. Richter was aware that the Wisconsin program could benefit from the exposure that might result from a book written by a nationally famous sportswriter and author. His curiosity piqued, Richter scheduled a meeting with Telander and Alvarez at the Madison Club.

"In the back of our minds, we were thinking he could write this book without us," Richter said. "Were we better off to give him access or not? I remember Barry asking him 'If I go into a recruit's home and see the book on the coffee table, how am I going to feel about it?' Telander basically said that if what we're doing here at Wisconsin is positive, then the book will be positive. We weren't necessarily crazy about it, but in the end we felt we were better off to be part of the process and not be confrontational about it."

For several months, Rick Telander had access to the inner operations at Camp Randall Stadium. He witnessed the saga of dropping sports, the discussions about the complaint filed with the Office of Civil Rights, and much more. "But we lost track of him and didn't hear anything for a long time," Richter said. "Then, we go to the Rose Bowl in 1994 and the book comes out."

The book, *From Red Ink to Roses: The Turbulent Transformation of a Big Ten Program*, was published by Simon and Schuster shortly after the 1994 Rose Bowl appearance by the Badgers. The promotional material noted that author Telander "goes behind the scenes in a Big Ten athletic department to reveal the human fallout from the necessary political and financial decisions that dominate college sports."

Thankfully for Richter and the Badgers, the book proved to be a good read for many Badger fans interested in hearing just about anything about their Rose Bowl heroes. But the book's overall tone and content were somewhat noncontroversial and provided few if any negative complications for the UW Athletic Department.

* * *

It was clear that the financial situation in the Athletic Department was almost entirely dependent upon the fortunes of the UW football program. Many doubted that the football team would be able to turn things around. Those who speculated that it could be done agreed that it wouldn't happen overnight. Still others didn't really care, and in fact, were hoping that the department's struggles continued.

Chancellor Shalala had appointed journalism professor Jim Hoyt to the Athletic Board in 1990. The following year, she would appoint him chair of the board. "I remember Donna saying to me then, 'OK, we've got the athletic director in position and we've got the football coach in position. Things are heading in the right direction. Now we need the faculty on board. Are you up for the job?' She knew there was reticence on the part of the faculty. They were starting to think there was too much attention being paid to athletics. There was almost—in some circles on the faculty—a perverse pride in the failures of the Athletic Department because in their eyes, that meant that it had to be a strong academic institution."

Hoyt's predecessor as Athletic Board chair was Roger Formisano; he agreed with Hoyt's assessment. "Part of the reason the department wasn't successful was the department itself," Formisano said. "But part of it also was the way the rest of campus viewed athletics with a 'Who needs it?' attitude."

As a faculty member in the UW School of Business, Formisano was asked by Shalala to provide expertise and assistance to the Athletic Department as it worked to solve the lingering financial struggles. Formisano spent a significant amount of planning time with Al Fish, the Athletic Department's chief administrative officer whom Shalala had appointed to serve in the department in Ade Sponberg's final months on the job. Fish, a former golfer at Luther College, had no previous athletic administration experience. He did, however, have extensive administrative experience in politics and in state government, where he worked for Governor Anthony Earl and for the state's Legislative Audit Bureau, which had recently completed an audit of the UW Athletic Department. In 1988, Fish sent a letter to Shalala's chief of staff, Harry Peterson, outlining what, in Fish's opinion, needed to be done to fix the Athletic Department.

Formisano and Fish, both given status and authority by the chancellor to forge ahead, spent many hours together to try and come up with a solution that might work.

"It became clear to both Al and I that in those sports that were being marginally funded, we were not doing those students any favors," Formisano said. "It seemed to me we should fund our sports to the point that they have a chance to be competitive in the Big Ten. Given the budget and the availability of funds over the next five years, we couldn't support all the teams we had. Something big had to go."

That seemed to be the consensus of the Badger coaches, too.

"When it came down to looking at our programs and the possibility that we were going to have to do something, we met with all the coaches of the programs," Richter said. "We wanted to hear from them. The tenor of the meetings was basically 'We can't continue like this. We can't continue to limp along with less and less money and expect us to be competitive. We're better off, even if someone's not here, to have a smaller program.' That was basically the talk."

As the discussions continued, it became clear that baseball would be among the sports targeted for elimination.

As a youngster, baseball had clearly been Pat Richter's favorite sport. When Richter was in college, many observers speculated that baseball was his best sport. At Wisconsin, he earned three letters in baseball, and some thought that Richter sacrificed a promising professional baseball career when he signed with the Washington Redskins of the National Football League.

"Pat was able to play a very significant role because of his connection with the baseball program," Hoyt recalled. "They couldn't argue that he was anti-baseball. He was somebody who understood the issue and he was able to handle the criticism of dropping that visible program. Although, in retrospect, it was nowhere near as visible as it was made out to be."

Because of his connection to the local baseball community, Richter ended up in the middle of several discussions with those who wanted to save baseball at Wisconsin. "There were some outside groups that were trying to change my mind about baseball, former players and teammates who came in my office to meet with me and try to change my mind. It was a very emotional issue. As a former player, I understood that.

"But the fact was, something had to go," Richter said. "The impact was going to be felt by some group of athletes regardless of what the sport was."

Internally, the decision was made to recommend to the UW Athletic Board to eliminate baseball, men's and women's fencing, and men's and women's gymnastics. And while the complaint filed with the Office of Civil Rights in 1989 had brought forth gender equity issues for the department, the decision to drop the five sports was motivated almost entirely by the department's efforts to regain its financial footing and to improve the overall quality of the program.

At the 1990 NCAA annual convention, Wisconsin track and field star Suzy Favor became the school's first winner of the Honda-Broderick Cup, awarded annually to the student-athlete who, by vote of athletic directors across the country, is judged most deserving of recognition as the Collegiate Woman Athlete of the Year. It was a time to celebrate Favor's accomplishments as an athlete at the University of Wisconsin. But at the time Favor was being honored, two issues of note were lurking in the background of the convention in Nashville: the 1989 complaint filed with the Office of Civil Rights and the pending recommendation to drop baseball at Wisconsin. Ironically, Favor's future husband, Mark Hamilton, whom she was dating at the time, was a member of the Badger baseball team.

It was during that convention that Shalala met with Richter, Fish, Formisano, and UW associate athletic director Cheryl Marra. At the meeting, the department outlined to Shalala its plan to eliminate baseball, men's and women's fencing, and men's and women's gymnastics. Upon hearing the department's plan at that meeting in Nashville, the chancellor approved it. The next step for the department was to present its plan to the UW Athletic Board and seek its approval.

It was a difficult argument to advance with the board. First, there were the emotions of the student-athletes, the coaches, and support staff in the affected sports. Second, there was political resistance on the board.

"There were clearly board members whose position was to save the sports at all costs," Hoyt recalled. "Cut whatever you need to cut to save the sports. And these were people who happened to be fairly articulate and were able to defend that position. In their view, we're in the business of providing opportunities for student-athletes, not in the business of eliminating them."

But according to Hoyt, Richter made a convincing case. "What convinced me and what I thought Pat handled very well at the time was that the cutting of sports was to free up budget money to do a number of things. Notably, it was done to pay down the debt in the department. Secondly, it was done so that we could reinvest in the teams that were remaining to provide them additional support so that they could compete at a higher level than they had competed at before.

"Gender equity was off in the wings," Hoyt said. "It was to reinvest; to provide more resources; to hire better coaches and pay more; to add assistant coaches in sports that didn't have them; to have full complements of scholarships in sports that before had only had partial scholarships; to provide more resources for the engine, the football program. The reinvestment into the ongoing program was quite persuasive. And Pat kept bringing that up, that we're not just cutting sports to save money. We're cutting sports to help with the deficit but to be more competitive."

"This was hard," Formisano recalled. "But Pat never ever wavered. He knew it was necessary. He didn't like it. He never really wanted to do it. But he knew that for the survival of the department and for it to be successful, something like this had to happen. Pat never pushed. He was brought along—he came along."

Some speculated at the time that eliminating baseball and the four other sports was not Pat's plan, but the work of Fish, Formisano, and others. Not so, said Richter.

"Pat knew that it was the right strategy from the beginning," Al Fish said. "We agreed that our credibility was at such a low point at that time we had to do something drastic to show that we were serious. It wasn't just about cutting back travel by 10 percent. Cutting sports really meant that we were serious. It was so dramatic that it was clear that we weren't just rearranging the deck chairs, this was a serious cut. You have to give credit to Pat, as hard as that was for him, and the process made it harder, he ended up sticking to his guns. It wasn't without having second thoughts, I'm sure. Before every meeting, we'd say, 'OK, are we ready to go do this again?' There would always be a pause, a deep breath, and then, 'Let's go.'"

"The fact is," said Richter, "we all went into this together."

It was a very long and contentious process. There were presentations made to Athletic Board committees and the full Athletic Board. There were meetings with the Board of Regents and its business and finance committee.

"It was something that split the Athletic Board wide open," said Hoyt. "It split the Athletic Department wide open. I think it split the campus wide open. It was a traumatic public break with tradition."

Most of the meetings were emotional and highly charged, with many of the affected student-athletes and coaches in attendance. The department would make its presentation and opponents would counter with their own presentation and their own recommended plan of action. On a couple of occasions, there were not enough faculty members present for a quorum, which meant no formal action could be taken at that meeting and that the department would once again need to state its case at a later time. That kept alive the hopes of those who wanted to retain the targeted sports. "Donna was furious because the board was starting to play games with us," Richter recalled.

Shalala took action and moved quickly to fill a vacant seat on the athletic board. Her appointment of Consumer Science professor Robin Douthitt established a faculty majority on the board and helped assure that the necessary quorum was established at future meetings.

Richter said the addition of Douthitt was a turning point. "Robin had done her homework," he said. "She was very well prepared to deal with it and even though she was one of the newer people on the board, she was one of the most informed. We went through at least two meetings with the larger group, so whenever we took action, the action stuck."

In April 1991, the department's plan to eliminate five sports, including baseball, was approved by a 10–7 vote of the UW Athletic Board.

On May 10, 1991, the Wisconsin baseball team played its final game before an estimated 2,000 fans at Guy Lowman Field. The team wore black undershirts, black stockings, and black caps. The Badgers defeated Purdue 5–2 in the first game of a doubleheader, but lost the second game 1–0.

The last Badger baseball team finished in last place in the Big Ten with a 6-22 record and was 16-36 overall. It marked the end of a tumultuous nine-week period of public debate and contentiousness, and the end of the school's 116-year baseball program.

Weeks later, there would be one final attempt to turn back the department's plan to eliminate the five sports. Faculty members on the Athletic Board asked the UW–Madison Faculty Senate to take up the issue, but that effort failed. "The chancellor told them that the train had already left the station," Hoyt said.

"We had spent a great deal of time on this," Richter said. "It wasn't something we moved into lightly. It was something that had been thoroughly thought out. Some programs were going to be eliminated. It didn't matter which sport. The impact was the same. Some student-athletes were not going to be able to fulfill the dreams they had when they first came here to be competitive and get an education. That was something that was going to be taken away from some student-athletes, regardless of the sport."

Throughout the troubling spring of 1991, Richter and the department stayed together, crossing a significant but painful hurdle in the process. "As a group, we were resolute that people didn't understand the financial fragility of the department," Richter said. "The intent was to show people that we were serious. We did have financial credibility in the back of our mind and we had to get that back in order to get the program back on track.

"I don't recall any internal disagreements of any substance," Richter said. "I think everybody realized that the situation was critical. I think everybody realized that we had thought it through thoroughly."

Richter vividly recalls leaving that final emotional meeting when the Athletic Board voted to eliminate the sports. "After that meeting was over, I'm walking along back down the long tunnel," Richter said. "I could hear someone walking behind me. I wasn't sure who it was. I wasn't sure if someone was going to jump me from behind. I started up the stairs and I could hear someone come up the stairs behind me. I turned around and it was [sports information director] Steve Malchow. 'People just don't understand,' he said. 'We don't have the tools and resources and material to do our own jobs. We don't have good typewriters, let alone word processors. People don't understand that things like this have to be done.'"

For years, as Pat Richter traveled the state talking about Badger athletics, one particular question came up again and again. "It was a hot issue for a long period of time," Richter said. "People were always asking about when baseball was coming back."

The troubling time also prompted Richter to conduct some self-evaluation of his work as the new UW athletic director and his ability to lead the program.

"You had to do a gut check and ask yourself are you the same person you were when you got into this," Richter said. "Or are you the nasty person that some are now saying that you are. I think you have to look in the mirror and say this is a tough decision, but sometimes those types of decisions have to be made.

Looking back, it's hard to say what kind of impact that decision had on where we are today. It gave us a little bit of breathing room financially. You had some immediate savings, but the greater impact came over time. It certainly was a way for us to demonstrate that we were intent on getting ourselves on solid footing and that we were committed to doing that. It demonstrated that athletics was not something that had an unlimited budget and unlimited resources. It allowed some breathing room to get football back where we needed it to be.

"I think those initial decisions gave us some credibility from downtown all the way to the UW System," Richter said. "Most people would understand you wouldn't go through that process if you didn't think it was worth it. It was just too agonizing and too difficult to go through it for minimal results. It had to be significant. It had to be major as far as impact."

Looking back, Richter recalled some words of advice he'd heard from Jerry Hiegel, former president at Oscar Mayer. Hiegel had talked about the decision-making process that he went through as president of a large company. "He basically said that every decision he made could have an impact on thousands of people," Richter recalled. "It wasn't something you take lightly. If you don't make what you think is the right decision, you subject everybody in the organization to risk. If you don't try to make it better, the whole enterprise can be subject to failure."

* * *

For Pat Richter and Barry Alvarez, the summer of 1991 was not unlike the summer of 1990. Golf outings, speaking engagements, and numerous other public appearances filled their calendars, all in an effort to tell the story about new leadership, new excitement, and a plan to turn around the fortunes of the UW Athletic Department.

With one football season under their belts, Alvarez and his staff were determined to improve upon the 1-10 record of 1990. The traditional roster turnover that is commonplace after a head coaching change was now completed, and the players that remained from the Morton era had made the commitment to the new staff and the new program. In addition, another group of Alvarez recruits was on board and the excitement and anticipation for Badger football continued to grow.

The Badgers did little to dampen that enthusiasm, winning their first three games of the season, with nonconference victories over Western Illinois, Iowa State, and Eastern Michigan. But a six-game losing streak dashed that early-season optimism, and despite two late-season conference victories, the first at Minnesota and the second at home against Northwestern, the team finished at 5-6. Still, the five victories represented a significant improvement over the previous season.

But while the on-field performance improved, the attendance numbers took a disappointing dip. General public season tickets dropped from 24,672 in 1990 to 22,080 in 1991. Student season tickets dropped from 5,977 in 1990 to 4,711 in 1991. Overall, the per-game attendance average dropped from 51,027 in 1990 to 49,676 in 1991.

It could have been worse, but for an unusual and innovative marketing ploy by UW Athletic Department officials. At the time, the Iowa football team, under Coach Hayden Fry, was selling out most of its Big Ten home games. In the wake of a 1990 Big Ten title and an appearance in the 1991 Rose Bowl, tickets to Hawkeye games in Iowa City were hard to find, and many Hawkeye fans had little opportunity to see their team play. Sensing an opportunity to sell tickets in the weeks leading up to Iowa's October 12 game at Camp Randall Stadium, the UW Athletic Department placed a series of advertisements in selected daily newspapers in Iowa, promoting the sale of tickets to the game in Madison. The strategy apparently worked, as thousands of Iowa fans filled the stands to watch the Hawkeyes edge out the Badgers 10–6 in an exciting and dramatic game. The crowd of 75,053 was the largest Camp Randall crowd since the 1986 season.

* * *

That fall, Steve Yoder was entering his 10th season as head men's basketball coach at the University of Wisconsin. In the history of Wisconsin basketball, only two coaches had held the job longer than Yoder. Bud Foster had coached the Badgers to three Big Ten titles and one NCAA title in his 25 years, and Walter Meanwell had won eight Western Conference titles in 20 years as head coach.

Yoder had been hired in the spring of 1982 when Wisconsin's search for a head basketball coach proved troublesome and frustrating. With athletic director Elroy Hirsch offshore on an alumni cruise, a lengthy search had led the UW to offer the job to longtime UW–Eau Claire coach Ken Anderson, who initially accepted the job, but then, just hours prior to his first press conference, announced that he had withdrawn his name from consideration.

At the suggestion of UW football coach Dave McClain, who had come to Wisconsin from Ball State, UW officials sought out Yoder, who had been head coach at Ball State during McClain's tenure there. Shortly thereafter, Yoder was hired.

Yoder's win-loss record was less than impressive in those early years; in his first two seasons, his teams finished with 8-20 records and won a total of just seven Big Ten Conference games.

Over the next four years, Yoder's teams never finished above .500 and never won more than six conference games in a year. Finally, in the 1988–89 season, the Badgers had a breakthrough of sorts, finishing 8-10 in conference and 18-12 overall and earning a berth in the National Invitation Tournament, the school's first postseason appearance since 1947. In two exciting games at the UW Field House, Wisconsin defeated New Orleans 63–61 in the first round, then lost 73–68 to Saint Louis in the second round.

After another disappointing season (14-17 overall, 4-14 in conference) in 1989–90, the Badgers once again made the postseason NIT in 1990–91, defeating Bowling Green in overtime 87–79, and losing to Stanford 80–72.

In nine years, Steve Yoder's teams had compiled a 115-147 record. And while his teams were entertaining at times, Richter wasn't comfortable with the status of the program.

"Football seemed like it was going in the right direction," Richter said. "As is human nature, you have a sense to think, 'Can we be better in basketball and some other things,' recognizing that we had some limitations. We went into that decision without any idea that we were going to be getting a new facility in the near future. Steve had kind of maintained the program. It hadn't really jumped out. He occasionally had some very good players. It just never seemed like his teams could compete for a title."

Associate athletic director Joel Maturi was the administrator in charge of men's basketball. He and Richter had several conversations about the status of the men's basketball program and about the possibility of a coaching change.

"Ultimately, it came down to the fact that for the last 10 years we were treading water, so to speak, and maybe it's time to make a change," Richter said. "We didn't have anybody in mind, but the program needed a jolt. We set up a meeting for the three of us prior to the end of the season. We thought we would get a leg up on the search process. There already had been some speculation starting to bubble up in terms of Steve not coming back, so we went ahead and told him that at the end of the season we were not going to renew the contract and that we were going to find somebody new."

On February 24, 1992, Richter held a press conference to announce that Steve Yoder's contract would not be renewed. "A change could bring us to a different level," Richter told reporters.

Yoder attended and participated in the press conference, one of those rare occasions where a coach who is being fired and the administrator who is doing the firing shared the same stage.

"There have been so many problems here," Yoder told reporters. "I have been through three college presidents, two chancellors and one acting chancellor, three athletic directors, and four football coaches. They've had their distractions over the last 10 years."

The following day, a *Wisconsin State Journal* editorial opined that "Whoever replaces Yoder should not come to Wisconsin expecting a basketball shrine to be built in his honor. State construction dollars for UW–Madison don't flow easily these days, and those that do make the trip down State Street were spoken for years ago.

"If the next coach is to outshine Yoder, he'll need to do so with the same arena, the same academic standards, and the same attention to the rules. That's not impossible, but it's not a high percentage shot, either."

Five days later, the Badgers played host to Michigan and their famed Fab Five. The Badgers, with their lame-duck coach on the sidelines, crushed the 17th-ranked Wolverines 96–78 before a boisterous crowd at the UW Field House. Following that game, the two teams headed in different directions. Wisconsin failed to win another game all season. Michigan, meanwhile, went on to the Final Four and won the national championship.

"It was the best game we had played," Richter said. "We came home that night and it was tough. Here you had let your coach go and then they go out and easily defeat the best team in the country. The phone rang; I answered it. There was this noisy background and the guy on the other end had obviously had too much to drink. He said, 'Geez, you must have your head up your ass. This guy's a great coach—a great coach.' And then he hung up."

Years later, there would be a series of revelations about the involvement of booster Ed Martin and the University of Michigan basketball team. There were allegations and rumors about Martin's gambling interests and the possibility that certain games may have been fixed.

"You get a little bit uneasy about going back and looking at that film in light of some of the things that have come out since that time about Ed Martin and Chris Webber and all those kinds of things and whether or not any cheating was involved," Richter said. "You hate to think of that, but the fact was, they were a hell of a basketball team and we beat them."

It was clear that Richter was comfortable with his decision to make the coaching change, but it wasn't easy. "Steve was really a good guy," Richter said. "I liked him very much. I likened his situation to [former football coach] John Jardine. John was the same kind of guy. People really liked him. John became very connected into the community. People knew him. He had a good circle of friends. But Steve kind of kept everything close to the vest and had a very tight-knit circle of friends. I had told him during the year that you have to get out and let people get to know you. It buys you time. If you don't do that, then people won't really have any emotional attachment to you and don't really care.

"Steve was Steve," Richter added. "Like I said, I liked him. I think he had a good heart and he meant well, but it just wasn't working out, so we decided to make a change."

Prior to making the coaching move, Richter had not spent a great deal of time researching possible candidates. Admittedly, he wasn't sure who was in the marketplace and, more importantly, what type of coach he wanted to hire. Still, he did have an advantage in that the Wisconsin vacancy was among the first on the market. And, just like the time he embarked on his search for a new football coach in December 1989, Richter quickly began to identify candidates.

Richter would soon find out that the Wisconsin basketball job was one of interest to many in the college basketball community. Rudy Martzke, a reporter for *USA Today* and a UW–Madison graduate, would call with information and anecdotes he had gathered. College basketball coaching legends George Raveling and Digger Phelps called. "Everybody was calling for a person they were backing," Richter said. "It was clear there was a good opportunity here."

Richter's March 1992 calendar book is filled with the names of young and promising coaching prospects.

On March 2, he met with Michigan State assistant coach Tom Izzo in Evanston, Illinois. "They were playing Northwestern and I met with him in the team hotel at about seven in the morning on game day," Richter said. "He and I had a really good conversation for a couple of hours. As we were walking out, we ran into Jud [Heathcote], who was walking by with a newspaper under his arm. Jud turned to Izzo and said, 'Hey Tom, did he tell you he's cutting basketball?'"

On March 7, Richter first met Stu Jackson. Jackson was a former player at Oregon who went on to work as an assistant coach for Rick Pitino at Providence College and recently had moved into a key administrative role with the National Basketball Association. Richter had not known of Jackson until recently, when he received a phone call from Rob Gooze of Madison, who knew Jackson from his days as a student manager at Oregon. Gooze told Richter that Jackson's wife had recently completed medical school and that Jackson, then the assistant vice president for operations in the NBA, might be ready to make a move. "The timing was right," Richter said. "I really hadn't run across his name anywhere. But in checking things out, he looked pretty good. We talked and had a nice conversation."

Richter and Jackson arranged a meeting in Madison on March 7. Jackson was heading west as part of his NBA duties, but interrupted that trip to visit with Richter and Shalala. "Given everything that I had seen and given everything that we had talked about on the phone, and given the fact that I thought he could be a very viable candidate, I had talked to Donna about seeing him," Richter said. "She was leaving town early the next day so we agreed to bring Stu over to see her late that evening."

Jackson arrived in Madison on Saturday night. Richter picked him up at the airport and they headed directly to the Olin House for a meeting with the chancellor. "We sat and chatted for a while," Richter said. "He was a very impressive guy. He carried himself well. He was very statuesque and had a good presence. Everything just seemed to be really squared away. And he had a good pedigree as far as coaching. [Rick] Pitino had called on his behalf. Stu had worked with Rick at Providence and had a lot of support."

The next day, Jackson and Richter met again at the home of Pat and Renee Richter. "We spent some time talking about different things and we agreed to stay in touch," Richter said. "I said at the time that if there was anything that would stand in his way, any problems, let me know, and vice versa. At that point, my thinking was that if it was OK from his standpoint, then for me, this seems to be the guy who fills the bill in terms of a jolt to the program."

In the meantime, there were other candidates and other conversations.

On March 9, there were meetings with John Williams and Ray McCallum, both assistant coaches under Yoder. Later in the day, Richter would meet with Butch Carter, an assistant coach in the NBA.

On March 13, he met with former Ohio State standout Jim Cleamons at the Hyatt Hotel in Deerfield, Illinois, and with Ken Burmeister of DePaul at the North Shore Hilton in Chicago.

On Sunday, March 15, he would meet with Ben Braun, a UW graduate who was then the head coach at Eastern Michigan. "I had scheduled a meeting with Ben on a Sunday in Milwaukee at the Moorland Road Best Western," Richter said. "I figured I wouldn't see anybody that I knew out there and we could keep the meeting quiet. Ben and I finished talking and we started to head outside to our cars and who do we bump into but Al McGuire, who looks at us, smiles, and says, 'Well, what do we have here?' It blew the cover right away."

On March 17, he met with Mike Brey at the Atlanta airport in the morning, and with Bo Ryan at Don Q Inn in Dodgeville in the afternoon. "A lot of people were supporting Bo," Richter said. "But in the back of my mind, I was thinking of something that was going to be a bit more dramatic; more of a shock."

On March 18, he again met with Jackson in Madison. On March 21, he met with Texas A&M coach Tony Barone in Saint Paul. And on March 22, he met with UW–Green Bay coach Dick Bennett in Oshkosh.

"I felt it was important to talk with Dick," Richter said. "He wasn't foremost in our minds at that time, nor do I really think he was interested in the Wisconsin job at that time. There were a lot of things on his mind. He was facing double hip surgery. He was really struggling with two of his players who had gotten in trouble with the law. I think timing-wise, he was not ready to bail from Green Bay with all that he had going on."

In the end, Richter continued to focus on Jackson, and ultimately, recommended his hiring to the Athletic Board, which gave its approval. On March 25, 1992, Stu Jackson became the 11th head coach in the history of the University of Wisconsin basketball program.

At a press conference that day, Jackson proclaimed that he would try to build upon what Yoder had accomplished. "There is no reason—no reason—that this program can't be on par with any program in America," Jackson said.

"I think in the basketball world, getting a guy like Stu Jackson was kind of a shock," Richter said. "It wasn't same old same old, willing to accept just being OK. A lot of people weren't aware of who Stu Jackson was, but when they found out what his credentials were and what he had done, they said, 'This guy's got a pretty good resume.'"

Again, Richter drew upon his corporate background in making a crucial personnel decision. "A lot of times when you change leaders, you change personalities," Richter said. "You're not just trying to succeed someone with another person who is quite similar. You look at Irv Shain and Donna Shalala and David Ward. There were differences there.

"With Stu Jackson, people started to take notice of Wisconsin basketball, especially when he took the team to the NCAA [Tournament]. He did a good job for us. And when you talk about the resurgence of the Wisconsin basketball program, you have to put his name right up there."

* * *

With the hiring of a new men's basketball coach completed in late March 1992, Richter and Badger fans turned their attention toward the Badger hockey team. The Badgers, who had won the NCAA championship as recently as 1990, had a number of veteran players on the 1991–92 team, and after a second-place finish in the regular season, had seemingly put things together and made a dramatic run, defeating New Hampshire, Saint Lawrence, and Michigan to the reach the championship game at the 1992 NCAA Frozen Four at the Knickerbocker Center in Albany, New York.

"It really wasn't a great place for a tournament," Richter recalled. "The venue was downtown, but there were no hotels to speak of near the arena so we ended up staying in the suburbs. It really was not like you see today or what you would see with the men's basketball tournament."

The championship game against Lake Superior State wasn't what the Badgers wanted to see, either. After Jason Zent's two goals gave the Badgers a 2–0 lead after one period, it appeared the Badgers were headed toward winning their sixth NCAA hockey championship and their second in three years. But then, a series of penalty calls against the Badgers changed the momentum of the game, and things began to unravel for the Badgers, who lost the game 5–3.

Sixteen penalties were called on the Badgers, including two 10-minute misconducts. On four different occasions, Lake Superior State skated with a 5-on-3 advantage.

"Sometimes, certain kinds of play, especially the Midwest style of play, are viewed differently by Eastern officials and vice versa, so the tendency is to perhaps call it a little bit tighter," Richter said. "Lake Superior State had a great team, but we had jumped out to a fairly good-sized lead, and then all of a sudden, things changed dramatically and the game began to start getting called a lot tighter. I think we played almost the last half of the contest with two men in the penalty box."

When Lake Superior State scored an empty-net goal with three seconds left, things got a bit nasty. Several UW players surrounded referee Tim McConaghy on the ice to protest his performance. And shortly after the game ended, there was a scuffle outside the officials' locker room involving UW graduate assistant coach Bill Zito and security personnel.

While the versions of the post-game incident varied, the NCAA eventually ruled that the UW lacked control of its team and staff. Zito was reprimanded and the UW was ordered to forfeit the tournament expense money. In addition, UW Head Coach Jeff Sauer was suspended for one game, which he served the following year.

"It was a very emotional moment," Richter said.

* * *

Richter's deep connections in the community meant that if something were going on around town, it wouldn't take long before he'd catch wind of it. And during 1994, there was a rumor going around that Richter's basketball coach, Stu Jackson, had been rude and unprofessional toward the waitstaff during a visit to one of Madison's finest restaurants, The Mariner's Inn.

"I think some people were not willing to accept a fellow like Stu Jackson because he was very polished, very professional, well-dressed, and he had a great presence," Richter said. "Regardless of what he was doing—there were times when he was abrasive—he was there to get the program back on track. There were various rumors that would fly around; you'd hear different things. There was one about going into the Mariner's and having some kind of flack with the ownership there. Something about Stu saying 'Don't you know who I am and what my position is?' I talked to him about that and he said he'd never even been to the Mariner's.

"It was too bad," Richter said. "He was trying to get himself into a position where he could make the program successful, but he was always fighting those kinds of little fires. Stu was very competitive and combative. He wasn't one to sit back and let people beat on him. He was a smart guy and had been around. He wasn't going to take things like that. And he did a good job here. He was very successful."

*　*　*

The 1992 football Badgers opened their season on the road against one of the top teams in the country, the Washington Huskies. The Badgers lost the game 27–10 to the second-ranked Huskies, but played a solid game and once again, gave their fans reason to hope for another step forward in 1992.

The following week, the Badgers won their home opener over Bowling Green 39–18. The attendance was 57,758, the largest home-opening crowd since 1986. One week later, the Badgers squeaked by Northern Illinois 18–17 before 50,688 at Camp Randall.

That set the stage for the team's Big Ten opener at home against Ohio State, when, much to the delight of the 72,203 fans at Camp Randall, the Badgers stunned the 12th-ranked Buckeyes 20–16.

In the postgame celebration, a photographer captured Alvarez and Richter hugging each other at midfield. A framed copy of that photo hung on the wall of Pat Richter's office until he retired. A souvenir game ball presented to Richter by Alvarez rested on a nearby shelf as well.

"I remember that as our first big win," Alvarez said. "And I remember how elated Pat was about it. He had a thing about Ohio State: he didn't like Ohio State. And that win was huge for him."

Inside the offices of the Athletic Department administration, the smiles produced by a strong performance at Washington and a remarkable upset of Ohio State lingered throughout the season. Despite the fact that the team lost four of its next five games, there clearly was an indication of a continued turnaround in attendance. The department's increased marketing activities and the team's on-field performance proved to be a solid and effective combination. Season tickets increased from 22,080 in 1991 to 25,078 in 1992. Student season tickets increased from 4,711 to 5,539. And overall attendance soared from a per-game average of 49,676 in 1991 to 61,378.

Entering the team's final game at Northwestern, Richter and Alvarez held out hope that a victory over the Wildcats would earn the Badgers a berth in a bowl game. Which bowl game, however, was the question.

Richter had been in conversation with organizers of the Freedom Bowl, played in Anaheim, California. The Freedom Bowl committee was talking to Wisconsin and to USC. Their hope was to put together a rematch of the 1963 Rose Bowl 30 years later.

Alvarez, meanwhile, had been in several separate conversations with representatives from the Independence Bowl.

"Barry and I had been talking to the bowl guys all during this time," Richter recalled. "That Friday night before the game, he had talked to Mike McCarthy from the Independence Bowl and told him, 'If we win this game and you want us, we're yours: we'll come to the Independence Bowl.' The next morning, we're at Northwestern and he mentions that conversation to me, that if we win, we're in the Independence Bowl."

That was good news, except that Richter had said nearly the same thing to the Freedom Bowl representatives. "From a publicity and game standpoint, how could you pass up a matchup like the one they were talking about; Wisconsin and USC, 30 years later?"

Wisconsin trailed Northwestern for most of the game. But thanks to two great touchdown receptions by Lee DeRamus, the Badgers rallied to pull within 27–25 with just over four minutes remaining in the game.

From his perch upstairs in the press box, Richter was excited about the comeback, but also was getting a bit edgy. "I could see the guy from the Freedom Bowl on the phone checking other scores and he said things were looking good," Richter said. "I was getting nervous about him getting me an offer, so I ducked out of the press box and went down on the sideline."

There, he watched as the Badgers moved in place for a last-minute field goal attempt. With less than a minute remaining and no timeouts, they had advanced the ball to the Northwestern 27-yard line. The Badgers called for one more running play to move the ball toward the center of the field to set up a 47-yard field goal attempt by Rich Thompson. Instead, a blitzing Northwestern linebacker knocked the ball loose from Badger running back Jason Burns and Northwestern recovered the ball with just 49 seconds remaining in the game.

With the two bowls bids waiting in the wings, the Badgers lost to Northwestern 27–25. There would be no bowl for the Badgers in 1992.

"It was very disappointing for all of us," Richter said. "But, there was no question it would have been a touchy situation for us. We certainly wanted to go to a bowl, but we were somewhat relieved as to the dilemma we had put ourselves in."

* * *

Stu Jackson's first season as men's basketball coach was off to a fast start. Led by Michael Finley and Tracy Webster, the Badgers won seven of their first nine games, including a 77–67 victory at Marquette. In one stretch, the Badgers defeated three ranked teams in a row: 19th ranked Minnesota, 24th ranked Ohio State, and 21st ranked Michigan State.

The team finished 14-14 overall and reached the NIT, losing a first-round game to Rice at the UW Field House. The average attendance numbers at the Field House had now reached 10,387, and there was big news on the recruiting front when Jackson landed a commitment from Chicago King's Rashard Griffith, a 6-11 center who was among the top high school players in the country.

The Badger men's hockey team, meanwhile, earned its sixth consecutive NCAA tournament bid, but lost 4–3 in overtime to Michigan and fell one game short of reaching the Frozen Four for the third time in the last four years.

CHAPTER TEN
THE ROAD
TO PASADENA

Perhaps the students at the University of Wisconsin had an inkling of things to come. How else might you explain the tremendous enthusiasm they showed in the summer and early fall of 1993? Coming off a second consecutive 5-6 season, there was no indication that the upcoming year would be anything but fun and entertaining, no reason for Badger fans to take the traditional "Rose Bowl!" chant seriously.

Still, UW students must have sensed something positive, because as Barry Alvarez prepared to begin his fourth season as head coach of the Badgers, nearly 12,000 UW students had purchased season tickets, more than double the amount sold in 1992.

It signaled the start of something special.

Nearly 67,000 fans watched the Badgers defeat Nevada 35–17 in their home opener, and after a come-from-behind road victory at SMU, the Badgers defeated Iowa State 28–7 before a capacity crowd of 77,745 at Camp Randall Stadium. It marked UW's first sellout since 1985.

The momentum continued as the Badgers rolled to three more victories and a date with Minnesota at the Metrodome in Minneapolis.

The 6-0 Badgers faced a key distraction going into that game. Earlier in the week, the Big Ten Conference announced that UW assistant coach Bill Callahan—who eventually led the Oakland Raiders to a Super Bowl as their head coach—would serve a one-game suspension for unsportsmanlike conduct and not be allowed to coach in the game.

Earlier in the season, Callahan had been scouting the Illinois at Purdue game in West Lafayette. "He was checking the visiting team booth to see where the guys would be sitting the next week when we played at Purdue," Richter said. "As he went in there, there were some depth charts on the wall, and obviously, they were for Illinois. He pulled the depth charts off the wall and was looking at them. Someone from Illinois sports information came along and asked if he could take those now, and he said, 'Sure' and gave them to they guy right away. They took the charts and that was it."

Shortly thereafter, Richter received a call from the Big Ten Conference. "They told me there had been a complaint lodged by Illinois Coach Lou Tepper, and [Commissioner Jim] Delany had characterized it as unsportsmanlike conduct, falling under a Big Ten rule that recently had been passed and called for a one-game suspension or a $10,000 fine," Richter said. "He called us about it and Barry and Bill and I kept going back and forth with Jim on the situation. Tepper never talked to his athletic director about it. He sent it right to Delany. We weren't even playing Illinois for another five or six weeks. We talked until we were blue in the face but we just couldn't get the Big Ten to understand and agree with our position.

"We just kept saying that it doesn't make any sense; it's a depth chart," Richter said. "It didn't rise to the level of unsportsmanlike conduct, in our opinion, so we appealed it and still nothing. We ultimately had to decide if it we would pay a $10,000 fine or have Bill sit out one game.

"Subsequently, there have been several instances where that could have been applied, but it just seemed like it was much more overblown that it should have. Had it gone through the proper channels where the two athletic directors talk directly and you don't go from football coach to conference commissioner, it may have been resolved. As it turned out, it may have cost us that game, which may have cost us a national championship."

With Callahan serving a one-game suspension, the Badgers stumbled and lost to the Gophers 28–21 at the Metrodome. But despite the loss, the Badgers were still in the hunt for the Big Ten title as they prepared for back-to-back home games against Michigan and Ohio State.

The two games were likely to be the most important back-to-back contests at Camp Randall Stadium in many years, and the excitement was building. On campus, much of the talk was among the students was about "storming the field" in the wake of a Badger victory over the Wolverines.

"It was a highly charged day," Richter recalled. "We hadn't been very successful against Michigan over the years, and here we were, 3-1 in conference and taking on mighty Michigan. It was a big game for us, a chance to continue what had been a relatively successful season to that point."

The Badgers didn't disappoint their fans. As the final seconds ticked off the clock, the Badgers shocked Michigan 13–10 and put themselves in good position for a shot at the conference title and a berth in the 1994 Rose Bowl.

Unfortunately, there was little time to celebrate the victory that day, as Camp Randall Stadium quickly turned from celebratory bedlam to fear and uncertainty.

"I remember when Darrell Bevell took a knee with about 25 seconds left, everybody kind of jumped because they didn't want to miss out on the celebration," Richter recalled. "I had headed into the locker room and really didn't notice anything unusual. I went into the postgame media conference, and as guys started coming in, they were saying that there was something going on out there. I started to head back out to the field and ran into a couple of players who were leaving the field and just shaking their head. I remember walking out the tunnel and looking out there—it was just surreal. There were various triages all around and someone said that we had four or five pulseless nonbreathers. I didn't necessarily know what that meant at the time, but you think, when you hear it, that somebody is dead."

According to later reports, for several days before the game, students anticipating a Badger victory had been spreading a call to rush onto the field to celebrate after the win. As the final seconds of the game ticked down and that victory was at hand, thousands of fans in the student sections of the stadium began to fill the aisles and press their way down to the perimeter fences. The crowd chant of the final ten seconds was joined by shouts of "Rush the field!" The enormous pressure of thousands of bodies pressing to get on to the field caused the safety fences to collapse. The crowd surged forward; some fans were carried along helplessly in the swell and others became pinned under the human tidal wave. Panic ensued, and police struggled desperately to rescue trapped fans as hundreds poured over them onto the field. In the end, 70 fans, most of them UW students, sustained injuries in the incident. Almost miraculously, there were no lives lost; but those in attendance that day would long remember the sight of ambulances on the playing field and the sound of the public address announcer pleading desperately with those celebrating victory to clear Camp Randall.

"The stadium was half empty and the lights were kind of down," Richter said. "You could see these various places on the field where people were being administered to and you just kind of got sick to your stomach."

In the wake of the October 30, 1993 Camp Randall crowd surge, Chancellor David Ward appointed Milwaukee businessman George Kaiser, a former state secretary for administration, to conduct a review of the incident and make recommendations for future crowd control and other game management issues. The Kaiser Report included 49 recommendations for stadium improvements, changes in student seating and ticketing, crowd safety management and increased ticket controls. Many of the recommendations were implemented immediately; others were added over the course of the next several seasons.

Just seven days after the Michigan game, the Badgers and their fans returned to the scene of the surge as UW and Ohio State battled in front of the fourth straight capacity crowd at Camp Randall Stadium. Eerily, the same scenario seemed to be playing out on the field, with the Badgers driving for a winning score late in the game in front of the student section. But Ohio State preempted any postgame celebration when it blocked UW's attempt at a game-winning field goal in the closing seconds, and the two teams tied, 14–14.

Following a 35–10 victory over Illinois in Champaign, the Badgers needed only to defeat Michigan State in their final Big Ten game of the year to tie for the league title and earn a berth in the 1994 Rose Bowl.

* * *

Wisconsin's Big Ten Conference game against Michigan State in 1993 was originally scheduled for October 2 in Madison. But 18 months before the game was to be played, officials of the Coca-Cola Bowl in Tokyo had approached the Big Ten and the UW and asked if the Badgers would consider moving their home game against the Spartans to a December 4 game in Tokyo.

"We felt at the time that it was a long-term investment in the program and in the long run would turn out to be a positive," Richter said. "We thought it would help us in our recruiting efforts to be able to tell a potential recruit that we were playing a game in Tokyo. We just felt it was right for the program."

In one sense, moving the game to December 4 in Tokyo gave the Badgers a competitive edge. With no game on the original October 2 date, Wisconsin was able to rest and recover early in the conference season. And, while the Badgers' last game before Tokyo was November 11 at Illinois, the Spartans played Penn State on November 25.

"At some point in time we had started ratcheting back the team's sleep habits an hour a day so that by the time we arrived they would almost be in sync with the time in Japan," Richter said. "The day we left, I think they practiced just before midnight, got onto the buses at 1:00 a.m., drove to Chicago, went to sleep at 4:00 a.m., got up at noon and took off about 3:00 p.m. On the plane ride over there, our guys were wide awake and all the Michigan State guys were sleeping. The plane was split right down the middle, with Michigan State on one side of the aisle and Wisconsin on the other. Most of our players were wide awake because when we landed it was going to be midnight over there. The Michigan State guys were tired."

"Once we arrived, the team was in sync with the time change, and I think that really helped us," Richter said. "It gave us an advantage."

Pat Richter and Barry Alvarez celebrate the UW victory of Michigan State that landed Wisconsin a berth in the 1994 Rose Bowl. Photo courtesy of the UW Athletic Department.

The well-rested Badgers had little trouble with Michigan State on December 4, whipping the Spartans 41–20. And what was Richter thinking as the on-field celebration started in Tokyo? "I'm thinking, here we are thousands and thousands of miles away from home. It would have been nice to have won this game in Madison. And I was wondering what was happening back in Madison."

Not surprisingly, back in Madison there was a crowd gathering on State Street. The celebration was well underway. The Big Ten champion Badgers were going to the Rose Bowl.

After the long plane ride home, the Badgers landed in Chicago and boarded their buses back to Madison. Along the way, they saw Badger fans waving from bridges above the highway and heard horns honking in celebration. With a police escort, the closer they got to Madison, the more people took notice. And as the buses drove the team onto the field at Camp Randall Stadium, an estimated 25,000 fans welcomed home their Rose Bowl–bound Badgers.

"That was probably one of the most gratifying things," Richter said. "It was a two-hour buildup, and then you come to the stadium and see all those people waiting there. You could feel that sense of appreciation and gratification as you got closer to the stadium."

* * *

With less than four weeks to prepare for Wisconsin's first Rose Bowl appearance in 31 years, the pace was rather hectic within the UW Athletic Department. And because the UW's last trip to Pasadena was in 1963, there wasn't a lot of institutional history to fall back upon.

"I had been there as a player in 1963," Richter said. "But as a player you really don't understand what goes into it. This time, there were so many more things going on that kept you busy. And of course, we hadn't been to a bowl game since we got there, let alone a Rose Bowl, so we really didn't know what to expect and what not to expect. We just went with the flow."

Fortunately, there were a few Badgers who had some knowledge about the process: Barry Alvarez and many of his staff had been to the Rose Bowl with the Iowa Hawkeyes. That limited knowledge came in handy during one of the bowl-planning sessions. With the football team and much of the UW's administrative staff in Tokyo for the game against Michigan State, Al Fish traveled to Pasadena to represent the UW in the advance-planning session for the Rose Bowl. The Badgers had not officially been designated as the Big Ten representative, because they needed to defeat Michigan State to earn the Rose Bowl berth. A representative from Ohio State also was in attendance, because the Buckeyes still had an outside shot.

"There were about 50 white-coated Rose Bowl people in the room and another 20 or so from UCLA," Fish recalled. "Then there are the two potential contenders from the Big Ten in the corner. At that time, they alternated locker rooms at the Rose Bowl, and this was the year that the Big Ten got the home locker room. UCLA had requested that since this was their home stadium, they wanted to stay in the home locker room. Barry knew they were going to ask this. He said 'Make sure you keep the home locker room and if there's a chance to throw a barb their way, go ahead and do it.' Those were my instructions. So the discussion came to the part about the locker room and the guy in the white coat on the podium says,

'UCLA has requested to have the home locker room because it's their normal home locker room and they wanted to know what the Big Ten position on this would be.' I stood up and said, 'No, we want to keep the home locker room, and by the way, we want to have anything that has UCLA or UCLA colors covered up.'"

Throughout the preparation process, Wisconsin officials were trying to learn as much about the Rose Bowl operations as quickly as possible. On the other hand, Rose Bowl officials knew little about Wisconsin, and they were searching for answers, too.

"When we went out there for the official press conference and meetings I happened to be riding with some Rose Bowl officials from the airport to Pasadena and on the drive, you could sense they had something on their mind," Richter said. "It felt as though there was something they wanted to ask but weren't asking. It was just one of those things where they seemed to be hedging and beating around the bush. Finally, one of them asked, 'Is it true your band brings a cannon?' They thought the band fired off a big cannon whenever we scored. I assured them that wasn't the case. Then they said, 'Tell us about the fifth quarter.'"

It was the beginning of long planning session, one in which Richter eased the concerns of the Rose Bowl committee and made sure the committee was comfortable with the UW band. It was just one of many logistical challenges that came with the new territory.

"I think the longer you are there the more you realize that the game is somewhat secondary to the parade," Richter said. "Obviously, for the teams and the fans, the game is the highlight. But for the Rose Bowl Committee and their people, the parade is huge. It's a massive undertaking. There are 100,000 people at the game and that's big, but there are millions and millions of people around the world watching that parade on television."

With most of the logistics in order, game time neared. And while Richter was aware of a strong demand for tickets, he was not aware of the severity of the crisis ahead.

"We had made calls around the Big Ten and tried get tickets from the other schools and we did get some," Richter said. "We tried to do the same with the Pac Ten schools but we found out later that those that had some extra tickets had already contacted the brokers, so we weren't able to get additional tickets from the Pac-Ten.

"Historically, the Big Ten hadn't sold all of its tickets," Richter said. "You have to remember when the Rose Bowl started, the only way Big Ten people could travel was by train, and most of the tickets went to the Pac Ten teams. So the ticket situation was way out of skew and now we have a team that hasn't been there in 31 years and here we go.

"You knew the tickets were hard to come by but you didn't realize what was going on—the scamming and things like that—until you got closer to game time when we got calls from people who said their tickets were supposed to be left under the door at midnight and other ticket horror stories like that.

"All of us were just trying to pick up tickets wherever we could," Richter said. "As you got to the game you could sense there were a lot more issues than you had been aware of prior to that."

Tickets to the game—with a face value of $48—were selling for $600 per seat. *Los Angeles Times* reporter David Wharton wrote that the thousands of Wisconsin fans seeking tickets to the game "started a run on tickets unlike anything Pasadena had ever seen."

A questionable ticket transaction between the UCLA Athletic Department and a Bruin booster undoubtedly added to the ticket frenzy. The booster was Angelo M. Mazzone III, a former Bruin equipment manager who had worked his way to up the administrative ladder in the UCLA Athletic Department before leaving to take a job in the private sector. Approximately 30 days prior to the 1994 Rose Bowl, Mazzone donated $100,000 to the UCLA athletic department for the right to purchase 4,000 tickets. Mazzone and his business partner, according to published reports, then made at least $400,000 reselling those tickets as part of tour packages for Wisconsin fans.

As game day drew closer, the demand for tickets intensified, and hundreds of Badger fans were unable to secure tickets at any price. Many fans who had flown to California expecting tickets ended up watched the game on television monitors set up outside the stadium or retreating back to their hotels.

With the ticket crisis as a backdrop, Richter arrived at the Rose Bowl to partake in the many pregame festivities for Badger fans. "As you went around the exterior part of the stadium, you could sense there were a lot of Wisconsin people there and a lot of Wisconsin things happening," Richter said. "There was so much excitement. We got stuck a little bit in the tunnel as we tried to enter the seating bowl. But as we got through, all of a sudden you look around and see all that red. It was amazing to me. That was the part of the experience that really stuck with me: to see all those Badgers fans there."

One of those Badger fans was Donna Shalala, who months earlier had been selected by President Bill Clinton to serve in his cabinet as Secretary of Health and Human Services. Even though she had been replaced by David Ward as UW chancellor and was busy getting oriented in her new job in Washington, D.C., Shalala wasn't about to miss the game in Pasadena. "I went with these secret service guys and when we walked into a Badger pregame pep rally, people started to chant 'Donna, Donna.' I thought they were going to die," Shalala said. "It became legendary back in Washington. It was a wonderful day. I felt a sense of great pride watching the Badgers that day."

With an estimated 60,000 Badger fans in the crowd of 101,237—and an estimated 2 million watching on television—the Badgers forced six turnovers and rushed for 250 yards to defeat UCLA, 21–16. Brent Moss gained 158 of those yards and scored two touchdowns. The Badgers took a 14-3 halftime lead, but the Bruins fought back and closed the gap to 14–10 in the fourth quarter. Then, an unlikely rushing hero emerged. Badger quarterback Darrell Bevell scrambled for a remarkable 21-yard touchdown run to give the Badgers a 21–10 lead. UCLA added another score to close to within 21–16, setting up a dramatic finish. As time wound down, the Bruins had advanced to the UW's 18-yard line and were threatening to score the game-winning touchdown, but UCLA quarterback Wayne Cook was tackled as time ran out. The Badgers had won their first Rose Bowl in the 105-year history of football at the University of Wisconsin–Madison.

Legendary Los Angeles sports columnist Jim Murray, recalling the week's worth of ticket controversy, seemed almost humored by the Badger victory:

> Ah, yes. The stingers got stung. The slickers outslickered. The bumpkins turned the tables on the wise guys. They turned over their hole cards and they were aces, and they said wickedly, "Are these any good?" They ran the table on the Fast Eddies. Sneaked their own dice into the game and faded the shooter. Sold their vegetable peelers to the guy on the corner. . .
>
> So, the guys from the place where they milk the cows and mow the hay had the last call. "I'll play these," they said, and UCLA had to fold. You had the feeling they had run in their own deck on the riverboat guys and every time the Bruins lost the ball—which was a lot—the "rubes" were the guys holding it up and saying sweetly, "Is this what you're looking for? Aw, too bad. You should take better care of it."

For Richter and the rest of the Badger family, the Rose Bowl victory was a joy to behold, a thing of beauty, a dream come true. But the impact that this single victory would have on the future of Wisconsin athletics had yet to impress itself on Richter.

"To me, we had made some gradual progress before this happened and I think had we known then what we know now about what the impact of [a win] would be, that would have made a big difference in the way we felt at the time," Richter said. "The Rose Bowl was good. It was where we wanted to be. We never really sat down and said, 'What just happened?' It was just a really good feeling."

CHAPTER ELEVEN
NOW WHAT?

So, now that we've won our first Rose Bowl, what's next?

That was the joke in and around the UW Athletic Department offices in early January. Life as they had known it had now changed. Where it would lead and what it would look like were unknowns.

"The one factor that cannot be underestimated is the Rose Bowl victory," said former Athletic Board chair Roger Formisano, who lent his business-school acumen to the administration and helped the department build a solid foundation. "Coming as soon as it did and as powerfully as it did, that washed a lot of rinse water over the dirty laundry that the Athletic Department had had to put up with, and it really set the stage for what we see today."

In the wake of the 1994 Rose Bowl, Richter and his staff were thankful that the department's situation had improved significantly over the past four years. And frankly, they all were a bit surprised with the amount of progress made. There was a sense of relief and a continued spirit of optimism and enthusiasm.

People enjoyed coming to work at 1440 Monroe Street. Much had been accomplished, but there was a lot more work to be done.

In Richter's mind, much of the success came as a result of an attitude that developed in the wake of the department's early efforts to solve the financial equation and its painful decision to eliminate five sports in 1991. "All of those things that happened early on gave us a certain toughness that if we can deal with those things, we'll be all right," Richter recalled. "What else could be out there that would be that much more difficult? It gave us a confidence to do what's right for the program. This is what we think is right and we did it that way. Once we dealt with those issues, there was very little to come later on that could be any more problematic.

"Some of the issues we dealt with—the financials, the cutting of sports, things like that—really weren't the things that others had gone through, either," Richter said. "For the most part, a lot of these things were a case of first impression for all of us. I think sometimes that's better when you move not on instincts alone but on beliefs and on what you think is right and on common sense. And I don't think that stopped. A lot of it is common sense. You deal from either personal experience or based on the fact that you just feel that this seems to be the fair and equitable way to go.

"You couldn't foresee what the impact of the Rose Bowl would be, but it did kind of reinforce the notion that this is what can happen when you're successful," Richter said. "You could see the confidence that people had, saying that these guys know where they've been and where they've come. And they realized that we were people who knew we couldn't afford to slip back and that we were making decisions deliberately knowing that this was the direction we wanted to go."

* * *

The euphoria of a Big Ten football championship and a Rose Bowl victory was quickly interrupted just 12 days after the UW's victory over UCLA in Pasadena, when the NCAA announced that the school's athletic program had been placed on two years of probation due to a series of rules violations in the wrestling program, most of which occurred prior to Richter's arrival as athletic director.

Among the rules violations were impermissible travel expenses provided to student-athletes, impermissible evaluations of prospective student-athletes, and impermissible payment made by the head coach to his assistant coaches.

The NCAA declared the violations to be major and placed the UW on two years' probation. Further, Wisconsin would now be subject to the NCAA's repeat violators rule, meaning that any additional major violations over the course of the next five years could potentially carry severe sanctions.

* * *

Meanwhile, at the UW Field House, Coach Stu Jackson's team was making a lot of noise and generating excitement for the state's basketball fans. With Michael Finley, Tracy Webster, and freshman center Rashard Griffith, the Badgers appeared to have the talent to break into the league's first division for the first time since 1973 and earn an NCAA tournament bid for the first time since 1947. The Badgers won their first 11 games of the season and went on to finish at 8-10 in the Big Ten, good for seventh place. More importantly, the team's regular season record of 17-10 earned an NCAA tournament bid. Remarkably, the UW Field House was now sold out for the season with an average attendance of 11,500 per game.

In the school's first NCAA tournament game since 1947, the Badgers defeated Cincinnati 80–72 in an NCAA west regional game at Ogden, Utah. Finley and Griffith each scored 22 points to lead the Badgers. Two days later, in a high-scoring shootout, the Badgers lost 109–96 to Missouri, despite 36 points from Finley and 27 from Webster.

But once again, the magic didn't last. Ninety days after leading his team to an historic NCAA tournament appearance, Jackson resigned to take a position with the Vancouver Grizzlies of the National Basketball Association.

"It was awkward timing," Richter said. "Some of the players had now had Yoder and Jackson and now were looking at another new coach. They came to me and said they wanted (assistant coach Stan Van Gundy) to be named coach. Quite frankly, at that time, naming Stan was more than just taking the easy way out. At that time of the year, you just don't go out and pick up a coach from someplace else. If they're the right kind of person, they're not going to leave a team in July, unless it's an unusual circumstance like in Stu's case."

Richter listened to the players, analyzed the options, and decided to elevate Stan Van Gundy to head coach. Publicly, Van Gundy was awarded a five-year contract. Privately, the university protected itself by including a one-year buyout limit, protecting the department in case the new coach didn't work out.

"Stan was a grinder," Richter said. "He worked hard and was a good guy. You could see how he'd have a great relationship with the players. In many cases, Stu had been in a perfect position for Stu's personality. Now, as the head guy, there really wasn't anyone there to fill that role."

As the season progressed, Richter was left with a feeling that things just weren't working out the way he had hoped. "Had this happened in the normal course of things, we would have gone out and tried to hire the best coach we could find," Richter said.

In March 1995, Richter announced that Van Gundy would not be retained. Local sports columnists ripped Richter for that decision, arguing that Van Gundy deserved more than one year on the job. Despite his disappointment with the move, things would eventually work out well for Van Gundy, who years later went on to become head coach of the Miami Heat of the National Basketball Association.

There was additional criticism for Richter when he and other administrative staff chose not to attend the team's annual banquet. "We thought that it might be best if we didn't attend so that the focus could be on the seniors and the rest of the kids," Richter said. "We ran that past a couple of the assistant coaches, and they agreed. So we didn't attend for that reason. But it came back to us that we were snubbing the team and the coaches by not going. Obviously, that's not what we were trying to do."

* * *

With the decision to release Stan Van Gundy from his contract, Richter decided that the program no longer needed a jolt like it did in 1992. Instead, Richter was hoping to land a coach that would provide some badly needed stability to the men's basketball program over a long period of time.

Etched in Richter's memory were his observations from the 1994 NCAA west regional in Ogden. That's where Jackson's team defeated Cincinnati, then lost to Missouri. Also competing at that Ogden regional were Dick Bennett and the UW–Green Bay Phoenix. And UW–Green Bay's opening-round game against California was a sight to see. Cal had a great team, including future NBA stars Jason Kidd and Lamond Murray. But Green Bay's tenacious defense and precise offense completely frustrated the Bears, as Green Bay upset Cal. Richter was present for that game and couldn't help but be impressed. And that, in great part, was why Dick Bennett had moved to the top of Richter's short list.

"We had to seek some greater stability and in the back of our mind, that boiled down to Dick Bennett," Richter said. "It was likely to be the last place he would coach. He was someone we wanted to talk to. We did talk to UW-Platteville coach Bo Ryan at that time. We at least made a call, as I remember. But we were thinking that we'd give Dick the first shot and see what happens."

During that time, Richter received a phone call from a former high school classmate at Madison East, Al Auby, who along with another Madisonian, Dave Shaw, was acting as an intermediary of Tubby Smith, then the head coach at Tulsa. Auby indicated that Smith would be interested in the job. "My thinking was that we were looking at Dick," Richter said. "And Tubby Smith, although a top candidate, was probably a secondary candidate at this point. They sent me information about Tubby. It was clear that Tubby didn't want to make it known that he was interested until the Dick Bennett thing played out."

Bennett's team was in the NCAA tournament again, so Richter had to wait until that was concluded. Richter called Dick Bennett late on a Sunday night and scheduled a meeting in Green Bay the following morning.

The plan was to meet at the Radisson Hotel near the Green Bay airport. But those plans changed when Bennett called Richter at home at 6:30 a.m. and suggested the two meet at the Bennetts' new house. "When the phone rang so early, I thought at first he was going to pull his name out of contention for the job," Richter said.

Bennett picked up Richter and drove to his house. "I remember driving through the area," Richter said. "It was beautiful. It was a brand-new house and they had just moved in. It was kind of a dream home. I was thinking that [Dick's wife] Anne Bennett was going to think I'm the worst son of a gun in the world for trying to get her husband to move from this dream home."

The two met most of the morning and into the early afternoon. "We talked in general terms about the stability," Richter said. "We technically couldn't offer him the job at that time. We talked about what we had, about our expectations. At that point, we had no clue that there was a new facility on the horizon at UW. The press later made a big deal that Herb Kohl didn't decide to make the gift until Dick Bennett was named coach. There was never any kind of tradeoff like that. Ann came into the discussions. It was obvious that they just loved Green Bay."

As Richter returned to the airport, he told Bennett that he would be out of town for a few days and suggested that Bennett call him on Thursday. There was no phone call on Thursday. Or Friday. Or Saturday. Or Sunday. "I wasn't going to call him back because I felt Dick was the kind of guy who you weren't going to force into a decision," Richter said. "I just knew that whenever he had made his decision, he would call."

The following Tuesday, Richter was working out during the lunch hour at the McClain Center on campus when he received word that Bennett was calling.

"I took the call and he said, 'Pat, I thought it through pretty thoroughly and I think it's best that I stay here.' I had gotten wind that there was a team meeting that afternoon, and I told him, 'Look, Dick, I know you've got a team meeting. Why don't we just wait and see what happens? Maybe something will be said at that meeting that will change your mind and we'll go from there.'"

Later that day, Richter was flying to Champaign, Illinois for a UW alumni function. As he was set to board the plane, Richter called Bennett. "I asked how the meeting went and Dick said, 'Well Pat, I discussed it with the players. They understood this was something that I was interested in and they gave me permission to seek the position. Now I have to talk to my recruits.'"

Meanwhile, Richter called Tubby Smith's intermediary and told him that Bennett was still at the forefront, but he would know more that night, after he had talked again with Bennett.

As Richter prepared to board the plane for his return flight to Madison, he called Bennett to see how his conversations with his recruits had gone. "He said the recruits were disappointed, but they understood," Richter said. "And he told me that he was going to throw his hat in the ring."

Once that happened, Richter and Bennett continued their conversations, and while he would continue talking with other candidates, Bennett clearly was the focus.

In their discussions, they talked about the timing of a press conference to announce the hiring. Both agreed that April 1 would not be advisable; neither wanted an April Fools' Day connection. Instead, a press conference to announce Bennett's hiring was scheduled for Friday, March 31.

On Friday morning, Pat Richter received a phone call from Sandy Wilcox, president of the University of Wisconsin Foundation, the fundraising arm of the university. Wilcox was calling to pass along some great news. Senator Herb Kohl was going to make a $25 million gift to begin the process for a new basketball facility on campus. The announcement—no fooling—would be on Saturday, April 1, 1995.

* * *

In the mid-1990s, it seemed as if everything was coming up roses for the UW Athletic Department. The football team's remarkable turnaround had a tremendously positive impact on the department's financial picture and had provided the type of morale boost to alumni that Donna Shalala had hoped for when she appointed Pat Richter to the job in 1989.

"When we beat Michigan State in Tokyo, you started to think about how we should capitalize on this," Richter recalled. "We felt like it wasn't just for the days immediately following the Rose Bowl. We had a feeling that it was going to be for a sustained period of time.

"We didn't really know what it was to arrive, but to say we were going to the Rose Bowl was huge. It was where you wanted to go, even if you didn't know what it was going to be like when you got there," Richter said.

The Rose Bowl appearance had a particularly strong impact on revenue generated by companies that manufacture goods bearing UW trademarks: hats, sweatshirts, T-shirts, and so forth. Those manufacturers pay a percentage of their sales to the owner of the trademark; in this case, the University of Wisconsin. The process worked like this: A screenprinter or embroiderer would register with the school's trademark licensing program and become an officially licensed manufacturer of Wisconsin logoed merchandise. That permitted the licensee to imprint or embroider a Wisconsin logo on a blank sweatshirt, for instance, and sell that product to a retail outlet, which then sold the product directly to consumers.

In the process, the licensee would pay the UW a small percentage of the wholesale price.

Trademark licensing was a relatively new phenomenon at the collegiate level, and in the late 1980s, the UW became one of the last large universities to get in that game. And while the new program generated a local debate—and legal action—over ownership of the Bucky Badger trademark, it did provide the Athletic Department with another new source of revenue when it was sorely needed.

In those early days of licensing, Badger fans often had to search long and hard to find a good selection of Badger merchandise. And as the university continued to grow the program, licensing revenue had reached the $350,000 mark in 1993.

But the licensing and merchandising world changed for the University of Wisconsin on December 4, 1993, when the Badgers defeated Michigan State in Tokyo and landed a berth in the 1994 Rose Bowl. Suddenly, merchandise bearing Wisconsin logos could be found everywhere: in the shopping malls and department stores, at gas stations and convenience stores, and on street corners in Madison and throughout the state.

Industry analysts compared the merchandise frenzy to the souvenir sales that followed the first world championship for the Chicago Bulls and Michael Jordan. Rose Bowl personnel in Pasadena said they had never seen anything like it. UW licensees and local retailers scrambled to keep up with the consumer demand for Badger products.

When the dust settled on that post-Rose Bowl merchandise frenzy, the trademark licensing revenue had soared to $1.4 million in 1994, an increase of over $1 million in just 12 months. Published reports estimated that the Badger merchandise frenzy had generated an estimated $40–$50 million in incremental retail sales of licensed goods.

The football team's success also positively impacted the school's efforts to secure a new shoe and apparel agreement. Previously, various head coaches at the UW had separate contracts with companies like Nike, Starter, Puma, Apex One, and others. In an effort to provide greater institutional control over these types of contracts, the Big Ten Conference passed legislation requiring the Athletic Department to be included as a third-party to such agreements. Additionally, the trend in the world of collegiate athletics was that Nike and Reebok were in hot competition with each other. That competition, and the fact that the UW football and basketball programs had made huge leaps forward, proved beneficial to Wisconsin.

University officials visited company headquarters at Nike and Reebok and, in the end, chose to accept a lucrative offer from Reebok. The contract provided that Reebok supply, at no cost to the university, all the shoes, apparel, and equipment needed by the department's 23 teams. In addition, Reebok paid the UW nearly $2 million over a five-year period, paid for international trips by the men's and women's basketball teams, and provided scholarships for low income youth to attend UW camps and clinics. The contract even provided that Reebok donate $25,000 to refurbish a city-owned playground in Madison.

The Athletic Department's desire to enter into the agreement with Reebok, however, raised several issues. First, two of the department's coaches, women's track and cross country coach Peter Tegen and men's track coach Ed Nuttycomb, publicly criticized the department's decision to sign with Reebok. Both questioned the quality of the Reebok product and the notion that the administration would dictate which shoes their athletes would wear. Additionally, campus activists protested language in the contract that, in their view, appeared to restrict the free speech rights of university employees. Finally, the issue of sweatshop labor practices overseas had started to surface nationwide and had become a local political issue as well.

Nonetheless, by June 1996, the contract approval process was nearly complete. Richter and other UW–Madison officials traveled to Milwaukee with a representative from Reebok, who, ironically, had attended UW and was in the same graduating class as Richter. They were attending a meeting of the UW Board of Regents on the UW–Milwaukee campus, and on the agenda for consideration was UW–Madison's proposed agreement with Reebok.

The meeting was open to the public and a few individuals had registered to speak before the Board of Regents. Among those was an elderly man who spoke passionately and eloquently about the contract being bad public policy for the state's flagship institution. The contract, he said, sent a negative signal to the working people of the state of Wisconsin because much of the Reebok product was produced overseas. At the conclusion of his presentation, the man turned and walked toward his seat in the rear of the room. On the way, he encountered Pat Richter, who was sitting in an aisle seat. The man leaned over, reached out to shake Richter's hand, and said, "Pat, I hope you don't take that personally. I just wanted to tell you, I thought you were great in that '63 Rose Bowl. That was the best game ever." Richter looked looked down at the man's new Reebok shoes and said, "Nice shoes!" The man replied, "They really are nice shoes."

Despite the many questions raised, the Regents approved the Reebok contract, effective July 1, 1996, and for the next five years, the UW Athletic Department benefited greatly from the arrangement.

Also at that time, the department rebid the rights to broadcast on radio the Badger football and basketball games. Ultimately, the department accepted an offer from Learfield Communications of Jefferson City, Missouri, an offer that significantly increased the revenue, and perhaps just as importantly, included an enormous amount of free radio advertising that the department would later utilize to promote ticket sales and special events in all sports. That advertising and the other promotional components of the radio agreement would continue to provide an effective tool to promote UW Athletics and help continue the attendance growth across the board in the years to come.

There were many other post-Rose Bowl milestones that signified a new world for UW. At the university's admissions office, the number of inquiries from high school students around the country soared. Those parents who years earlier had told Shalala that they weren't going to let their sons and daughters attend UW–Madison, were taking a new look and giving the school a second chance. Attendance at alumni functions around the country increased, and conversations with university donors and potential donors were ever more pleasant.

"I think there was a certain euphoria and excitement—bragging rights." Richter said. "To be able to puff your chest a little bit, like the fellow in Chicago who sent me a letter after we defeated Michigan State in Tokyo to go to the Rose Bowl. He said, 'Thank you, thank you, thank you. I now have bragging rights in my own office.' And he included a check to the UW Athletic Department for $10,000. I think there was a lot of that, not so much a mindset of, 'Let's make sure we do this for the next 10 years.' It was just a certain sense of relief that something good had happened, and we were enjoying it."

But in the back of his mind, Richter was indeed thinking about the next steps: What could be done to sustain the rapid upward climb experienced by the UW Athletic Department in just four short years?

"I always kept thinking, and used it as a measuring stick, that when I was in school, Michigan was nothing special," Richter said. "They were just like anybody else. But then they built an athletic program that was nationally prominent and importantly, then they maintained it. Institutionally and otherwise, it was important for Michigan to be Big Blue and be successful. Not just in athletics, but the whole institution."

Richter clearly began to see a difference between getting there and staying there. "You may get to that point where you go to a big bowl, yet, if you don't maintain it, you really haven't achieved much," he said. "You always felt that once you reached a certain level, that to maintain that level was going to be very difficult. Now people see you as a different kind of competitor.

"Once we got to that level, we knew that everybody's expectations would be elevated and there are different kinds of pressures that come about. I don't think any of us could have imagined what it was going to mean. But you started to see the opportunities. Licensing: we found out that the trip to the Rose bowl was worth $1 million in licensing revenue. Shoe and apparel. Ultimately, your multi-media rights. You can start to see that by being competitive and successful, you get to enjoy some of those opportunities. And those are the things that save you money and those are the things that the better athletic programs are enjoying. And you can see how that helps them."

* * *

In the days between the UW football's historic victory in Tokyo and its 1994 Rose Bowl appearance, a letter from the Office of Civil Rights arrived at the University of Wisconsin Athletic Department.

Four years prior, a complaint had been filed with the Chicago branch of the OCR, alleging that the Athletic Department had been discriminating against women in the manner in which it funded sports at Wisconsin.

In 1991, university officials compiled a response to the complaint and sent that in to the Office of Civil Rights. The response outlined the Athletic Department's history of expanding opportunities for women athletes and articulated the department's plan for continued expansion.

"We heard nothing from them," Pat Richter said. "It was nearly 30 months later, in December of 1993, and all of a sudden someone must have observed that Wisconsin is going to the Rose Bowl or whatever. We get their response back, and it said 'We don't think this is enough. We want you to add women's gymnastics and women's fencing within the next 30 days.' It was obvious that they didn't really understand our situation, let alone athletics in general; that you could add a sport back within 30 days. It just didn't make any sense at all. We weren't prepared to do that and we weren't going to do that."

Fortunately, Richter and the Athletic Department had the backing of then chancellor David Ward, who had succeeded Shalala when she left to join President Bill Clinton's cabinet. "I think Chancellor Ward was a little bit taken aback that OCR thought we weren't doing a very good job with women's athletics," Richter said. "He was very strong in his support for what we were trying to do and was standing up to some of the things the Chicago office of OCR had said."

The UW dug in its heels, claiming that it had a strong history of expanding opportunities for women athletes and continued to provide the necessary support for those athletes. In addition, the UW had a plan for continued expansion and for roster management.

"Pat did not take this hook, line and sinker," said Marra, who worked closely with Richter on gender equity issues throughout the years. "He did not just say, 'OK, we're going to add this because you told us to.' When we had our meeting with them, I'll tell you what, Pat went toe-to-toe with the people they sent here, as did Chancellor Ward. The people from OCR said we must have plenty of money since we went to the Rose Bowl and that we should have no problem adding these things. I think he learned pretty fast about what Title IX was all about."

Richter felt the complaint-based method of enforcement put the UW Athletic Department at a competitive disadvantage. And he felt strongly that the OCR was not operating as it should. "It became clear to me that we were being led along to be made an example," Richter said. "I think they were going to get us to a certain point and then go out and say, 'Look, here's where Wisconsin is and you're going to have to get to that point.'"

Richter said the UW's plan was to add one sport, possibly two, to get the participation numbers closer to 50-50. Over the years, the number of opportunities for women athletes continued to grow, as did the amount of funding to support those efforts. The UW eventually would add three women's sports: softball, lightweight crew, and hockey.

In addition, in order to get the participation numbers in line with the percentage of women enrolled at UW–Madison, the department embarked on its aggressive roster management program, capping the number of participants in some men's sports and expanding the number of roster spots in some women's sports.

It was a long and sometimes frustrating process. But in the end, their efforts were rewarded in November 2001, when the Office of Civil Rights notified UW–Madison that it was in compliance with federal law.

"I think we did what was right for Wisconsin," Richter said. "There were never any strong disagreements among the staff. It wasn't a male versus female thing at all. It's what is right under our system. We were all interested in what was right. We weren't interested in just falling over and doing all of what they said we should do.

"The fact is that we had a plan," Richter said "There was a plan in place to add sports, to do that gradually in a financially prudent manner so that you didn't have to eliminate any other sports. That was the reality."

Looking back, Richter feels strongly that the UW reached it goals not because the federal government was hovering over it, but because it was the right thing to do for Wisconsin. And he is proud of the manner in which it happened. "It was a collective effort," he said. "It wasn't somebody pushing an agenda. It evolved over time. It took 10 years, but what we have today is a very solid program that's supported and has everybody's backing. There's recognition that it's the right thing to do, but that there indeed are other horses that have to carry that wagon."

The endeavor to advance gender equity became part of Richter's life in the UW Athletic Department. And his efforts bore fruit: In 1992, 34 percent of UW–Madison's 614 student-athletes were women. In 2001, nearly 52 percent of the 751 student-athletes were women.

Along the way, there were a variety of special moments in women's athletics. When the Badger volleyball team hosted arch-rival Illinois in an NCAA match on November 30, 1990, nearly 11,000 fans attended. Said Marra: "The people just kept coming and coming and coming." Three years later, when the department hosted the 1993 NCAA Women's Volleyball Division I Championships at the UW Field House, it was the most successful volleyball championship in NCAA history. Nearly 10,000 fans attended the semifinals and another 11,155 watched the championship match. The two-night attendance total shattered existing tournament record and along with the 10,935 who attended the Illinois match in 1990, meant that UW had three of the top five crowds in NCAA tournament history.

Fourteen months later, on February 12, 1995, the department achieved another milestone, when 11,500 watched the Wisconsin women's basketball team play Michigan State at the UW Field House. It marked the first time a Badger women's basketball game had been sold out. For the next five seasons, the UW women's basketball team drew over 100,000 fans to their home games each year.

Pat and Renee Richter were often among those in the crowd at women's athletic events, showing their support and enjoying the competition just like everyone else in attendance.

In January, 2005, when the UW Athletic Department celebrated 30 years of women's athletics, Pat Richter was among the honored guests participating in the festivities.

"He became a very strong advocate of gender equity," observed Jim Hoyt. "I think early on, gender equity was just something that he had to deal with. But by the end, it was something that he was dealing with because he was committed to it."

* * *

In September 1995, Pat Richter was gearing up for a Badger football weekend. On the morning of the game, there was a scheduled meeting of a group of Badger donors at the UW Foundation offices, just a couple of blocks west of Camp Randall Stadium.

Over the years, Richter had been troubled by a painful hip, and occasionally took an over-the-counter pain reliever. At the start of the week, he golfed in Milwaukee with businessman Burleigh Jacobs, a former UW golfing great in the late '30s and '40s. He told Jacobs about his hip pain, and Jacobs suggested that two of the pain relievers are better than one. Four days later, prior to a Friday afternoon meeting of the UW Athletic Board, Richter's hip was hurting again after a noon workout, and he took he took two pain relievers on an empty stomach. During the night, he felt a bit nauseated and weak, and got up several times. He became concerned, but nothing seemed urgent. To be safe, he decided that he would stop to see UW team doctor Greg Landry on Saturday morning prior to the football game.

"I stopped at my office in the Stadium and then walked over to the Foundation," Richter said. "I just felt lethargic and listless and kind of sick to my stomach. When I got to the meeting, I exchanged pleasantries and so forth, and then sat down because I felt tired. Ken Kruska and some other guys came in and I stood up to shake hands, and when I stood up I got a bit dizzy and finally said, 'There's something going wrong here and let's not ignore it any longer.' So I asked Kenny, 'How about if you take me to the hospital. I just don't feel good.'

"We went to University Hospital and they did some checking and found out that there was a bleeding ulcer that was probably caused by the ibuprofen and not having enough food in my stomach," Richter said. "They kept me in the hospital overnight and I missed the game. By the time they cauterized it, I had lost about four units of blood. Things seemed to be getting better, but they suggested that I not travel the next week to Penn State."

He missed a good game: the Badgers defeated sixth-ranked Penn State 17–9 in Happy Valley. "We won the game and their athletic director, Tim Curley, called me right away after the game to congratulate us on the win and wish me well," Richter said. "I thought it was a real classy thing to do."

* * *

The late Chris Farley, of Saturday Night Live fame, was a neighbor of the Richters in the village of Maple Bluff on Madison's Near East Side. Farley was a friend of the Richter children, and throughout the years of his rising stardom, he would stop and visit, and if it was Christmastime, he might bring cookies with his mother, Mary Anne.

"When he came back to Madison, I knew that Barry always liked to have famous people talk to the football team," Richter said. "I called up Chris and invited him to speak to the football team. I brought him out there and he did his Matt Foley stuff and he had a ball.

"Later on, when we were going to the Rose Bowl, I called his mother, to see if Chris was going to be in California for the Rose Bowl. We decided to get him hooked up for the Big Ten Dinner and do a comedy routine that night as part of the program. When I introduced him, I acted somewhat serious and said that there are times in our lives when we have a chance to meet some great motivators, the Norman Vincent Peales of the world, the Billy Grahams of the world. And I said, 'Tonight, we have such an opportunity, a real gem of a motivator. Please welcome Matt Foley.' The place just broke up.

"Chris was in the back of the auditorium, drinking coffee and getting wired up to go. We introduced him and he came in the back door and tumbled down the stairs. On stage, he did a cartwheel and danced around, hitched up his belt, laughed heartily and said, 'I ripped my suit.' He had ripped the crotch out of his brand-new suit. Everybody had a great time that night."

"He joined us for the parade the next day," Richter said. "He looked like Busby Berkeley. He had white pants and white shoes, a white shirt with a red cardigan sweater over it. He had a red tam. He thoroughly enjoyed it."

* * *

On December 10, 1995, the University of Wisconsin men's soccer team shocked the national soccer community by defeating Duke 2–0 before 21,319 at Richmond Stadium in Richmond, Virginia, to win the NCAA championship.

It had been a remarkable run for the Badgers. Entering the championship contest, the UW had held six straight opponents scoreless. It would be no different in the title game.

Senior Lars Hansen and junior Chad Cole each scored goals. Senior goalie Jon Belskis, continuing to fill in for the injured Todd Wilson, earned his third shutout in three career starts to lead the Badgers to victory.

"This is the best feeling of my life," Cole told a reporter for the *Wisconsin State Journal*.

Other news from the soccer program was not to be as glorious. In the summer of 1997, according to NCAA records, an assistant men's soccer coach requested a financial contribution from the university's soccer booster club through two representatives of the university's athletics interests to support a youth soccer association for the development of a soccer park. As a result, on June 24, 1997, a cashier's check for $35,000 was drawn on a booster account payable to an area youth soccer association. The contribution went toward the building of Reddan Field in Verona; a good cause, but as would be discovered later, an NCAA violation.

The $35,000 donation made in June 1997 seemed rather innocent at the time. The money was sitting in a UW soccer booster fund account. The new youth soccer complex was being named after retired UW coach Bill Reddan, a man whose tireless efforts helped youth soccer grow at a dramatic rate in the Madison area. And while it was a much-needed boost in the efforts to build the youth complex, the booster club donation would become part of the department's second major NCAA violation in five years.

Just two months before that donation was made, Melany Newby, the UW's vice-chancellor for legal and executive affairs, had begun to review the checking account records of the department's booster organizations. The purpose of the review, according to NCAA records, was to "evaluate potential changes in the relationship with the institution's athletics letter-winner organization and to confirm the accuracy of policies and procedures concerning the booster account, which were developed and implemented following a previous NCAA infractions case in 1994 involving the institution's wrestling program."

What eventually followed that internal review was the conclusion that the some of the activities in question were indeed violations, but that overall, the violations were categorized as secondary in nature. In most cases, it was simply a matter of not seeking advance institutional approval for reimbursements that likely would have been approved.

NCAA staff who investigated the case concurred, and they, too, categorized the infractions as secondary in their summary. However, in a somewhat surprising move, the NCAA Committee on Infractions ruled on March 24, 1999, that the case was not a secondary violation, but in fact was a major violation.

The NCAA concluded that:
- Numerous athletics department staff members received athletically related supplemental income and benefits from sources outside the institution without obtaining prior written approval from the university's chief executive officer. In most cases this supplemental income covered normal and reasonable business expenses in excess of state reimbursement limits and would have been approved if requested.

- The institution's name was utilized in endorsements for personal gain without prior written approval.

- A university booster club made a substantial financial contribution to a local youth athletics association.

- The university failed to adequately monitor its athletics program as to various booster organization funds and other compensation to athletics department staff persons.

The university was placed on NCAA probation for another two years. It was the second major violation in the past five years and as such, the department once again became subject to the NCAA's five-year repeat violator rules.

It was not one of Richter's fondest memories.

"This was one that Barry and I were really upset about because of the way it was portrayed," Richter said. "It made it appear as if we got money for something that we shouldn't have gotten. From day one—and this was not a policy change that we put into place when we got there—if you went on a trip and you stayed in a hotel that was $100 a night and the authorized state payment was $75, then you filed an expense [report]. The $25 over the state's authorized amount went to the W Club and you were reimbursed for that $25. You were reimbursed for what you actually spent. If you spent $100, you were reimbursed for $100."

Alvarez recalls a conversation about it with Chancellor Ward. "I remember going over to the chancellor's office," Alvarez said. "I was so upset at the time. My mother had just sent me a newspaper article from the Pittsburgh paper back home. I showed the chancellor and said 'Here's the headlines. My mother wants to know if I'm stealing something.' The headline read 'Alvarez, Richter Receive Illegal Funds.' It made us sound like we were crooks."

In Richter's opinion, it was the volume of information that overwhelmed the NCAA Infractions Committee. "The problem was that once they went back over a four- and five-year period, you can imagine how many banquets, trips, etc., that we did over that period of time," Richter said. "The volume of that material was more imposing than anything. When we went to the NCAA, I'm not sure they fully understood what was involved. I think because we were already on probation, that this triggered it again.

"Subsequently, I ran into Tom Yeager, who was on the Infractions Committee and later was chair of that group," Richter said. "I got the impression from him that the case was so unusual—they had never seen anything like it—that they actually changed the rules afterward so that it wouldn't be a problem anymore because it was a technicality."

The issue would surface during a conversation with an NCAA official in 2001. "We sat and talked about it later at the Shoe Box thing," Alvarez recalled. "Someone from the NCAA, when I'm on the conference call, he's reading about this other issue back in 1999. And someone from the NCAA says, 'I've never heard of this before.'"

Nonetheless, the fact that it was the department's second major NCAA violation in the past five years would haunt them later.

CHAPTER TWELVE
NEVER A DULL
MOMENT

Following its triumphant appearance in the 1994 Rose Bowl, the Wisconsin football team did not immediately return to Pasadena, but there were plenty of other bowl trips and successes along the way.

Rose Bowl or no Rose Bowl, Wisconsin football fans continued to display their strong support for the program. Average attendance had surpassed 77,000 in 1994 and would remain above that level through the balance of Pat Richter's career as athletic director.

The 1994 Badgers had an opportunity to make another mark on the national college football landscape when they headed to Boulder to meet highly ranked Colorado in the UW's second game of the season. Unfortunately, they were humiliated by Colorado 55–17 at Folsom Stadium in Boulder. Still, the team managed to finish 7-3-1 and earned a berth in the Hall of Fame Bowl in Tampa, where the Badgers soundly defeated Duke 34–20.

The following season, there was another early-season loss to Colorado, this time, a 43–7 defeat in front of a capacity crowd at Camp Randall Stadium and a national television audience. The 1995 Badgers never seemed to fully recover from that loss, struggled to a 4-5-2 mark, and did not earn a bowl berth.

In 1996, freshman Ron Dayne led the Badgers to an 8-5 record, including a 38–10 victory over Utah in the Copper Bowl in Tucson, Arizona.

In 1997, the Badgers again finished 8-5, but were defeated by Georgia 33–6 in the Outback Bowl.

It was the 1998 Badger football team that rekindled those memories of Pasadena when it won its first nine games of the season. And, after a disappointing 27–10 loss at Michigan, the Badgers came home to defeat Penn State 24–3 and earn a berth in the 1999 Rose Bowl, where the Badgers again were matched up with UCLA and the Bruins' high-powered offense. Instead, it was the Badger defense that prevailed, as freshman Wendell Bryant sacked UCLA quarterback Cade McNown as time ran out in the UW's 38–31 victory.

The 1998 Badgers finished the season with an 11-1 record and ranked sixth in the country. It was the most victories in a season in the history of UW football. Wisconsin's Tom Burke led the nation in sacks, and cornerback Jamar Fletcher led the nation in interceptions. Those two defensive standouts, in combination with an efficient and productive offense, helped Wisconsin lead the nation in turnover margin.

The success would continue for the 1999 Badgers, although at the start of the season, things weren't looking rosy at all. Ranked eighth in the country, Wisconsin lost its third game of the season at Cincinnati 17–12, and then lost its home opener to Michigan 21–16.

Then, a turning point. The struggling Badgers traveled to Ohio State to play the 12th-ranked Buckeyes. The Badgers' new starting quarterback that day was Brooks Bollinger, a redshirt freshman. Prior to the game, Richter was the guest speaker at the Wisconsin Alumni Association's pregame Badger Huddle on the Ohio State campus. He told the assembled Badger fans that day to "keep an eye on number five, because he may prove to be one of the best quarterbacks in Wisconsin history."

It was a difficult start for Bollinger, as the Badgers fell behind 17–0. But suddenly, the tide turned. Led by Bollinger and Dayne, the Badgers stormed from behind to defeat the Buckeyes 42–17 at Ohio Stadium in Columbus.

After the game, Richter surprised Coach Barry Alvarez and asked if he could speak to the team in the locker room. It was the first and only time Richter had made such a request to Alvarez. "I'll always remember that," Alvarez said. "He really has a spot in his heart for Ohio State. I don't know if there is anybody he enjoys beating quite like Ohio State. The emotion that he showed in that locker room to that team that night certainly is a memory for life."

"I don't like to get into the middle of things," said Richter, "but that particular game, you felt like you represented all the alumni in North America because of what they had done. These young men had come back from such great adversity against a very good team. You just felt so proud of them. It was such a pleasure to talk with them."

Following that dramatic road victory, the Badgers went on to win their next seven games. Wisconsin's final game of the regular season was at home against Iowa, and there was much at stake. First, a UW victory, combined with a Penn State loss that same day, would give the Badgers the Big Ten title and put them back into the Rose Bowl. Second, Dayne was within striking distance of setting an

NCAA career-rushing record, and he continued to be the front-runner in the race for the Heisman Trophy.

On a sunny and unseasonably warm November day, everything fell into place for the Badgers. Just prior to kickoff, the Badgers learned that Penn State had lost their game, which meant a UW victory would bring a Big Ten title and a Rose Bowl berth. In the middle of the second quarter, Dayne set the NCAA career-rushing record. And the Badgers defeated the Hawkeyes 41–3 to win the Big Ten title and earn a second consecutive berth in the Rose Bowl; their third in just six years. In a memorable postgame celebration, the Big Ten awarded the championship trophy, the Rose Bowl extended a formal invitation, and the UW unveiled its placement of "33 Ron Dayne" on the façade of the upper deck as thousands of Badger fans waved souvenir towels commemorating the historic day.

"It was a beautiful day," Richter said. "Nothing could have happened any better than it did that day."

Six weeks later, the Badgers defeated Stanford 17–9 in the 2000 Rose Bowl. The team ended the season ranked fourth in the country. Dayne won the Heisman Trophy and was the consensus national player of the year. Teammates Chris McIntosh and Jamar Fletcher also were named first team All-Americans.

Pat Richter and Ron Dayne celebrate Dayne's NCAA rushing record and the Badger's berth in the 2000 Rose Bowl. Photo courtesy of the UW Athletic Department.

Nearly nine years after hiring Barry Alvarez, the football program's success had exceeded all expectations. "When we hired Barry, we knew he had come from winning programs," Richter said. "He has a great deal of confidence, a certain swagger. Some people don't like that, but I think with all successful coaches there's an ego. They, more than anyone else, understand that the successful coaches in this business do very, very well, and the ones who aren't successful are looking for a job and they're bouncing around. There is a tremendous motivation to be successful.

"Barry had seen Bob Devaney at Nebraska, Lou Holtz at Notre Dame, and Hayden Fry at Iowa," Richter said. "He knew how those successful coaches operated and he was confident enough in his abilities to understand that if you surround yourself with good people, a lot of good things will happen."

With the victory over Stanford in the 2000 Rose Bowl, Wisconsin became the first Big Ten Conference school to win back-to-back Rose Bowls. Not Ohio State. Not Michigan. But Wisconsin.

"The 1999 Rose Bowl was so significant because it proved that 1994 wasn't just a one-shot deal," Richter said. "It was a sign that there was some solid football going on here and that under the right circumstances and the right chemistry, our teams can go to the Rose Bowl. Then, to repeat in 2000, that was even more incredible because no one repeated at the Rose Bowl, much less Wisconsin. It really kicked everything up a notch and everybody's expectations are different now because of that."

* * *

There was more excitement to come for Wisconsin Badger fans. And it would come from an unlikely source—the Badger men's basketball team.

The 1999–2000 Badgers were an unheralded cast of hard-working players who had learned the system of their coach, Dick Bennett, but weren't always executing it the way it had been taught. As the team headed into the final stages of the Big Ten season, it carried a 14-13 record—just 5-8 in the Big Ten— and there was talk of a postseason tournament bid, but a bid to the NIT, not the NCAA.

But after a thrilling come-from-behind victory at Iowa and another road victory at Northwestern, the Badgers played their final regular season game of the season against the 14th-ranked Indiana Hoosiers in a nationally televised game in Madison. And in a tense game before a capacity crowd at the Kohl Center, the Badgers defeated Indiana 56–53. The victory seemed to be enough for the Badgers to earn an NCAA tournament bid. Still, an additional victory or two at the upcoming Big Ten tournament wouldn't hurt.

The Badgers then defeated Northwestern and Purdue in the Big Ten Tournament at the United Center in Chicago, before losing 55–46 to Michigan

State in the tournament championship. It was the third time the Badgers had lost to the Spartans that season, but it wouldn't be the last.

The Badgers earned a berth in the NCAA's west regional and traveled to Salt Lake City to meet Fresno State in the first round. After a surprisingly easy 66–56 victory over Fresno, the Badgers played top-seeded Arizona in the second-round game. Arizona, ranked fourth in the country, couldn't solve the Badger defense and lost 66–59.

That put the Badgers into the Sweet Sixteen, where they traveled to Albuquerque to play 10th-ranked LSU. If Arizona was frustrated with Wisconsin's defense, LSU was positively befuddled as it lost 61–48 to the Badgers.

Now, it was down to one game. The winner would head to the Final Four and the loser would head home. The opponent was a familiar one, the Purdue Boilermakers, coached by Gene Keady. Just 15 days earlier, Wisconsin had defeated Purdue in their third meeting of the season. Keady, an accomplished veteran coach who had led his teams to three Big Ten titles in the 1980s, had never reached a Final Four.

The Badgers, behind the continued hot shooting of guard Jon

Pat Richter helps cut down the nets after the Badger men's basketball team defeated Purdue to earn a berth in the 2000 Final Four. Photo courtesy of the UW Athletic Department.

Bryant, defeated Purdue 64–60, and Wisconsin was headed to the Final Four.

Within 90 days of celebrating Wisconsin's second straight Rose Bowl victory, Richter and Badger fans everywhere were celebrating the school's first appearance in a Final Four since 1941. Upon the team's return to Madison late that Saturday night, an estimated 25,000 fans came to Camp Randall to celebrate the team's accomplishments at a welcome home celebration.

"That generated some tremendous euphoria," Richter said. "It was so improbable. The Final Four had never even been in our vocabulary."

Wisconsin's opponent in the NCAA semifinal in Indianapolis was all too familiar—Michigan State. The Spartans had defeated the Badgers on three previous occasions that season, and in a hard-fought defensive struggle, the Badgers lost 53–41 to end their improbable dream.

"The Final Four really was everything it was cracked up to be," Richter said. "It really was the spectacle that everybody said it was. And for us to be there, it was something special. It really was."

It was also something special for Coach Dick Bennett, who had been a tremendously successful coach at UW–Stevens Point and UW–Green Bay prior to joining the Badger staff. "I think in the Big Ten he was able to work with a little higher-skilled athlete," Richter said. "But he was able to instill in them the defensive spirit and intensity and the aggressiveness and work ethic. It's a great example of showing what you can accomplish as a team. The sum of the parts is greater than the individual parts. Individually, other than Kirk Penney, they may not have been blessed with great shooting ability, but together they played so well. With [Andy] Kowske and [Mike] Kelley and those guys, they were good athletes, but when they played together, at times, they were unstoppable."

At that UW Athletic Board's final meeting of the 1999–2000 academic year, Richter summarized the performances of Badger teams that year.

The football team won the Big Ten title and the Rose Bowl. Ron Dayne became the second player in UW football history to win the Heisman Trophy. The men's hockey team won the WCHA regular season championship. The men's basketball team reached the Final Four. The women's basketball team won the WNIT championship. The women's cross country team placed fourth in the country and Erica Palmer was the NCAA individual champion. The women's swimming team was 11th in the country. The wrestling team placed 9th in the NCAA and Dan Pritzlaff won an NCAA individual title at 165 pounds.

No doubt, it was a fabulous year.

* * *

Following that magical run to the NCAA Final Four in April 2000, there was considerable off-season speculation that Wisconsin coach Dick Bennett would retire. He had, after all, accomplished what he had hoped for when he took the job five years ago. Pat Richter had talked about that with Bennett, but over the summer of 2000, there had been no hint of retirement from Bennett.

During the summer, the Badger basketball team had an opportunity to participate in an overseas tour, and Pat and Renee Richter joined Bennett and the basketball Badgers on the team's European tour.

"In watching the games and Dick's demeanor on that trip," Richter said, "I noticed a real intensity in him and I thought, 'Boy, he's really fired up for the season.' I thought, 'Gee, he's really into it.'"

As the season started, any talk of Bennett's retirement had long passed. Practice had opened and the season was underway. Wisconsin opened with a 66–58 loss at Tennessee, then edged Northern Illinois 68–64 in the home opener at the Kohl Center. The following week, associate athletic director Cheryl Marra, the sport administrator for men's basketball, called Richter and said that Bennett wanted to meet with them in the morning.

"I kind of sensed that there really was no other reason to meet," Richter said.

The following morning, Bennett came over to Richter's office in Camp Randall Stadium to meet with Richter and Marra, and it didn't take long to figure out Bennett's intentions. "You could just tell from his facial expression that this was it," Richter said. "There may have been something leading up to that, but nothing of any great concern. He came in and said that he was going to step down, that this was it."

Richter brought up the European trip, the intensity and energy that Bennett had shown earlier in the summer. "I said, 'Gee, I thought you were really cranked up in Europe.' And he said, 'That's what kind of got me thinking, because I wasn't doing it naturally. I had to bring the

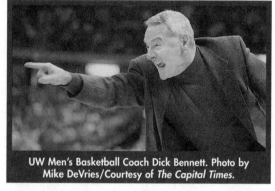

UW Men's Basketball Coach Dick Bennett. Photo by Mike DeVries/Courtesy of *The Capital Times.*

anger and fire myself up artificially. I just wasn't into the passion or interests or whatever.' He said he just wasn't able to do it.

"I think he sensed that he was bringing more anger than actual motivation and desire for the game, and I think that was concerning him," Richter said. "I think he was probably right, because you look at that and some of the games before that and maybe that's what he sensed when he came in— there was an anguish in him that you could sense that fall."

Bennett told Richter and Marra that the Maryland game—the ACC Challenge game played at the Bradley Center in Milwaukee later that week— would be his final game, and the three agreed to keep the news to themselves.

"It was a very intense game," Richter recalled. "I could remember thinking in the back of my mind that I hope it doesn't get to the point of him doing something that he's going to regret. There was one time on television where he gave the choke sign. That was misinterpreted on television. Basically, that was the choke defense. He told Jon Bryant, 'I told you to play the choke-up defense!' Everybody thought he was saying, 'You choked' but that wasn't it at all. But still, there was a real intensity, just hoping to get through the game without an incident. It was great that he could win that game and go out on such a wonderful victory."

The Badgers did win the game, defeating 13th-ranked Maryland 78–75 in overtime. The following day, November 30, 2000, Bennett announced his retirement. Assistant coach Brad Soderberg was named interim head coach for the remainder of the season.

"The natural thing was to let Brad take over," Richter said. "Whether that was part of Dick's plan, I'm not sure."

While he was clearly hoping the move would lead to continued success, Richter admitted he had some early doubts. "You caught yourself thinking that if you were going to start from scratch, would you hire somebody that is in Dick's mold," Richter said. "Dick is such a unique guy, an unusual guy, and a special guy. It's pretty hard for somebody to be just like him and carry on like nothing happened."

Publicly, Richter maintained a wait-and-see approach. He refused to comment to the media for fear of fueling speculation and placing added pressure on Soderberg, his staff, and most importantly, the student-athletes.

During that time, Richter received inquiries about the position and whether it would be available at a later date. One of those contacts indicated that if the job became available, Rick Majerus would have an interest. In December, following Bennett's resignation, Richter met Majerus and talked at length about the position. "At that point, I just told him 'I'm not sure I'm going to make a change. And I'm not going to make a change unless there's reason to make a change.'"

"As we went through the season, my feeling was that the farther we got away from Dick's influence, the more we seemed to kind of slip a bit," Richter said. "It wasn't the same team. To Brad's credit, he tried to keep that style. I don't think he's doing that at Saint Louis. He's probably done something differently. But trying to continue it that season, it was harder to keep that together because Dick was Dick and somebody else just couldn't do it the same way as Dick did."

The Badgers finished the regular season with an 18-10 record and 9-7 in the Big Ten, earning another NCAA tournament bid. Their first opponent was Georgia State, coached by former Maryland coach Lefty Driesell, in the first-round regional at Boise, Idaho. Still uncertain about his upcoming coaching decision, Richter watched every move and analyzed every maneuver, hoping for clues during his decision-making process.

He wondered to himself, if the team wins its first round game, did that eliminate or reduce his options? Ultimately, the season ended on a down note when the Badgers were upset by Georgia State 50–49. "It was time to pull all of those things together and make a decision," Richter said.

After the game, Richter chatted briefly with Tony Bennett, Dick's son, who was a UW assistant coach at the time. "I told Tony that regardless of which way we went, he would be an important piece," Richter said. "I told him that he'd done a good job and that regardless of what we do, we'd like to have him be part of some continuation here at Wisconsin."

As the team traveled back to Madison, Richter was still uncertain, but he was beginning to lean toward making a change. "The more I thought about it, Brad wasn't the same as Dick," Richter said. "Dick was unique and special. Just talking to a lot of people at that time, even though we won, it was still hard work. From a fan's perspective, if you were starting from scratch, would that be the way that you'd go, given that you've been to the Final Four?"

Richter had decided to make the change and informed Soderberg the following day. And once again, Richter was in the market for a new men's basketball coach. This time, it would be the last time.

* * *

After agonizing over his decision regarding Brad Soderberg, Pat Richter decided to renew his conversations with Rick Majerus. Now that the job was available, would Majerus still have an interest?

"We didn't make a change because we wanted Rick Majerus," Richter said. "We made it because of what we thought was best for the program."

Still, Rick Majerus would have been an interesting choice. A Milwaukee native who served as an assistant to Marquette's Al McGuire and Hank Raymonds, he had a successful head coaching career at Marquette, Ball State, and most recently, at Utah, where he had become truly a big name in the collegiate coaching ranks.

If someone with the stature of Rick Majerus might still be interested, Pat Richter was going to let it run its course. "Not knowing much about his situation, I was thinking that this would be one of those things that would be attractive to him," Richter said. "We then re-connected. There was a lot of speculation about him in the media. Some people had speculated that we were looking for a big-name coach, a national coach. We just didn't want to get it out too soon that we were meeting. He was at the Pfister Hotel and we had an arrangement that I would come in to the parking lot, take the elevator to a certain floor, cross over to the next tower, and so on. We made it hard for someone to follow me in, not that they were doing that anyway."

Over a two-day period, Richter and Majerus talked basketball. "He had watched tapes of our team," Richter said. "He went down the roster player by player. He was noncommittal at that time. He discussed some of his health issues and some of the things he had to do."

At the time, Majerus was on leave from Utah. He had been spending considerable time in Milwaukee helping to care for his mother, who was ill. "I just said if you have any questions about how we operate, just give Barry [Alvarez] a phone call. I said we'll touch base in a couple of days or whatever."

The following day, Majerus called and left a message with then-Director of Football Operations John Chadima indicating that he was coming to Madison to visit and might want to meet with Barry Alvarez. "John called me and was somewhat excited and I brought him down a bit when I said I bet he's coming over over here to tell me he doesn't want to take the job,'" Richter said. "There was no other reason for him to drive here at that time. I told Renee that he's coming over here to bail out."

During the days since he announced his decision to make a coaching change, Richter had conversations with many of the same people who talked with him during previous searches—Rudy Martzke, Sonny Vaccaro, Leslie Visser, Digger Phelps. "Digger had a few guys he was calling for, but the others were telling me that the word is that Majerus is just stringing you along," Richter said. "Rick does this, they said. He goes along with it and then bails out. I said, 'All I can tell you is that we're still talking to him and he hasn't said that yet.' All of them were great conversations, and I said, 'You would have thought the guy would have said no,' so I was going to pursue it until it runs its course."

Majerus arrived at the Richter residence on a Sunday afternoon. There, they watched NCAA basketball and talked about Wisconsin athletics and other topics. "The conversation was rather upbeat and I thought maybe he'd changed his mind," Richter recalled. "He didn't sound like or look like a guy who was going to give you some bad news."

Moments later, though, Majerus gave Richter the final verdict. "He said, 'I appreciate everything, but I just can't take it.'"

For Richter, it was time to re-group, time to focus on other candidates for the head coaching position at the University of Wisconsin. His attempt to hire Majerus had failed, and it left him open to criticism in the local media. Still, he had few regrets.

"I think it was worth the try," Richter said. "It was fascinating talking with him. He's a interesting guy. He was very well read, very bright and intuitive. There was maybe a five to ten percent chance that it was going to work out, but if it does, then terrific. It wasn't a surprise nor was it utter disappointment. It was worth a try."

Richter came into his office that following day and it was if he was starting from scratch. He had not contacted many other candidates during the Majerus courtship. Now, it was time to look closely at other candidates.

"Ben Braun was always of interest, but California had stepped up and gave him a good package and there was no way that we were going to get him out of there," Richter said.

"We were in conversation with the Big Ten at the time just to make sure we were in sync and not stepping on anybody else's toes because Michigan was looking for a head basketball coach," Richter said. "That's when you [the author] and I ran down the list of names and you said, 'What about Bo Ryan?' That's kind of the way it was. I don't know that we felt at the moment that that was the answer, but it was worth a conversation."

Richter called Bud Haidet, Athletic Director at UW-Milwaukee to get permission to talk with Bo Ryan, then the head coach at UW–Milwaukee. He then scheduled a meeting with Ryan. "We had a great meeting," Richter said. "After the meeting, we just asked ourselves, 'What are the negatives?' We couldn't think of any. So we said, let's think about it overnight and come back the next morning and talk about it again and see if we had identified any negatives. There really were none."

There were, however, plenty of positives. "The people in Wisconsin knew him," Richter said. "There was going to be a reaction one way or another to him being the coach. In most cases, it probably would be positive. He had a great following at UW–Platteville and had been very successful at UWM. There was familiarity—roots. In that sense, he was like Mike Eaves, and like Barry, who later had developed such strong connections to Madison and *wanted* to be here, and didn't want to disappoint people here. So there was a motivation for him to be successful."

Ryan also had a significant amount of coaching experience, although at a different level.

"When you've coached that many basketball games, you've seen pretty much everything they can throw at you, regardless of level," Richter said. "He had been successful at every level. Personality-wise, you thought here's someone who can be successful with his Midwest experience and a Philadelphia upbringing."

Among those Richter called at the time was Big Ten commissioner Jim Delany. Richter told Delany that he was likely going to hire Bo Ryan. Hearing that news, Delany relayed a conversation he had with associate Big Ten commissioner Rich Falk, who upon hearing the news that Dick Bennett had resigned last November, said two words to Delany: Bo Ryan.

"Falk told Delany that Bo, like Ben Braun, is the kind of coach we need in the Big Ten," Richter said. "He said Bo is a teacher, a student of the game. He's the kind you need to keep in the Big Ten because they are good solid coaches."

The more Richter talked to others about Ryan, the more he liked what he heard. "He had more of a national presence and awareness than people really knew," Richter said.

"We just felt he was the best guy for what we were going to do and we had somebody who would be successful and be here for a long time because of those connections," Richter said.

"When we hired him, he was probably in the lower half of coaching salaries in the conference," Richter said. "But we said, 'If you do some good things, we'll take care of you.' To this day, even with the success that he's had, he's well paid but he's certainly not at the top of the ladder. It's been fair and equitable, I think, and he's been very appreciative of the opportunity."

Bo Ryan (left) and Pat Richter address the media on March 29, 2001, after Ryan was introduced as the new UW men's basketball coach. Photo by David Sandell/Courtesy of *The Capital Times*.

In April 2001, Bo Ryan was hired to be head coach. The press conference held in the Nicholas-Johnson Pavilion was more like a family reunion than a media event. Ryan shook a lot of hands, burned through a lot of reporters' cassette tapes, and reunited with a lot of friends and former colleagues.

"The press conference went a little longer than planned, which now, we're used to with Bo," Richter said. "We went downstairs to the locker room for a team meeting. Bo started the meeting by asking if anyone had a tattoo. Then he said, 'Hey guys, how about we take our caps off. When we're indoors, this is our work area. When we're outside, that's a little bit different.'

"That to me showed a little bit of discipline," Richter said. "Most people would think that Dick and the others were very disciplined, and this was one thing that I thought was a bit unusual and that it was important to Bo. In the process of the conversation, he would say things that seemed a little bit outrageous and say something that was a little bit off the wall and get a reaction from the players. Then he'd say, 'I'm just kind of kidding' and just trying to keep them off balance.

"He told the players that he knew most of them not by name but by uniform number. You're so and so, you made that shot from the arc against so and so, or you drove the lane against us. He got to Dave Mader and said, 'I saw on television that you're working on that elbow when you shoot free throws. You have to get that elbow up a little higher. But you're a pretty good free throw shooter aren't you?' He said yeah. And as he said that, I looked over to the bulletin board and they had the free throw stats, and Dave Mader was listed on the board as number two.

"Bo kept them off balance and it seemed like a very comfortable conversation," Richter said. "It was a good meeting and the players felt very good about it. Most of the players felt good about the previous staff and felt bad about the situation."

While there was excitement in the air that day, no one, including Richter, could have predicted the early results—two regular season conference titles, a conference tournament championship, a Sweet Sixteen, and an Elite Eight appearance in Ryan's first four years at Wisconsin. During that time, the Badgers put together a streak of 38 straight victories at the Kohl Center.

"Basketball wasn't on the front burner for a lot of people here," Richter said. "Stu and Dick and Brad had gotten it started with a good solid base. But I don't think anybody thought that we'd see what we saw those first few years. It's just been very, very solid.

The Kohl Center winning streak. The fan interest. It's been fun and it's been enjoyable—and you don't get headaches. It's not hard work!"

* * *

On more than a couple occasions, especially following some of the football team's more successful seasons, Coach Barry Alvarez's name was mentioned as job vacancies occurred at other colleges or in the National Football League. Most of the time, the speculation and the rumors didn't lead very far. But on one occasion, the feeling was that Alvarez was seriously considering a move.

It was 2001, and Donna Shalala had recently been named president at the University of Miami in Coral Gables, Florida. Butch Davis, the Hurricanes' football coach who had led his team to a number two ranking in 2000, had left Miami to become head coach with the Cleveland Browns.

At first, Richter didn't give credence to the rumors of a possible Alvarez departure to Miami. "From my situation, if you're number two in the country, would you go outside the organization given the fact that you're only one spot from the top?" Richter asked. "From Chancellor Shalala's perspective, do you run the risk of going out and bringing in someone from around the country, versus somebody on the staff where this thing is very close to being the best in the country? That's a big risk. You're starting your tenure there; that's not the way to start out. If they were number three or four, that's different.

"But from Barry's view, the fact that it was a southern school, given the connection with Donna, given the fact that it's one of the top teams in the country, he's probably got an interest."

"From our viewpoint, we were starting to get moving on the Camp Randall renovation project at the time and it was important to keep him around here," Richter said. "So we started having some conversations about what was happening in Miami. When it came down to crunch time, Barry was dealing with an agent, Neal Cornrich."

Barry Alvarez, flanked by UW Chancellor John Wiley (left) and Pat Richter, tells the press on February 2, 2001, that Alvarez will stay in Madison and coach the Badgers. Photo by Mike DeVries/Courtesy of *The Capital Times.*

Richter said the unofficial word out of the Miami camp was that Miami was going to go to $1.4 million and that was it. "That's what they had offered Butch Davis when he left, and that's where they were," Richter said. "I think what happened is that the agent got his starting point and started to look at other things like bonuses and staff, and he nibbled it to try and get more."

Richter called Miami athletic director Paul Dee to get the straight scoop. "We knew basically where they were, that they were dropping out," Richter said. "They were not going to be flexible. They were not going to change. At that point, we knew Miami had bowed out."

"Cornrich was coming back to us, too, and asking us for more and we basically said, 'No, that's it.' This is what we were going to do and that was it. By that afternoon, we had talked to Barry and he said that he was going to stay."

During that time, Richter and first-year chancellor John Wiley went to the home of Barry and Cindy Alvarez to let them both know that they were wanted and needed at the University of Wisconsin. "We went out to their house and talked about Camp Randall and about how we thought this was one of the better jobs in the country, especially in the college ranks," Richter said. "With John Wiley coming in new, I think Barry wanted to find out a little bit what he was about, and of course, he was very supportive.

"We knew we were going to be competitive, and he knew we had pretty much taken care of him during his time here," Richter said. "I'm not sure if they would have said, '$1.4 million and that's it,' whether he would have taken the job or not. It appeared to me that there was a lot more activity and action in that situation than others."

* * *

Indeed, 2000 was a remarkable year for the University of Wisconsin Athletic Department. A Rose Bowl victory. A Final Four appearance. The WHCA's McNaughton Cup. The list of accomplishments was long, but as the celebration was winding down during the early summer months, there was another controversy heating up.

On July 9, 2000, the *Wisconsin State Journal* first reported that the newspaper's two-month investigative work had found that many UW student-athletes had accepted unadvertised shoe discounts and in some cases received no-interest credit arrangements at the Shoe Box, located in Black Earth, just west of Madison. If true, the discounts and credits were likely in violation of NCAA rules.

An internal UW investigation quickly followed the newspaper report, and as football training camp began, there were a lot of unanswered questions about the possible impact of the case.

As the investigation grew, so did the anticipation, particularly in the football offices. The Badgers had won the conference title and the Rose Bowl the past two seasons, and with a strong corps of returning players, there was reason to believe the team could be a contender for a third consecutive Big Ten championship. In the preseason Associated Press college football poll, the Badgers ranked fourth, the highest preseason ranking ever for a UW football team.

Training camp had opened in early August, and from all reports, the camp was going well, with few injuries and great enthusiasm. The first game was to be played a few days earlier than normal, on Thursday night, August 31, against Western Michigan, a strong Mid-American Conference opponent. But any training-camp momentum was squashed when Coach Barry Alvarez was informed of the scope of the investigation and about the possible impact it could have on his team.

The results of the university's early investigation indicated that nearly 50 football players and a number of athletes from other sports had received improper discounts or credit at the Shoe Box. Using a self-made formula that combined the frequency of transactions with the total value of the discounts, university investigators placed the affected student-athletes into three different levels of violations. Those with the more frequent transactions and with the higher dollar amount of credit were subject to the greater penalties.

On the morning of the opening game, UW officials gathered in a conference room at the Best Western InnTowner Hotel, just west of campus. There, in a two-hour teleconference with NCAA officials, the UW argued that only five players should be suspended.

Following the teleconference, the NCAA committee huddled to make its determination on the eligibility of the players in question. Shortly after the lunch hour, Richter received a phone call from the NCAA, and the news was not good. Twenty-six football players had been suspended by the NCAA for one to three games each.

"No one's ever had to go through anything like that as far as preparation for a game," Alvarez said. "That—more than anything else since I've been here—really bothered me. It was our best team. No one had ever won back-to-back Rose Bowls and here we had a chance to win a third. I felt we were as good as anyone in the country. We have all the kids back. We have a great camp. A week before the game I'm notified that all these players have been suspended. At one point, I had an understanding that five kids were going to be suspended. The next thing I know, we're sitting in a meeting on the morning of the game, and then we had to go tell our players four hours before the game that 20-some players are suspended, some for three games, some for two, some for one. Some are going play this game, some the next."

The opponent on opening day, Western Michigan, was no patsy. They had played in their conference championship game the previous year, and on a hot, muggy late summer night, they made life difficult for the short-handed Badgers, who played the game without 20 of their players.

"It really disrupted the squad," Alvarez said. "Our quarterback (Brooks Bollinger) got killed in that game because our tackles hadn't played before and they couldn't block very well. They were back up tackles and hadn't had the reps they needed in training camp. It just about killed Brooks. He was never the same after that game. Some of our other linemen got hurt from all the switching and all the disruption. It was ridiculous."

The Badgers defeated Western Michigan 19–7 in the home opener. And it was a struggle.

"This may be the longest day I've ever had to go through in coaching," a weary Alvarez told the media after the game.

The lineup juggling would continue for two more weeks. In another home game, the Badgers edged Oregon and star quarterback Joey Harrington in a thriller, 27–23, to improve to 2-0. Then, with just one more week of roster juggling remaining, the Badgers defeated visiting Cincinnati 28–25 in overtime.

With a full roster for the first time all season, the Badgers hosted Northwestern in their Big Ten opener at Camp Randall. Unfortunately, the Wildcats stunned the Badgers 47–44 in two overtimes. Wisconsin would lose three of the next four games, and what had started out as a season with great potential turned into a season of disruption and disappointment. Still, the Badgers managed to finish with a 9-4 record, including a 21–20 victory over UCLA in the 2000 Sun Bowl.

Pat Richter had first found out about the Shoe Box and a potential problem when the department's compliance officer, Tim Bald, visited him in the fall of 1999. "He told me that somebody had mentioned something to him and he said he was going to go out and talk to this guy at the Shoe Box [owner Steve Schmitt] and tell him the do's and don'ts and see what's going on out there. Tim came back and said he had been out there and talked to this guy, and Tim said he wasn't sure Schmitt understood the rules. So I basically said to Tim, 'Well, keep an eye on it.' By that time, all of this had already occurred and the owner never did change his story throughout. He never thought he did anything wrong. It wasn't like giving somebody money to sign. I mean, nobody's going to come to a school because you get a discount at a shoe place.

"But this one, because of the magnitude of it and in some cases—it was titillating and interesting—it got huge publicity," Richter said. "I know from talking to my counterparts around the country, they spoke tongue in cheek and would say, 'You've got to be kidding me.'"

"There was such a life to this thing," Richter recalled. "Probably the most difficult was the timing with football. It was really hard to quantify how this affected us or hurt us. It was a constant point of discussion. The Shoe Box this and that."

"The thing that upset me most throughout the whole deal was at the press conference we had announcing the deal and I was asked the question, 'Did you kind of notice the thing in November but let it slide into January because of the Rose Bowl?' I said, 'Well, then you don't know me because something like that doesn't even deserve an answer.' To try to infer that we had tried to push this under the rug because of the Rose Bowl or the Heisman—not knowing at that point if or how much Ron Dayne was even involved in it."

In April, 2001, the university announced the results of its internal investigation. The findings indicated that 157 current student-athletes received store credits or discounts that nonathletes did not receive.

As a result, Chancellor John Wiley announced that the university put itself on a three-year period of probation with the NCAA.

The university's athletic program was already on probation with the NCAA because of a 1999 determination that Athletic Department staffers accepted income from outside sources without receiving proper approval, and that the department did not properly monitor its booster organizations' funds.

Wiley also announced that UW would pay $150,000 to the NCAA, which was about the amount of net revenue received by the university for postseason tournament appearances made in 1999 and 2000 by the men's basketball team.

In addition, the self-imposed sanctions included a reduction in scholarships in football and men's basketball, and put limits in place on the number of coaches permitted to recruit off campus the next year.

Wiley announced that David McDonald, the chairman of the UW Athletic Board, would leave that position to become deputy athletic director and report directly to Wiley. Bernice Durand, a professor of physics, would take over as chair of the Athletic Board.

UW also dissociated itself with Shoe Box owner Steve Schmitt for five years. Schmitt was considered a booster of UW sports, having once bought season basketball tickets. That connection made the student-athlete discounts an NCAA violation, Wiley said.

Six months later, the NCAA Committee on Infractions announced in October 2001 that it had increased the scholarship reductions and that it had placed the University of Wisconsin on five years' probation.

"I've said all along that I would take 50 Shoe Box situations compared to one of the academic type of things that went on at Minnesota or some of the things that are came out recently at Ohio State. They're entirely different. You're not necessarily cheating somebody else. Even though we've now had three majors, I think you really have to look at them in the context of say, the Chris Webber situation at Michigan. Those things are a lot different. You never want to have a major, but compared to what they're involved with, you just have to say, 'We're there, but it's just an entirely unique situation.'

"In the inner circles of athletics, that became a thing we were kidded about, given the nature of it," Richter said. "Others might have been cheating academically or financially, and ours was shoes!

"Ultimately, though, it's clear that the buck stops here," Richter said.

* * *

In January of 2002, Wisconsin's Jeff Sauer held a press conference announcing his retirement, and Pat Richter was back at the coaching search game.

In the years leading up to Sauer's announcement, Richter had been disappointed with the team's performances. "Obviously, Wisconsin had great history and legacy with John Riley and Bob Johnson and Jeff Sauer," Richter said. "We won the NCAA championship in 1990. The feeling was that since that time, things had started to go a bit downhill. We weren't as successful as we had wanted to be and

Pat Richter introduces former UW hockey player Mike Eaves as the new Badger hockey coach on March 19, 2002. Eaves replaced Jeff Sauer, who had coached Wisconsin for 20 years. Photo by Mike DeVries/Courtesy of *The Capital Times.*

again, we were kind of in a position of being in the middle of the pack. The feeling was that once the Kohl Center was built, why shouldn't we able to attract the best players?"

"Jeff had done a great job for such a long time," Richter said. "We started talking about a possible coaching change a couple of years before we actually made the change, especially when women's hockey came on board. We talked about the possibility of being a director of hockey operations."

Once the search began, a lot of candidates surfaced, including Mark Osieki, Don Granato, Tom Carroll, Bob Mancini, and Jeff Jackson. Two current assistant coaches, Mark Johnson and Pat Ford, were strong candidates, too.

Richter also knew about former Badger Mike Eaves, who had extensive coaching experience and was coaching the U.S. National Development Team in Ann Arbor, Michigan. "I had met Mike some time ago," Richter said. "He was a first-rate individual and I made a contact with him, flew over to Detroit, and met with him for a couple of hours in the Detroit airport. It just kind of confirmed what I had thought. He seemed like an intense coach, very competitive. Obviously he was successful as a player, very successful in the professional ranks. He had coached at a prep school in Finland. He had sons who were excellent players. And importantly, he had that connection to Wisconsin. He had been a player here. His wife, Beth, was from Madison. His father-in-law was a student-athlete and a coach here as well. If an opportunity came along for Mike, that's something we never ruled out. Still, it would have to be an excellent opportunity for Mike to make that break, and if it did happen, it's more than likely that he would have put us on a track to a successful rebuilding of the program.

"We wanted to make sure we protected ourselves from a fan attendance standpoint," Richter said. "Even though we were at or near the top in attendance in the country, there was still room to grow. We had Mike on the back burner for quite a while. We spent a lot of time talking to a lot of other people about the position. I remember being in Jeff's office and calling in [assistant coaches] Pat Ford and Mark Johnson to inform then that I was going to go with Mike Eaves. They were very disappointed. There were a lot of people who supported Mark. He has tremendous experience. He had much the same connections as Mike, and Pat did too. I just felt more comfortable with Mike in terms of where I thought the program should go. Even though in some circles, it would not be a popular decision, I felt that was the best direction for the program."

On March 19, 2002, the UW Athletic Department announced that Mike Eaves had been hired as the new head coach of the UW men's hockey program.

* * *

The men's basketball program, meanwhile, continued to defy the odds. And as the years passed, Richter's reputation of successful head coaching hires would be greatly enhanced, as his choice of Bo Ryan was now golden.

The Badgers, who had not won a Big Ten basketball championship since 1947, shocked the college basketball world by winning the Big Ten Conference title in 2002. The following season, they once again won the conference title and advanced to the NCAA's Sweet Sixteen. In 2004, the Badgers won the Big Ten Conference basketball tournament. And in 2005, they advanced to the Elite Eight and nearly knocked off top-seeded and eventual national champion North Carolina.

"No one could have anticipated those things," Richter said. "In fact, probably no one was even hoping for those things to happen. We just were never known as a basketball school. The last 40 years we had just kind of, well, played. The accomplishments of basketball were just as gratifying as any of the football successes and each in their own way signified a tremendous accomplishment, something we never anticipated nor expected. It had a lot to with our financial stability, with our overall effort in building a solid program and in our ability to build and renovate facilities. Each in their own way allowed us to do certain things in our program."

"He's a great tactician," Richter said of Bo Ryan. "He has great people around him and they each know what they're supposed to do. One thing about Bo, he's basically the same person all the time. You really can't tell whether it's a win or loss. I think he understands that he's put everything into it and he's given the kids as much preparation as they could possibly have for the game, and once the game starts, it is a game played by young people and certain things happen beyond your control and you can't dwell on it. I think he knows the right buttons to push and when to push them."

* * *

Pat Richter got to know former Milwaukee Brewers owner and current baseball commissioner Bud Selig when the UW Athletic Department began hosting Badger outings in the Milwaukee area. Each year, Selig seemed to show up at the outings and typically spent time chatting with Richter and other Badger boosters in attendance. Selig, a UW alumnus, always seemed comfortable talking with Richter about the Badgers.

"I didn't know Bud very well until I took the job as athletic director," Richter said. "But he became a good friend over the years. He was always very accommodating with his time. We had a lot of conversations during the September 11 time when we were all trying to figure out next steps. Ironically, everybody seemed to be taking the lead from the NFL because they were first up. Bud had kind of gotten the word that they initially were going to play but that changed. We talked about security issues and so forth.

"We talked a lot about revenue sharing, because the Big Ten has it and major league baseball didn't," Richter said. "He never mentioned anything to me about the fact that we dropped baseball in 1991."

Selig, who served with Richter on the Board of Directors of the Green Bay Packers, attended Richter's retirement party in March 2004. Unbeknown to most, it was a time when some behind-the-scenes trouble was brewing in the world of major league baseball.

"He said to me 'It's going to start to hit the fan tonight.' It was the beginning of the steroids controversy," Richter said.

The annual outreach efforts by the UW Athletic Department led to another growing relationship, this one between Richter and Packer President Bob Harlan. The Packers hosted an annual steak fry on behalf of the Badgers at Lambeau Field, and over the years, that served to strengthen the relationship between Harlan and Richter. Eventually, Richter was appointed to the Packer board. His timing was good. The year of his appointment to the board, the team won the Super Bowl.

"We kidded ourselves about the fact that we have some of the same personality traits, as well as the same birthday," Richter said. "Again, we talked a lot about revenue sharing, and, with the Packers in the middle of a renovation, we had a lot of conversations about that. We talked about trying to sell the program in the political process. There were a lot of people beating up on him in the press and some of the same things had happened to us on occasion over a decision that you make. I told Bob, you kind of look in the mirror and see that you're the same person and that you haven't changed, it was the decision. It was almost like kissing babies and being a politician. And it worked. He did a great job. Since that time, we've talked about retirement and our future plans."

* * *

On two separate occasions during Pat Richter's nearly 15 years as UW athletic director, the Big Ten Conference and the University of Notre Dame entered into lengthy discussions about the Fighting Irish joining the Big Ten.

And while it didn't pan out on either occasion, it always made great sense to Richter.

"We knew it was always going to be difficult with football being the dominating sport there," Richter said. "The studies that we had indicated that if you were going to expand from 11 to 12 schools, there really was only one school that made sense, and that was Notre Dame. Otherwise, I think you'd have to add three schools and go to 14."

Unlike any other university in Divison 1-A, Notre Dame had its own foot-ball television contract with a major network—in this case, with NBC. Because of that—and the fact that when and if Notre Dame advanced to a Bowl Championship Series game, it did not have to share the revenue with any fellow conference members, since the Fighting Irish football team was not a member of a conference. Because of the potential for huge revenue gained from the televi-sion contract and the Bowl Championship Series, most felt that Notre Dame's move to the Big Ten would not make financial sense for the Fighting Irish.

Not so, said Richter. "We felt the numbers—publicly it was talked about that they had this separate NBC contract and couldn't make the move—the numbers over a long-term basis were pretty much the same. If they go to the BCS, they don't have to share the bowl revenue with anybody. But the fact is, they haven't been to a BCS game for a while."

The first time, when Notre Dame finally decided not to move forward, Richter said it appeared as if the Big Ten was begging them to come in. "It was never that way at all," he said. "There was a perception in the public. I think [Big Ten commissioner] Jim Delany's point at the time was that, 'Hey, we're not out there on our hands and knees. We think it works for everybody, but if someone is not a willing partner, we're not going to plead with them.' So that's why the next time it kind of popped up, it was really played as more of a neutral. If it works, fine. But it's up to them. We didn't want to take a chance of getting egg on our face again."

Richter said the faculty at Notre Dame was excited about the move to the Big Ten because of the research nature of all the Big Ten institutions. "That would bring them into a different type of academic environment," he said. "I think there was a quote from a professor at Notre Dame at the time who said, 'It's difficult to overcome ignorance and stupidity in a very short time,' referring to the people at Notre Dame who didn't want the move to happen. From an academic standpoint, it appeared that this was of very much interest to them. But basically, as general-ly happens, it boiled down to a football decision. The perception, the history, being Notre Dame was too huge and too much to overcome."

CHAPTER THIRTEEN
INTO THE SUNSET

Pat Richter's accomplishments will be measured in many ways, but perhaps the longest lasting of those will be the long list of new or renovated Athletic Department facilities.

In 1991, the UW opened the University Ridge golf facility, and from the beginning, it has been wildly popular. The course was built just southwest of Madison and features a wide-open front nine and a back nine carved out of the woods. In 1992, University Ridge was ranked third nationally in *Golf Digest*'s Best New Public Golf Courses. The rave reviews have continued through the years.

In 1993, the Athletic Department completed a $2 million resurfacing project to improve and update the Dan McClimon Memorial Track and Soccer Complex, which serves as the home for the Wisconsin soccer and track and field teams. The complex, named after the late Dan McClimon, a former UW track and field coach who died in a plane crash while returning from a recruiting trip, includes an Olympic-sized natural-grass soccer field.

In 1997, the new $1.6 million Fetzer Student-Athlete Academic Center was opened in the basement of the McClain Facility on the UW campus. The 15,000-square-foot facility, named after lead donors Wade and Bev Fetzer, includes 11 study rooms, a 55-seat auditorium, and computer labs. Since the day it opened, it has served UW student-athletes well.

Also in 1997, the department opened its new Talbot Wrestling Complex, located underneath the east grandstand in Camp Randall Stadium. The facility, named after lead donor Tom Talbot, serves as the training facility for the UW wrestling team.

In 1999, the department's state-of-the-art softball facility was opened. Long-time Madisonians Robert and Irwin Goodman contributed $500,000 toward the $1.2 million project, which would be called the Goodman Diamond.

In 2005, the new three-story Porter Boathouse was dedicated on the site of the old crew house at the end of Babcock Drive along the shore of Lake Mendota. The new 52,000-square-foot facility, named after former rower and lead donor Ben Porter, will house both men's and women's rowing teams.

Richter is especially proud of the Fetzer Academic Center and its positive impact on the academic experience of the student-athletes. Richter remembered well what the academic facilities were like during his undergraduate days at Wisconsin. And from the moment he took the job as athletic director, he wanted to improve the learning environment for the student-athletes.

"I think the feeling early on when we first got there from a recruiting standpoint, we needed to do a few things in this area," Richter said. "The reason it caught my eye is that it really was no different than when I was in school. Basically, it was in the same part of the stadium. It was an old, decrepit, miserable environment. I felt it would be difficult to get anyone to come here with that kind of academic facility. So if you're were a coach, I could see the difficulty they faced.

"Building the Fetzer Academic Center was the right thing to do and one of the best things that we've done in terms of upgrading and providing a good environment," Richter said. "The people who worked there felt the same way, and it enhanced the way they approached their jobs as well."

The two most visible projects were the Kohl Center and the renovation of historic Camp Randall Stadium.

Sen. Herb Kohl addresses the opening day crowd at the new Kohl Center in January, 1998. Pat Richter (far right) is joined by Mark Bugher from the Wisconsin Department of Administration, Chancellor David Ward, Ab and Nancy Nicholas, Jack Kellner Sr., and Jack Kellner Jr. Photo courtesy of the UW Athletic Department.

The $79 million Kohl Center was opened in January, 1998. The building is named for U.S. Senator Herb Kohl (D-Wisconsin), a 1956 graduate of the UW–Madison who donated $25 million to the project. At the time, Kohl's gift was the single largest private donation in University history. Former all-Big Ten basketball player Albert (Ab) Nicholas and his wife, Nancy Johnson Nicholas, pledged $10 million toward the project. The facility's practice gymnasium is named the Nicholas-Johnson Pavilion and Plaza. And the Kellner family—Jack F. and his sons, Ted and Jack W. of Milwaukee—donated $2.5 million to the project. Richter and the department proudly point out that the facility was built without the use of state taxpayer dollars.

"It really served as a symbol of success for this department," Richter said. "You don't build something like that unless things are going well. We are tremendously indebted to Sen. Kohl, the Nicholases, and the Kellners for providing the financial leadership on the project. As it began to take shape, you could see that it was going to be an outstanding facility. It became a psychological positive for everybody. We were able to complete something and absorb the debt and to fund it. Many years from now, it will still be serving the needs of our teams and our fans."

Richter remembers the angst displayed by a lot of loyal Badger fans as the basketball team prepared to leave the Field House for its new home on Dayton Street. "A lot of people were concerned about the move," Richer recalled. "The faithful 5,000, of which we've run into about 15,000 over the years, were concerned that the Kohl Center would never be the same; it would never be as loud. The fact is that you have to try to upgrade and move things up whenever you can. I think it's been proven that the Kohl Center is just as loud as the Field House ever was. It's a comfortable facility and has turned out to be a home court advantage and people are now taking great pride in that. It's our house now and we want to protect it."

The renovation of Camp Randall Stadium was a major undertaking as well, becoming the costliest project ever tackled by the Athletic Department. First built in 1917, Camp Randall is the fourth-oldest college football stadium in the country. Over the years, there had been several additions and repairs to the facility, but there had never been any major renovation. "It needed to be improved," Richter said. "And as you began to ask people for more money, the expectations of what they get in return were getting more prevalent, but you have a facility that's 85 years old."

The project first received approval from the Board of Regents in 2000. The underground utilities portion of the infrastructure construction project was completed in August 2002, and after a delay in the project, the construction began in earnest in March 2003. The project was partially completed in time for the 2004 season and fully completed in August 2005. The final cost of the renovation was $109 million.

The renovation included an impressive new structure on the east side of the stadium that houses 72 suites and 900 club seats. Some criticized the department for including those new seating areas in the project, arguing that suites and club seats belong in the professional ranks, not in collegiate facilities. Richter disagreed.

"You just couldn't do the things that needed to get done without building other things that could pay for them," Richter said. "You had to get the restrooms and concessions and the infrastructure, but you have to find a way to pay for them. And the only way to pay for them would be the suites and club seats. Frankly, that really was the key. If we hadn't had those, it wouldn't have worked, because all the money from the suites and club seats drops right to the bottom line and allows you to fund the rest of the facility."

In his final three years as athletic director, the construction crews were hard at work immediately outside Richter's second-floor office window. He watched closely as the project unfolded. "Seeing it progress and develop day by day, you could sense that it was going to be special," he said. "Given the limited footprint that we had here at the stadium, you could only do so much. And what they built was remarkable.

"Again, it was another very visible symbol of what's happened with the program," Richter said. "And anytime that happens, people want to be a part of that; they want to get caught up in that. That's a very positive thing."

* * *

From the moment Pat Richter accepted the position as athletic director, he had a plan for retirement. That's why the original contract signed by Richter said that he could not provide one-year's notice until 2003, which, in fact, is exactly what he did.

"Basically, my timetable had always been around age 62," Richter said. "It wasn't any particular event or anything like that. It was just the time I had been looking at all along. Looking back, it was a good time because things were in pretty good shape. You weren't walking out on a problem or leaving the department in a tough situation. This was more of a personal timetable that had been established a long time ago."

Richter said that age 62 always felt like the right time, especially as he neared that age. "I felt good. I felt healthy," he said. "There are so many things you just don't get to see and do when you're involved in these things.

"Basically, I'll just step out of the limelight and have a chance to be a regular person again," Richter said. "Nothing gave me a bigger kick than going to last fall's football game wearing shorts. I went to some tailgate parties and so forth. You still want the team to win and have all things be successful, but you just don't have that pressure."

There was also an indication that Richter had grown somewhat weary of the daily battles that must be fought to advance the program in the complicated world of intercollegiate athletics at a major research institution. "There is a certain amount of bureaucracy that you're dealing with because of the nature of the institution," he said. "That's just the way it is. With a state organization and a lot of bosses, there are some inefficiencies that are built in because that's the way it's set up, with lots of checks and balances."

Richter pointed to the department's efforts to secure lucrative shoe and apparel contracts, first with Reebok and later with Adidas. "We're in a competitive environment," Richter said. "Other schools aren't worrying about those things; not that we shouldn't, but the fact is, you are expected to compete and win, and sometimes it feels like you're playing the game with one arm tied behind your back."

* * *

On the afternoon of February 14, 2003, Pat Richter announced his intentions to retire as athletic director effective April 1, 2004.

"I simply did the best I could in directing a very complex organization in an ever-changing world," Richter told the assembled media and a live radio and television audience. "As a Madison native, I'm especially proud of the job my administration has done because my family could enjoy it too. Hopefully we made things better for those who compete in or cheer for Badger athletics."

"I've been a blessed man both professionally and personally," Richter added. "It's especially gratifying because the important people in my life have been able to share the joys with me. Renee and I look forward to spending time with our family, and this includes the Badgers."

In retirement, Richter said he'll continue attend Badger games and play golf. He is dabbling in some consulting work. Most of all, he'll be spending more time with Renee and their family.

Oldest son, Scott, and his wife, Khaki, and their two sons, James Patrick and Nicholas, live in Richmond, Virginia. Son Brad and his wife, Chrissy, live in Waunakee, Wisconsin, with their two children, Max and Samantha. Son Barry and his wife, Kim, spend time in Switzerland during Barry's professional hockey season, and then return to Madison, where they live with their children, Blake and Alexandra. The Richters' youngest son, Tim, lives in Madison.

* * *

Among the many compliments paid to Pat Richter was one from Chancellor John Wiley, who praised Richter for his leadership and noted: "I think Pat will be remembered as a builder." And while there were indeed a number of new buildings built and old buildings renovated during Richter's time, there was a lot of other building going on, too.

"Not necessarily in the sense of bricks and mortar but building in the sense of the overall program," Richter said. "We started out in debt and we tried to build a good solid foundation by cutting some programs and tightening things up a bit. But then as football became successful and then basketball and ultimately hockey chimed in, and the other programs were being very competitive, you could say it was building the department block by block. In that sense, we were building an organization as well as the bricks and mortar to house that organization."

Wisconsin State Journal sportswriter Tom Butler, who covered much of Richter's athletic career at UW, was not surprised by the organization that Richter built. Still, just like the Badger football program and the Final Four and more, Richter's success on the job exceeded nearly everyone's expectations. "I knew that he'd be a good athletic director," Butler said. "But who ever thought it would turn around like that? Look at what he did. Who is ever going to top that? Not in our lifetime. He just had the right manner. He could convince people. They respected him."

"He was exactly what the Athletic Department needed at the time Donna hired him," said Jim Hoyt. "We needed somebody who could travel the state, fly the flag, and engender confidence in the program. I think the feeling among alumni and around the state from day one was that the Athletic Department was in good hands, that it was going to turn around. I don't think there was much public doubt that he was absolutely the right person for the job."

Looking back, there was something special about the combination of three very different individuals who teamed together to achieve that early success: Richter, the local legend; Alvarez, the confident and hard-working football coach; and Shalala, the dynamic leader of the institution. "The thing the three of us had is that we trusted one another," Alvarez said. "I never looked over my shoulder. I think Pat believed that I was trying to do the right thing. We weren't trying to pull the wool over anybody's eyes. We weren't trying to out-slick anyone. We were trying to out-work people. He certainly wasn't concerned. And I think he welcomed Donna's involvement. He was very comfortable with her."

"Pat's career is the stuff of legends," said Shalala. "What Pat did better than anyone else is that he hired good coaches. And he had the credibility in the community. I think he was such a natural, and even though you couldn't tell it when you sat down and talked with him, there's no question that he had the golden touch."

"Pat was a guy who hired people that he trusted," Alvarez said. "He gave you a job and he let you do it. I just tried to do my job and he understood that. He would show up whenever there were issues. If I had lost a tough game, I could count on Pat showing up to visit with me or getting a call from him. He was a guy who let you do your job. If he had concerns, he may just come down and sit with you and visit to see where you're coming from. He always wanted to know what's going on and wanted to know what the issues were, but he was always supportive. And you always felt that he was on your side. He always could understand your view and would be supportive of it.

"Pat has a tremendous name," Alvarez said. "People know the name Pat Richter. That's what he gave this university, much like Elroy. His name gives you credibility because of what he stands for. He was a great athlete and an outstanding person. He was the true scholar-athlete."

* * *

Al Fish recalled the management team's repeated references to "the letter from Lodi" during Richter's years as athletic director. "Pat had always been really influenced by what the general public thinks, not only about himself, but about the Athletic Department," Fish recalled. "From a staff standpoint, we would always discount it and say, 'It's just one guy writing a letter in.' But Pat took all these things very seriously. I remember one time we had a very critical policy issue that we were thinking about and we put in what we thought was a very reasoned and fully comprehensive argument. We put all that out there and Pat pulls out this letter from a guy from Lodi and says, 'Well, he doesn't think so, and here's his thinking.' It was like they were of equal weight and you had to be able to respond to that.

"And while we may have laughed about it or at times were frustrated by it, it turns out that it was one of the reasons that Pat was strong," Fish said. "He had his ear to the ground. He thinks and cares about what people think about Wisconsin, and people knew that. There were hundreds of people over the years who we saw come up to Pat and say, 'Thank you for responding to my letter. Thanks for returning my phone call.' A lot of athletic directors don't do that or don't care. While we joked about it, I think it was an insight into his character there that helped make him so successful."

* * *

On the night of March 2, 2004, hundreds of friends and colleagues of Pat and Renee Richter gathered at Madison's Monona Terrace to celebrate Pat Richter's retirement as athletic director.

The evening included tributes from Major League Baseball Commissioner Bud Selig; from Bob Harlan, president of the Green Bay Packers; from Merritt Norvell, a former Badger teammate of Richter's who went on to become athletic director at Michigan State; and from incoming athletic director Barry Alvarez.

The three chancellors during the Richter era, Donna Shalala, David Ward, and John Wiley, also paid tribute. There were other dignitaries, relatives, and a smattering of old East Side friends. There was a video tribute to Richter and souvenir Pat Richter bobbleheads. It clearly was a festive affair, and it became even more so when those gathered to celebrate with the Richters watched on large television screens as the Badger men's basketball team upset Michigan State in overtime.

Donna Shalala traveled from Florida to be there. She, like everyone else who spoke that night, heaped praise on the retiring athletic director. "People give money all the time to their alma mater." Shalala said. "Some of them give advice to their chancellors or presidents. But once in a while, someone who loves their university steps up, drops everything that they're doing, and sacrifices both personally and professionally for a dream. Pat Richter, All-American, son of Wisconsin, gave of himself to restore glory to his alma mater. In the process, he improved the university, not only athletically but academically; we were able to recruit better students and better scholars. He is a graceful, enormously talented, and wonderful man. I value him as a friend and a colleague. Pat, you're a class act and it's a pleasure to be here tonight to celebrate your 15 years."

Alvarez spoke of the many great moments spent with Richter, including the postgame celebration after Wisconsin's historic victory over Michigan State in Tokyo. "I'll never forget the euphoric feeling that Pat and I had that night in Tokyo," Alvarez said. "We were on cloud nine and went to a famous Japanese restaurant with a number of our friends to celebrate, and we had a wonderful Japanese meal—at Tony Roma's!

Pat and Renee Richter enjoy a laugh together at Pat's retirement dinner on March 2, 2003. Photo courtesy of the UW Atheltic Department.

"At the start of every football season," Alvarez told the crowd, "I always talk to my football team about focusing on the legacy that they want to leave—something they can look back on and be very proud of. Pat, through your dedicated service and tireless efforts, you left the greatest legacy of all. You brought back the UW Athletic Department.

"Pat, I feel blessed to have served under you and under your direction," Alvarez continued. "I thank you for giving me the chance to run my own program in my own way with your total support. And I thank you even more so for leaving an Athletic Department in such good shape. You forever raised the bar for Badger athletics, and I promise I will do all that I can to protect and grow the legacy that you've created."

After listening to all the guest speakers that night, Pat Richter took center stage for the final time in his career as athletic director. As expected, he handled it with class, dignity, and humility.

"I'm truly overwhelmed and humbled by all of this," Richter told the crowd. "You think of the movie *It's a Wonderful Life* because it really has been a wonderful life. It's hard to imagine as you begin to reflect on all these things."

"Before I took this job I remember in 1989, we'd go to the football games with John and Renee Moore and we'd go sit in the south end zone and stretch out on the bleachers," Richter said. "If the Badgers got a first down in their first series of the second half, we'd stay. And if they didn't, we'd head home and do some yard work. It wasn't much fun, but the yard looked great.

"I was fortunate to have been grounded in basic values essential to good leadership by my parents, teachers, teammates, coaches, and colleagues,"

Pat Richter greets his former boss, Donna Shalala, at a March 2, 2003 gala celebration at Monona Terrace. Photo by Michelle Stocker/courtesy of *The Capital Times*.

Richter said. "When I assumed the Wisconsin AD position, I never forgot those precepts. Hire good people. Treat them with dignity. Establish objectives. Set a good example. And get the hell out of their way and let them do what they're supposed to do.

"The most compelling reason for coming back to UW was to try and make it enjoyable for the student-athletes, for the fans to have fun watching them, and to make it fashionable again to be a Badger fan.

"For the past couple of weeks we've pored over scads of pictures and clippings and memorabilia," Richter said. "There was one particular clipping that really caught me off guard. There was an article in a company newsletter about a man who had passed away suddenly while at work at the young age of 43. The writer wrote that he was devoted to his wife and family and dedicated to his work. Loyal, faithful, conscientious— he symbolized the company in the truest sense of the word. He was modest, proud of the accomplishments of his children. He was a builder of a wonderful family and of his church. He was a builder of America through his work at the company. His fellow members of the Gisholt family knew he was all this and much more. He always pointed out the best in people. He was quick to rise to the defense of his friends and those he knew were in the right. He was always ready to help his fellow man, even though it may have meant personal sacrifice. He was truly a builder among men, doing his very best to build for his employer and his loved ones.

"This was written about my father at his passing more than 40 years ago," Richter said. "I can only hope they'll say the same thing about his son."

QUICK FACTS
PAT RICHTER

Alma Mater: Wisconsin, B.S. in Landscape Architecture, 1964; Wisconsin, J.D., 1971.

Family: wife Renee; sons Scott (wife, Khaki, and grandsons J.P. and Cole), Brad (wife, Crissy, grandson, Max, and granddaughter, Samantha), Barry (wife, Kim, grandson, Blake, and granddaughter, Alexandra), and Tim.

Playing Career: Lettered three times each in football, basketball, and baseball; All-American tight end in 1961 and 1962; Academic All-American in 1962; led the Big Ten in receiving yards twice and topped the nation as a junior; set a Rose Bowl record catching 11 passes for 163 yards vs. No. 1-ranked USC in 1963; All-Big Ten first baseman at UW; received his UW scholarship to play basketball; first round NFL draft pick of the Washington Redskins in 1963; played eight seasons for the Redskins.

Awards: 1963 Big Ten Medal of Honor recipient (academic and athletic excellence); 1997 inductee into the National Football Foundation College Football Hall of Fame; given an NCAA Silver Anniversary Award for postcollegiate accomplishment in 1988; member of the inaugural class of inductees into the UW Athletic Department's Hall of Fame in 1991; inducted into the Rose Bowl Hall of Fame in 1994; gained induction into the Verizon Academic All-America Hall of Fame in 1995; named "Executive of the Year" by the Sales & Executives of Madison in 1997; member of both the Wisconsin State Athletic and Madison Sports Halls of Fame.

NCAA and Big Ten committee service: Former chair of the Big Ten and Western Collegiate Hockey Association athletic directors; formerly served on the NCAA Football Issues Committee, the Big Ten Compliance Committee, the Rose Bowl Management Committee, the NCAA Division I-A Ice Hockey Committee and the Agent/Student-Athlete Special Committee.

Noteworthy UW-Madison item: Richter and his wife, Renee, have made a generous charitable gifts to the Kohl Center project. Two of the trophy cases on the main concourse have been named in their honor.

INDEX

MORE GREAT
SPORT TITLES FROM
TRAILS BOOKS &
PRAIRIE OAK PRESS

Baseball in Beertown: America's Pastime in Milwaukee, *Todd Mishler*

Before They Were The Packers, *Denis J. Gullickson & Carl Hanson*

Cold Wars: 40+ Years of Packer-Viking Rivalry, *Todd Mishler*

Downfield: Untold Stories of the Green Bay Packers, *Jerry Poling*

Great Moments in Wisconsin Sports, *Todd Mishler*

Green Bay Packers Titletown Trivia Teasers, *Don Davenport*

Mean on Sunday: The Autobiography of Ray Nitschke, *Robert W. Wells*

Mudbaths and Bloodbaths: The Inside Story of the Bears-Packers Rivalry, *Gary D'Amato & Cliff Christl*

Packers By the Numbers: Jersey Numbers and the Players Who Wore Them, *John Maxymuk*

For a free catalog, phone, write, or e-mail us.

Trails Books
P.O. Box 317, Black Earth, WI 53515
(800) 236-8088 • e-mail: books@wistrails.com • www.trailsbooks.com